BLAKE IN THE NINETIES

Blake in the Nineties

Edited by

Steve Clark

and

David Worrall

First published in Great Britain 1999 by
MACMILLAN PRESS LTD
Houndmills, Basingstoke, Hampshire RG21 6XS and London
Companies and representatives throughout the world

A catalogue record for this book is available from the British Library.

ISBN 0–333–68160–6

First published in the United States of America 1999 by
ST. MARTIN'S PRESS, INC.,
Scholarly and Reference Division,
175 Fifth Avenue, New York, N.Y. 10010

ISBN 0–312–22054–5

Library of Congress Cataloging-in-Publication Data
Blake in the nineties / edited by Steve Clark and David Worrall.
p. cm.
Includes bibliographical references and index.
ISBN 0–312–22054–5 (cloth)
1. Blake, William, 1757–1827—Criticism and interpretation.
I. Clark, S. H. (Steven H.), 1957– . II. Worrall, David, 1950–
.
PR4147.B46   1999
821'.7—dc21   98–50735
                                                      CIP

This book is printed on paper suitable for recycling and made from fully managed and
sustained forest sources.

10   9   8   7   6   5   4   3   2   1
08   07   06   05   04   03   02   01   00   99

Printed and bound in Great Britain by
Antony Rowe Ltd, Chippenham, Wiltshire

Contents

List of Figures

Preface

The essays collected here are based upon the conference 'Blake in the Nineties', held at St Mary's University College, Strawberry Hill, in July 1994. Our thanks are due to Charmian Hearne and her colleagues at Macmillan for their support for this project. All the errors contained within are the responsibility of the editors.

Steve Clark and David Worrall

Notes on the Contributors

Stephen C. Behrendt is George Holmes Distinguished Professor of English at University of Nebraska-Lincoln. Amongst his publications are *Reading William Blake* (1992) and *Royal Mourning and Regency Culture: Elegies and Memorials of Princess Charlotte* (1997).

Steve Clark is currently Visiting Fellow at the Centre for English Studies, University of London. He is the co-editor of *Historicizing Blake* (1994). His publications include *Sordid Images: the Poetry of Masculine Desire* (1994).

Keri Davies is a doctoral student at St Mary's University College researching collectors of Blake. He is Chair of the Blake Society of St James's, Piccadilly and has contributed to *Blake/An Illustrated Quarterly*.

Robert N. Essick is Professor of English at the University of California, Riverside. He is a co-editor of two volumes in the recent Blake Trust series and is currently working on the on-line Blake Archive with Morris Eaves and Joseph Viscomi. He is an avid collector of Blake and his circle.

Angela Esterhammer teaches at the University of Western Ontario. As well as articles and translations, she has published *Creating States: Studies in the Performative Language of John Milton and William Blake* (1994).

Michael Ferber teaches at the University of New Hampshire. Amongst his publications are *The Social Vision of William Blake* (1985) and *The Poetry of William Blake: Penguin Critical Studies* (1991).

Nelson Hilton is Professor of English at the University of Athens, Georgia. As well as being review editor of *Blake/An Illustrated Quarterly*, he is co-editor (with Thomas A. Vogler) of *Unnam'd Forms: Blake and Textuality* (1986) and the author of *Literal Imagination: Blake's Vision of Words* (1983).

Edward Larrissy is Professor of English at the University of Leeds. His publications include *William Blake* (1985) and *Yeats the Poet: the Measures of Difference* (1994).

Marsha Keith Schuchard is an independent scholar in Atlanta, Georgia. She has published numerous articles on the alternative Enlightenment and a recent study *Restoring the Temple of Vision: Cabalistic Freemasonry and British Literature* (1997).

Joseph Viscomi teaches at the University of North Carolina. He is a co-editor to two volumes in the recent Blake Trust series and is currently working on the on-line Blake Archive with Morris Eaves and Robert N. Essick. His publications include *Blake and the Idea of the Book* (1993).

David Worrall teaches at St Mary's University College, Strawberry Hill. He is the author of *Radical Culture* (1992), co-editor of *Historicizing Blake* (1994) and he edited one of the books in the Blake Trust series.

Abbreviations and Short Titles

Unless otherwise indicated, all references to Blake's texts are to page and plate numbers in David Erdman, *The Complete Poetry and Prose of William Blake*, rev. edn. (Berkeley: University of California Press, 1982), and to plate numbers in *The Illuminated Blake*, rev. edn. (New York: Dover, 1974).

A	*America America a Prophecy*
AH	*Ahania The Book of Ahania*
ARO	*All Religions Are One*
BL	*The Book of Los*
DC	*Descriptive Catalogue*
E	Erdman, ed. *William Blake, The Complete Poetry and Prose*
E	*Europe Europe a Prophecy*
EG	*Everlasting Gospel*
FR	*The French Revolution*
FZ	*The Four Zoas*
G	*The Gates of Paradise*
IB	*The Illuminated Blake.* David Erdman
J	*Jerusalem Jerusalem the Emanation of the Giant Albion*
Job	*Illuminations for the Book of Job*
LBD	*A Large Book of Designs*
M	*Milton Milton a Poem*
MHH	*Marriage The Marriage of Heaven and Hell*
NNR	*No Natural Religion There is No Natural Religion*
NT	*Night Thoughts*
PL	*Milton, Paradise Regained*
SE	*Songs of Experience*
SI	*Songs of Innocence*
SBD	*A Small Book of Designs*
SL	*The Song of Los*
T	*Thel The Book of Los*
Ti	*Tiriel*
BofU	*Urizen The (First) Book of Urizen*
VDA	*Visions Visions of the Daughters of Albion*
VLJ	*A Vision of The Last Judgment*

Introduction

Steve Clark and David Worrall

Blake in the Nineties is an assessment of Blake's own work in the 1790s but also a consideration of critical debates during the 1990s. It draws on three main traditions of Blake criticism over the past decade: editorial, hermeneutic and historical. The third component was the primary concern of an earlier volume, *Historicizing Blake* (1994), which was intended to provide a broadly cultural-materialist reorientation to then current theoretical preoccupations.

The William Blake Trust facsimiles of the illuminated books are both the cause and symptom of a renewed interest in bibliographical analysis of Blake's *oeuvre*. To a non-specialist audience, it may perhaps seem of limited interest, for example, that the composite orderings of *The Book of Urizen* by Keynes and Erdman have been abandoned as purely speculative, but the fact that Blake's most famous lyric has been consigned to an appendix is, at the very least, indicative of a new climate of opinion. (The preface including 'And did those feet' occurs only in copies A and B of *Milton* and is therefore omitted from Essick's and Viscomi's edition, which uses C as copy-text.)

The illuminated books cannot but produce multiple readings: issues of variant copies, different orderings and text-design interplay have to be confronted before even beginning to address verbal, narrative or typological ironies. Criticism has tended to celebrate the meaning-making capacity of the visionary imagination in the abstract, but in its specific readings to make it manageable through appeals to symbolic system, genre and archetypes. A celebration of indeterminacy has it almost too easy on Blake's texts. The 1990s has witnessed a curious mutation of deconstruction into a fastidious bibliographical ultra-empiricism. This has, somewhat unexpectedly, resulted in interpretative curtailment rather than textual licence: rigorous examination of the particular artefact sharply reduces the sphere of hypothesis. *Blake in the Nineties* seeks to explore the parameters of this editorial revisionism and also its

1

broader implications evident in a more general mood of hermeneutic asceticism.

Robert Essick's essay opens by seeking to arbitrate between two poles of the new bibliography: Morris Eaves's *The Counter-Arts Conspiracy* (1992) and Joseph Viscomi's *Blake and the Idea of the Book* (1993). Essick sees a choice between interpreting according to what Blake writes – the stress on transcendent forms – and what he does – the material constraints of the working practitioner. This in turn may be restated in terms of traditional philosophical opposi-tions between Platonic ideas and Aristotelian praxis, deductive and inductive reasoning, and so on. A preference is stated for the latter view, but rather than succumb to the temptation to offer a final adjudication, the terms of debate are shifted to another polarity: linear versus tonal art, and conception versus execution. It is the collector, committed to pleasure in (rather than critical arguments about) the artefact, who is capable of rethinking this divide, rein-stating the authority of the connoisseur.

There have always been arguments about the form in which Blake's illuminated books should be encountered: purists have demanded nothing but the original artefact (Essick's insistence on the uniqueness of copy C of *Jerusalem*), though for most purposes critics have come to rely on Erdman. The high quality of the William Blake Trust/Tate facsimiles goes some distance towards offering a middle way. Joseph Viscomi's meticulous empirical investigation and reconstruction of the physical process of print-making allows chronologies of composition to be convincingly established. For the first time, it becomes possible to witness Blake's texts evolving along the lines of the multiple versions of Wordsworth's *Prelude*. Patient excavation of the genealogy of production allows the recon-struction of an original four-plate work, forming a response to Swedenborg, which quickly evolved into the *Marriage*. In his essay, the third of a series, Viscomi explores the consequences of this origi-nal intention in the relation between Swedenborg and the dramati-zation of illuminated printing within the *Marriage* itself.

Edward Larrissy's essay takes up the theme of the formal self-reflexivity of the artefact, and explores at length the multiple connotations of technical terms such as imposition, reversal and reflexion. These are given an existential rather than an aesthetic inflection: the emphasis is not on revealing the infinite, but rather on the temporality of the process of production, whose gaps, ellipses and duplications may be read in terms of either mechanical or positive forms of repetition. This in turn is linked to a tradition of Protestant theology, most forcefully exemplified in Kierkegaard, in which the fallen world itself may be redeemed through a transformed concept of time as a moment of crisis and conversion. Larrissy concludes by suggesting that this narrative of differentiation, which nevertheless reclaims the past, is most clearly evident in Blake's *Illustrations of the Book of Job*.

Stephen Behrendt gives a more phenomenological and reception-oriented account of the problematic relation between text and design in Blake. He advances a model in which the process of internalization of meaning becomes both sacramental yet oddly physical, recalcitrantly particular. The illuminated books are situated within the contexts of early traditions of manuscript ornamentation, book-illustration and canvases containing verbal collage (Hogarth, Rowlandson). The relative simultaneity of response to the painted image is contrasted with the linear, disjunctive and problem-solving aspect of decoding written text. An extended reading of 'The Tyger' is offered as an example of the continually stimulating and elusive meta-text produced by Blake's utilization of both sets of conventions.

This leads on to three essays more concerned with the interpretation of specific texts, though with reference to earlier contexts of Protestant devotional writing, Miltonic speech acts and Lockean metaphor. Nelson Hilton offers a genre study of the *Songs* in the context of eighteenth-century hymnody. One might have thought it an unlikely choice of subject for a broadly semiotic model of reading, but such an approach has notable advantages in this area. Defenders of hymnody, notably Donald Davie, have tended to demand a prior theological commitment – understanding through belief; Blake critics investigating this relation have preferred to see the relation as one of simple ideological inversion.[1] Hilton shows an appropriate respect for rhetorical complexity of the form, its purely linguistic resources; Blake utilizes these at least as much as he parodies them, and in 'To Tirzah' produces a kind of limit-case to both the genre of hymnody and of the *Songs* themselves, prefiguring both the greater speculative range and elements of potential grotesquerie of the longer prophecies.

Angela Esterhammer's essay deals with the performative aspect of Blake's rhetoric, centring on *The Book of Urizen*. In both Genesis and *Paradise Lost*, its two major precursor texts, the power of calling forth has an intrinsic ambiguity. It serves as inaugural moment of creation in producing a phenomenal world and simultaneously imposes a set of potentially oppressive socio-political relations. A comparable awareness of the political dimension of divine language may be discerned in late eighteenth-century biblical scholarship, in such otherwise antithetical figures such as Lowth and Paine. *The Book of Urizen*, with its slippages between literal and figural, dramatization of the equivocal consequences of naming, and vertiginous summonings and dispersals of world-contexts, represents a sustained exploration of language as action, in both productive and repressive capacities.

Steve Clark also stresses the productive power of *The Book of Urizen*, in a similar move back to seventeenth-century antecedents, here Locke rather than Milton. In line with recent historiography his essay emphasizes the philosopher's political activism, theological radicalism and symbolic resonances, and seeks to establish areas of continuity with Blake's work rather than accept the customary polarity between them. Through analyses of *There is No Natural Religion*, the *Marriage* and the figure of Urizen, it is argued that Blake reactivates the metaphorical substratum of Locke's *Essay on Human Understanding*, notably its ethic of labour and imperative of self-confinement, and that his work is most compelling when drawing on its apparent adversary most directly.

The next four essays seek to extend and qualify our sense of Blake's complex embeddedness. David Worrall's recovery of the diverse signifying practices of radical subcultures in the period amply confirms the extent to which they permeate Blake's work. Potential contexts of reception are established with sufficient precision to refute the traditional objection to his solipsistic isolation. The essay raises the broader problem of dealing with plebeian culture of the period. Discourse theory, whether defined in Foucauldian or Bakhtinian terms, allows attractive homologies to be established between Blake and various forms of popular culture, but its synchronic model resists assimilation to a diachronic idea of historical progression through intentional agents.

Michael Ferber concentrates on the position of the Romantic writer in wartime, preoccupied with, yet simultaneously estranged from, the experience of the battlefield. The point of an intrinsic impotence, however, could be extended to active influence in public history of any kind. The bold decision to stress the failure of Blake's work, its inability to achieve a significant apparent audience of any kind, makes inevitable frustration its central motivation. Hence the ambivalence of Blake's utilization of the pacificist tradition of the two swords: forswearing aggression becomes a means of giving vent to it. This raises the possibility that the appeal of Blake's poetry, for all its later ethic of forgiveness, resides in its compensatory projection of anger, wrath and vengefulness. The emphasis on the defeatism of Blake's texts may perhaps be regarded as premature; but the question posed remains central: in what other kind of broader historical narrative are they to be inserted?

Reconstruction of schism within the Swedenborgian New Jerusalem Church during Blake's membership in the late 1780s has long been occluded by gaps and suppressions in the documentary record. Marsha Keith Schuchard uses extensive research in parallel archives uncovered in Sweden and America to reconstruct its internal politics. In contrast to Viscomi's emphasis on specifically textual debts in the *Marriage*, Blake's allusions are shown to involve specific acts of self-positioning within the intrigues of the movement. It is now evident that it was dominated not by urban artisans, as traditionally presumed, but by complex factional rivalries within an exotic international cast of Illuminati and Freemasons. Much of what looks most recondite, if not bizarre, in his work can thus be located within the mainstream of the Alternative Enlightenment: indeed in comparison to a figure such as Cagliostro, one is struck by the comparative sobriety of Blake's speculations.

Blake himself was in no straightforward way proletarian: a self-taught, independent craftsman committed to ideals of high art, with no clear identification with popular activism. For the first time, Keri Davis's research succeeds in establishing precise points of mediation with the radical intelligentsia, which has tended to be somewhat loosely assumed on the basis of apocryphal evidence (for example, the warning to Paine of impending arrest) (Erdman 1977, pp. 154–77). More unexpectedly, his reconstruction of the milieu of Blake's first known collector, Rebekah Bliss, intervenes powerfully in contemporary discussion of the issue of his sexual representations, now widely regarded as problematic. In this context, it is salutary to learn that at least one part of his primary audience was female, and depending on the degree of intensity one ascribes to its communal ethic of friendship, arguably lesbian.

There is evidently still room for a new Blake for a new century.

Note

1.   Donald Davie, *The Eighteenth Century Hymn in England* (Cambridge: Cambridge University Press, 1993).

1

Blake and the Production of Meaning

Robert N. Essick

Opening acts of self-situating have become a cliché of modern literary criticism.[1] Yet I feel compelled to indulge briefly in that mode, given the perspectives of the authors appearing in this volume and of the participants in the conference from which it emerged. My colleagues in both contexts are literary scholars and art historians; their relationship to Blake's works is determined in many respects by those professional roles. Although I have from time to time masqueraded as both an art historian and a literary critic, I relate myself to Blake primarily as a collector of prints and drawings.[2] Since my presence here at least hints at a social or institutional anomaly, I have taken the anomalous – in its etymological sense of 'difference' – as my theme. I want to explore the ways different cultural and institutional contexts create different perspectives on Blake which in turn produce not just different interpretations, but different conceptions of the grounds and constituents of meaning – or at least what constitutes meaning's next-of-kin, significance.[3] I will pursue this issue in light of two recent – and I believe extremely important – books about Blake, but I also want to delve into some differences within Blake's canon of pictures and texts. My final goal will be to call to the bar one of Blake's fundamental principles: the unity of conception and execution.

Book reviews are not a conventional part of volumes such as this. None the less, a brief excursion into that genre provides me with a way of quietly asserting how an old and now undervalued concept, the 'eye of the connoisseur', relates to current concerns in Blake criticism. The two books I intend to review – or at least misuse for my own advantage – are Morris Eaves's *Counter-Arts Conspiracy* (1992) and Joseph Viscomi's *Blake and the Idea of the Book* (1993).[4] Although there is much to praise in both volumes, my initial

7

approach will be antithetical. The opposition I have in mind is less between this reviewer and the books at issue and more between the two books – their fundamentally different approaches to Blake's writings and how they relate to Blake's art.

Who would have thought, in the wake of deconstruction, feminist criticism, postmodernism, postcolonialism, queer theory, the hermeneutics of despair and a player to be named later, that the liveliest arena of Blake criticism would be that valley of dry bones, bibliography? Yet I would contend that this is indeed the case thanks to Viscomi's *Blake and the Idea of the Book*. His recovery of the edition-printing and colouring of the illuminated books, and the chronology of these sessions, will have – or at least should have – consequences far beyond the bibliographical. I have qualified my prophecy because I fear that many people who should read Viscomi will not, because they resist reading a text in which every other sentence presents what, in a pre-Nietzschean world, were called 'facts'. But the pursuit of those consequences, intended and otherwise, will have to wait for another time or mind, for my focus here will not be on the major thrust of Viscomi's discoveries but on one of his leitmotifs.

At key junctures, Viscomi turns to the relationship between conception and execution in Blake's graphic works. But I must immediately emend my sentence: Viscomi usually (and cleverly) avoids my word 'conception', and favours the word Blake uses with slightly greater frequency, 'invention'. Viscomi thereby shifts his own discursive frame from the verbally or transcendentally conceptual and towards material activity, indicated in part by rendering otiose that most abstract of nonentities, a preposition. We conceive *of* ideas about 'truth' or 'justice', but we can invent – in the sense of materially create – washing machines and radios without prepositional intermediation.[5] The preposition also places conception in the realm of representation, as though a concept is a sign of something else 'of' which it is not. Acts of material invention unfold as – in a special sense – 'insignificant' activities because they may create signifiers but, as activities, they are not themselves representations of something else.

But what about pictures? Do they begin as mental concepts, images 'of' something else, or do they evolve only within material acts? Viscomi opts for the latter – what he calls 'an idea of invention grounded in execution' (370) – and refers to Blake's practices more than his writings for authorization. That practice typically takes the form of 'drawing' – either on paper or on a copper plate – in which, as Viscomi puts it, 'invention and execution are organically inter- twined' (370). From this perspective, 'form and meaning evolve from the continual interactive relationship between … invention and execution' (42) – an interaction that finally takes on a 'sense of oneness between subject and object' (43). Finally, for Viscomi, the words 'invention' and 'execution' record a distinction in theory without a difference in practice.

Viscomi's reference to a subject/object 'oneness' exemplifies a view Eaves directly criticizes in *Counter-Arts Conspiracy*, although I suspect that the composition of his critique preceded this particular example. Eaves mildly, patiently, chastises both Viscomi and Essick for replicating the romantic ideology: we 'tend to sentimentalize "the medium"', thus confusing Blake's Platonistic if not Platonic theorizing with the kind of Wordsworthian naturalism that pro- motes the deep engagements of human subjects with natural objects' (184).[6] Eaves has a point, given Viscomi's use of terms such as 'organically' and 'oneness' of the 'subject and object'. Further, Eaves's displacement of the context for our brand of romanticism from artistic production to nature worship gives it an anti-Blakean twist. In defence, I would point to the difference between 'concep- tion' as theory – for example, the unity of subject and object – and 'conception' as the invention of particular images that give the artist a 'sense' of that unity. Viscomi implies this same point in his only reference to the same dead Greek invoked by Eaves: 'Art-making of the kind practiced by Blake is inherently Aristotelian, while discus- sions of art, including Blake's, tend toward the Platonic' (43). Yet simply to claim that Eaves and Viscomi are talking about different things – lexis for one, praxis for the other – divides conception- as-theory from invention-as-drawing in a way that threatens the basic consanguinity of conception and execution accepted by both our critics, however differently they hierarchize them, and at the same time elides very real differences.

We can begin to delineate those differences with just two further quotations from Eaves. Can we imagine Viscomi ever saying any- thing even close to the following: 'Execution is only the *result* of Invention' (Eaves 1992, 179). Unfortunately for Viscomi, and for me, Eaves is quoting Blake's 'Public Address' (E576) when he writes these words in support of his contention that 'Blake's value system is strongly at work orienting the items in the series [that is, concep- tion, drawing, and execution] toward conception and away from

execution, toward the "Mental" and away from the "Corporeal"'
(179). One might also cite Blake's *Vision of the Last Judgment:* 'Mental
Things are alone Real' (E565). Thankfully, Blake never said what I
find to be Eaves's most telling two sentences on this topic: 'All tools
signify compromises that This World makes necessary. There are
no burins in eternity' (185).[7] Is this why, when Blake could have
followed Emanuel Swedenborg in his imaginary journeys to
heaven, he went instead to hell in *The Marriage of Heaven and Hell*?
And might corporeal burins become 'Mental Things' when used to
produce art?

The fundamental differences between the Eavesian and Viscomian
perspectives evolve from their different personal and institutional
contexts and devolve into a different idea of the ratio (in Blake's
sense) between theories couched in words and practices signified
by their products. Both men hold university positions as English
professors, but only one is *really* an English professor. By a real
English professor I mean someone who accepts, as an unconscious
modus operandi if not a self-conscious ideology, the hegemony of the
word over other forms of semiosis, and particularly over those with
an unseemly dependence on representational modes that trumpet
their secondariness – in relationship to both ideas and the objects
represented – in a way words do not.

The real English professor, as defined above, is of course Morris
Eaves. He was a student of the word before he starting mucking
about with drawings and engravings. The focus of his studies, even
those richly and tellingly illustrated, is on what Blake and others
have *said* about pictures. Only in the realm of language can visual
images be elevated out of their gross particularity and transformed
by the abstract substantives of general conceptualization. If the
romanticism of Viscomi and Essick is excessively organic and incarnational, Eaves's romanticism is resolutely transcendental. Remember,
no burins in heaven.

Viscomi isn't *really* an English professor. He needs language as
much as Eaves to conceptualize his understanding of visual images,
but the latter's privileging of the word need not follow from that
necessity. Viscomi was an artist before falling into the linguistic
trap of a PhD in English. A good deal of artistic materialism,
the immediate engagement with objects, clings to the hem of his
rhetoric – all those 'facts' I mentioned earlier – and shapes his
romantic sense of the mutually engendering intercourse between
invention and execution.[8]

Let me now turn to another perspective on these issues, one associated with collectors like myself, those 'Cunning sures & the Aim at yours', as Blake called them in his *Notebook* (E510). Collectors are generally not thought of as constituting an interpretive community, as producers of meaning. What they generate is a shared set of arbitrary and ever-shifting attitudes, which both mystify and commodify objects. This object-specific materialism and its attendant Aristotelian rage for cataloguing small differences make the collector a natural ally of Viscomi's emphasis on praxis. Matters of taste, and aesthetics in general, have been widely neglected in academic discourse, except as a vehicle for historicizing and demystifying class distinctions, capitalism and the shards of aristocratic tyrannies.[9] Connoisseurship has in some circles become the love that cannot speak its name. Eaves has indicated how Viscomi and Essick have romanticized the relation of conception and execution. The following personal narrative will similarly romanticize the synergy of collecting and the production of meaning.

The most important sale of Blake's prints since the dispersal of Frances White Emerson's illuminated books in 1958 took place in Christie's King Street rooms on 30 November 1993. This was the auction of the small but choice collection formed by Frank Rinder early in the century. For many years, the collection was owned by Rinder's daughter, Esther Harvey, who lived in the Somerset village of Curry Rivel, about 25 minutes by car from Taunton. These circumstances prevented easy access by Blake scholars, only a very few of whom made the pilgrimage to Mrs Harvey's home. When I journeyed to Curry Rivel in 1979, I had hoped to see what was by far the most important work in her possession, copy C of *Jerusalem*. The separate plates I had specifically asked to study were kept in a box with family photos, letters and other odd bits, but *Jerusalem* was in a bank vault in Taunton. I had missed my chance. My consolation was that we all had the 1952 Blake Trust reproduction of copy C, and thus knew what the book looked like. Or so I thought.

The Rinder sale provided a window of opportunity for several interested parties to study *Jerusalem* and other treasures in the collection. The marketplace was at least a momentary friend to scholarship before the book disappeared into a private American collection. My first reaction, upon opening the fine vellum binding housing the Rinder *Jerusalem*, had more to do with the collector's sensibilities than the scholar's. I was immediately struck by the difference between what I had expected to see, based on the Blake

Trust reproduction, and what I found. I knew the dimensions of the original from Bentley's *Blake Books*, but this relatively abstract bit of information was insufficient to overcome the visual presence of the Trust volume and its close-cropped margins. The reproduction was claustrophobic; the original, with its wide margins, expansive.

My next reaction centred on the quality of the printing. From the reproduction I had learned that copy C was a mess, particularly in its second chapter. The whites were terribly ink-splattered, even by Blake's unconventional standards. His occasional attempts to wipe away these blemishes and add a few touches of barely visible grey wash here and there seemed insufficient attempts at correction and improvement. The overall effect remained excessively accidental and disturbingly awkward.

The original immediately gave me a very different impression. What seemed sloppy in the reproduction appeared to be intriguing and less haphazard in the original. Obscuring veils of ink-splatter became intermediate tones. The sheer variety of effects, achieved at both the etching and inking stages of production, now appeared boldly innovative and a challenge to my fundamental conceptions of Blake as a graphic artist. While the context of a linear and primitivist aesthetic remained relevant, the traditions of mezzotint and aquatint suddenly became more companionable than oppositional.[10] I seemed to be holding in my hands a great work of early nineteenth-century *tonal* printmaking.

I did not have a copy of the Blake Trust reproduction with me in Christie's rooms. My first thought was that the photographic process used by the Trust had the characteristics of a low-grade xerox, one that converts an image to black and white without intermediate tones. When I did return to the reproduction, my eyes tended to confirm this supposition. But something else happened when I put the Blake Trust volume side by side with photographs of copy C, or even with the reproductions in Christie's catalogue. I could now see in the Trust volume almost everything I had seen in the original. The differences were very slight, once my eyes had been instructed by the original.

My cautionary tale has several morals. One is a fundamental principle of traditional connoisseurship: study originals, not reproductions. To this we can add an Eavesian corollary about how every system of production or reproduction mediates images according to its own machinery. Or we could turn to W. J. T. Mitchell's witty phrase, 'no representation without taxation'.[11] But to these I would add a third observation that returns to my earlier concern with the relationship between conception and execution. Both Eaves and Viscomi concentrate, in their different ways, on the nature of that relationship within the process of original production. My experiences with *Jerusalem* led to a concern with the reception of pictures – that is, with how they are perceived and understood. General theories about Blake's art, particularly the doctrine of line, predetermined the way my eyes responded to his images.[12] In such circumstances, conception becomes a form of proleptic mediation which, like all media, lends its peculiar distortions to our perceptions. Only a confrontation with the original illuminated book provided sufficient visual stimulus to shake off my preconceptions.

My coda makes me a little hesitant to reproduce *Jerusalem*; photographs in books may offer only another filtering grid that belies my response to the original. But I'll run the risk and attempt to use a combination of visual and verbal mediation to buttress my contention that the first printing of *Jerusalem* was dedicated to the production of tonal prints. The clearly inked and printed impression of the title page in copy A (British Museum) offers one of the best examples of tonality established at the etching stage. In the past, I have urged fellow Blakeans *not* to allow these fine hatching and crosshatching patterns to sink below the threshold of visual apperception – as though part of Blake's meaning was to reveal the tricks of his trade.[13] I'm now asking readers to consider the traditional purpose of such tricks – the illusion of tone – and its relevance to our perception, and finally our understanding, of this print. Blake went to considerable trouble to hatch and crosshatch what would otherwise be an empty whiteness serving as the ground – or rather sky – out of which his letters and figures rise in black relief. The combination of white- and black-line techniques for the delineation of the images, including the letters of 'Jerusalem', provides further subtle gradations. Much as the living forms pictured here hover between the human and the lepidopterous, large areas of the plate intermediate between the absolutes of black and white.

Many plates in copy C demonstrate Blake's addition of tone at the inking, printing and hand-tinting stages. Three examples should suffice to indicate the techniques and their stylistic results. On plate 46, many of the whites, even in the lower reaches of the text cloud, have been sprayed with a fine mist of ink, a graphic corollary to Vala and her veil pictured on the left. Although chance played a large role in where the individual specks of ink would fall, it is difficult to envisage how Blake's inking ball, accidently slipping into etched valleys, could produce this effect. I suspect that Blake used some splattering technique, such as shaking a brush loaded with ink over selected areas of the plate. The result is the relief equivalent of tonal processes such as stipple, mezzotint or aquatint.

Before printing, Blake scratched away some of the ink mist from the whites surrounding the woman's raised right hand, upper right in the design. The patterns created indicate that this work was executed with a round-pointed instrument. The final stage of tonal addition was applied to the individual impression: grey washes, even in areas wiped of the ink mist, and a few pencil lines on the thighs of the central figure. Blake seems to be searching for a variety of tonal gradations through both additive and subtractive techniques, much as his late pencil sketches show him searching for the right outline by drawing multiple alternatives.

Plate 47 in copy C repeats the techniques we have seen in the previous examples, including fine etched hatching, an even heavier ink mist, and touches of grey wash. But the most interesting tonal feature is the bold wiping Blake deployed to create white highlights on the figures. The technique is a relief-printing analogue to the burnishing Blake used late in life to revise several of his earlier intaglio plates.[14]

Albion, slumping into a Urizenic posture on plate 37, bears on his skin heavy ink splatters and grey washes. Ink dots are clustered together to emphasize his shoulder and lower-arm muscles, just as a stipple engraver reduces the space between incised points to create dark passages. But the overall effect here is not the refinement of stipple work but something more akin to the sore boils covering Job, or the rough scales covering his tormentor, in Blake's sixth Job engraving. Albion, enervated and englobed by despair, is covered with the dirt of the earth his fallen and fragmented body will become.

As I consider these images in reproduction, I am once again conscious of their difference from the original and how you may be suspicious that I am engaging in Bond Street connoisseurship devoid of interpretive significance. A final personal narrative may help in this regard. *Jerusalem* plate 76 in copy C, when viewed in the Blake Trust volume, reinforces preconceptions about Blake's bold, binary and linearist graphic style. The original reveals tonal subtleties masked by all reproductions I have seen. The quality of light, at once crepuscular and dazzling, is rendered at the etching stage through the thin white lines of what Blake called 'Woodcut on Copper' (*Notebook*, E694), and at the printing stage through the warmth of the ink, the dense delicacy of its application, and the colour of the paper. If we went in search of similar effects produced by Blake's contemporaries, I would begin with the mezzotinters.

I have already made a few, tentative suggestions about how we might thematize the tonalities of copy C. More expansively, the gendering that unfolds in Blake's own writings on the arts may offer a means for locating the nexus between the graphic and textual dynamics of *Jerusalem*.[15] The poem's gestures towards prelapsarian androgyny, and its far more frequent plunges into the contentions of masculine and feminine polarities of fallen time and space, may also be at work in the tensions and harmonies of line and tone in the visible body of the book. But I will leave such matters to the experts – *real* English professors – and attempt instead to contextualize what I see in *Jerusalem* copy C, first within Blake's career as a printmaker, and then within a broader history of graphic techniques and tastes.

Looking back from the perspective generated by *Jerusalem*, we can perceive Blake's considerable investment in tonal graphics. On the commercial side, there are of course the early stipple prints after Watteau, Stothard and Morland.[16] These are first-rate examples of the technique, just as Blake's 'Beggar's Opera, Act III' after Hogarth (1788–90) is a masterful display of linear patterns and shading with a stipple burin. This too is a rendering of space, light and dramatic action through tone – although the point is lost if we study only progressively later and poorer impressions. As collectors know well, wear on a plate converts a continuum into a binarism – that is, the intermediate tones fade and the opposition between black and white increases.

Two arguments can be marshalled against the sort of evidence I have been presenting on behalf of William Blake, Tonal Printmaker. One is chronological, the other generic. Both types of conventional wisdom can be summarized as follows. The stipple prints come early in Blake's career; they do not represent his mature intaglio practices. Further, these are commercial prints in which Blake had to follow the tastes of the publishers whether he agreed with them or not. His original, self-published prints, and particularly the illuminated books, are a rejection of such tastes and bear a thoroughly antithetical relationship to them.

The generic argument is the hardest to overcome. Several of us have found it convenient to construct, or simply assume, the legitimacy of yet another binarism – commercial versus original graphics. As in so many other circumstances, this enabling fiction rigidifies historical flux into a categorical absolute. I think we can begin to dissolve the barriers between commercial and original productions, and the concomitant distinction between popular graphics and Blake's, by turning first to the chronological objection. Blake continued to produce stipple and other sorts of tonal prints throughout his career. 'The Right Honourable Earl Spencer' dates from 1813, 'Revd. Robert Hawker' from 1820, and 'Wilson Lowry' from 1824. All show Blake's skill at deploying sophisticated tonal processes through the full range possible in intaglio printmaking. Perhaps the most startling example is 'The Child of Nature' of 1818, a plate in which the stipple shading is so small, in proportion to the size of the image, that it approaches the appearance of aquatint. Yet this unBlakean print offers a bridge to Blake's original graphics where public tastes and market forces are supposed to play a greatly diminished role. About five years before 'The Child of Nature', Blake etched 'The Chaining of Orc'. This very small plate has resisted all attempts to determine its precise medium. The discovery of a second impression in 1990 (private collection), with the dots of shading positioned as in the previously known Rosenwald impression (National Gallery of Art, Washington), proved that the tones were produced at the etching stage and are not the result of ink splatter of the sort decorating the first printing of *Jerusalem*. But whatever the techniques Blake used, 'The Chaining of Orc' is about as close as one could get to aquatint in a relief print.

Turning to the illuminated books, we can find further precedents for the tonal textures displayed by *Jerusalem* copy C. Blake may have begun using ink-splatter techniques as early as 1795 when printing copies of *Songs of Innocence and of Experience* in black or dark brown ink. In *Songs of Experience* copy N (Huntington Library, San Marino), 'The Sick Rose' shows clusters of ink dots in etched whites, while 'The Little Vagabond' bears both ink mist in the whites and heavy reticulations on the relief surfaces defining the image. These effects in illuminated prints of the mid-1790s may be accidental, but Blake found such impressions acceptable for inclusion in copies of his books. When hand-tinted, as in *Experience* copy N, the veil of ink dots adds its own darker tonalities beneath the colours, much as different grain sizes affect colour aquatints.

We can be more certain of our inferences about Blake's intention to produce tonal prints when inking accords with the breakdown of continuous relief surfaces at the etching stage. Plate 38 from *Milton*, particularly in the uncoloured impression from the Rinder sale (Figure 1.1), is a good example of white-line etching used to

Figure 1.1   William Blake. *Milton*, plate 38, separate impression. White-line etching (Essick collection).

produce surface tone. While the distinction between relief and bitten surfaces is retained, just at or below the threshold of vision, both sorts of surfaces are broken into such small bits and pieces that the general effect is of a grey day at the seashore. This quality of light is crucial in establishing the emotional tenor of the print.

Plate 38 is not an isolated example. Indeed, if the etching of *Milton* preceded *Jerusalem*, then the former marks a dramatic inclusion of tonal techniques within illuminated printmaking. For the first time, Blake made extensive use of the 'Woodcut on Copper' and 'Woodcut on Pewter' techniques he described in his *Notebook* (E694). Plate 38 exemplifies 'Woodcut on Copper'. 'Woodcut on Pewter' is bolder and closer in appearance to relief etching than the white-line hatchings of 'Woodcut on Copper', but I think it too is an attempt to achieve a variety of lighting effects in relief processes. Dark outlines seem to emerge from a lighted cavern, as in *Milton* plate 29, the dramatic self-portrait of 'William' Blake arching backwards in pain or ecstasy as Milton, in the form of a falling star, descends into his left foot. The technique is flexible enough to permit just the opposite impression – lighted forms emerging from darkness – as on plate 33, the 'Robert' design, a contrary companion in both lighting and bilateral symmetry to 'William'. Although partly masked by hand colouring in all extant impressions, the 'Robert' plate also reveals the use of a technique first noticed by Viscomi.[17] Blake seems to have splattered his etching ground onto the plate in a rough imitation of aquatint, or purposely allowed the ground to lift or otherwise decay while immersed in acid. The results, clearly visible above Urizen's right arm on plate 15 of *Milton*, are pitted surfaces that create tonal variations. When handtinted, the printed base adds density and texture to the colours. Blake could thus replicate the surface qualities of colour printing without the labour that process would have required in books of 50 or 100 plates.

Blake's typically reticulated inking in his later illuminated books continues the dispersal of continuous lines and surfaces for the sake of intermediate tonalities. Posthumous pulls show how different the effect is when less grainy relief ink is used to print relief etchings. Posthumous impressions are bolder than Blake's own in their contrasts between relief and etched surfaces, and consequently give more emphasis to bounding lines. If you are looking for Linear Blake in the later illuminated books, look at Posthumous Blake.

Let me now turn again to *Jerusalem* copy C and its history. I have argued elsewhere that Blake's revival of intaglio graphics in the last decade of his life, and in particular the use of burnishing to revise many of his earlier separate plates, was greatly influenced by John Linnell.[18] Even in the stipple plate of 'Mirth' (*c.* 1816–20), these revisions are dedicated to the dramatization of light more than line (second state, *c.* 1820–7). Burnishing has added to this plate an intaglio equivalent of the play of light and dark in *Jerusalem* plate 76 or what Blake had attempted, as early as 1805, in his white-line etching of 'Deaths Door'. The Job plates of 1823–6 bring the drama of light to its culmination. If, indeed, Linnell was a crucial stimulus in this final realization of tone in Blake's monochrome graphics, then it may be no accident that he purchased *Jerusalem* copy C. The first section delivered was chapter 2, heretofore considered the most flawed in its inking.[19] It has always been something of a mystery as to why Blake would sell such a supposedly messy copy to his new chief patron. The price was less than that fetched by other copies of *Jerusalem*, but Linnell received similar discounts on other illuminated books. Once we see *Jerusalem* copy C not as a poor piece of linear art, but rather as one of Blake's most advanced experiments in the inclusion of tonal variety in illuminated printing, then the sale to Linnell makes sense. His skill at creating subtle intermediate tones and shimmering reflected light in his own line engravings and mezzotints made him the ideal customer for Blake's attempts at similar effects in another graphic medium.

Linnell's patronage and influence cannot be the sole reason for Blake's development of intermediate tones in his illuminated prints. That process had already begun before the two men met in 1818. Blake's life-long penchant for technical experimentation, coupled with a desire for a monochrome replacement for hand tinting and colour printing, may have provided their own internal impetus. Yet, external forces cannot be ignored, including perceived market pressures and the internalization of popular tastes in spite of theoretical opposition to them. Blake's experiences under William Hayley's patronage may have offered just such a negative, or at least two-edged, influence. The insistence by Hayley and his female friends on softening revisions in the engravings he commissioned from Blake, coupled with the latter's belief that he had learned much about business practices from Hayley, may have worked their subtle insinuation into Blake's graphic practices.[20] His replacement, as Hayley's chief engraver, by Caroline Watson seems

to have heightened Blake's sensitivities to the incursions of feminine tonalities into a masculine vision based on line, but his
responses as a practising printmaker seem, on the face of it, less
oppositional than inclusive.[21] Moses Haughton's large stipple and
aquatint plates of Fuseli's paintings may have demonstrated to
Blake that such tonal techniques were not antithetical to sublimity.[22]
What was demonized in Blake's writings on the arts was incorpo-
rated into his printmaking activities, even when producing his late
illuminated books.

Blake's gradual inclusion of tonal processes, even in his most personal graphic expressions, accords with the broad history of
engraved and etched representational images in Europe. That history is in large measure shaped by a search for techniques that
could represent intermediate tones in printable images. Blake's
graphic theory is *retardataire* in relation to that evolution. His graphic
practices, however, show a complex intertwining of resistance to,
and exploitation of, tonality.

I have been opening a gap between theory and practice, between
conception and execution. Not 'conception' as the invention of an
image; on that point my Viscomian romanticism remains intact. My
concern is with 'conception' as aesthetic theory – what Eaves calls
'the conception of conception' (256) – and its relationship to aesthetic practice. These have been heading in opposite directions for
the last several pages of this essay; I'll try to push them a bit further
down their diverging paths.

This is certainly not the first time someone has noticed a difference between Blake's doctrine of line and his artistic habits. In her
1974 book, *Blake's Human Form Divine*, Anne Mellor found a tension
between textual denunciations of the enclosed human body and
Blake's rendering of it in his designs of the mid-1790s. More
recently, in a review of Eaves's *Counter-Arts Conspiracy*, Martin
Butlin (with an eye trained on Turner as much as Blake) has
pointed to the 'fact' (as he calls it) that 'however much Blake may
have insisted on the clearness and sharpness of the outline as
embodying inspiration, his own practice did not always live up to
this', at least in his early drawings.[23]

Such observations indirectly question the premise, shared by
Viscomi and Eaves, that conception and execution are intertwined
(even if one term always predominates). In *Counter-Arts Conspiracy*
we are told that 'the technical features of illuminated printing correlate well with ... such polemical defenses as the *Public Address*'

(186), while Viscomi, in his final sentence, hopes that his book will assist 'in revealing how profoundly Blake's theories of art and imagination are grounded in practice' (374). But other comments in *Blake and the Idea of the Book* indicate at least slight fissures in the marriage of idea and act. Blake's late drawing style, in Viscomi's view, 'included both the indeterminate and determinate' (40). The same could be said for Blake's colour printing, a process that produced little more than blots and blurs until given definite form with pen and ink. One might still argue that in these examples the indeterminate is merely a necessary stage in the search for determinate outline, but Viscomi implies something more general, and less easily explained away, with his claim that 'the technical evidence demonstrates that Blake was far more catholic … and far more practical and efficient – and less symbolic – in his printmaking than has been heretofore imagined' (176).

The statements I have been quoting hover at the margins of the conclusion I wish to draw. If indeed Blake, from let us say 1804 onwards, became an increasingly tonal printmaker, and if the copy of his greatest illuminated book he sold to the major patron of his later years records the deep incursion of intermediate tonality into his most personal graphic media, then neither a chronological nor a generic argument can heal the breach between graphic execution and the doctrine of line. Tonal practices in his late graphics and the linearist aesthetic propounded in writings such as *A Descriptive Catalogue* (1809) and the *Public Address* (c. 1810) are contemporaneous phenomena. They contradict each other; in turn, that contradiction sunders Blake's other central aesthetic principle, the unity of conception – at least as general theory or principle – and execution. Blake's linearist conceptualization of what constitutes 'true' art is inconsistent with his increasingly tonal methods of execution.

Let me offer one final exemplification of my view. In the last year of his life, Blake wrote to George Cumberland that 'a great majority of Englishmen are fond of The Indefinite which they Measure by Newtons Doctrine of the Fluxions of an Atom. A Thing that does not Exist. … For a Line or Lineament is not formed by Chance a Line is a Line in its Minutest Subdivision[s] Strait or Crooked It is Itself & Not Intermeasurable with or by an Thing Else' (12 April 1827, E783). Now let us consider Blake's outline engravings. Those he produced for the recipient of this letter fit comfortably within the aesthetic and epistemology of line. And so too do all the outline engravings by various hands of John Flaxman's classical compositions – with one

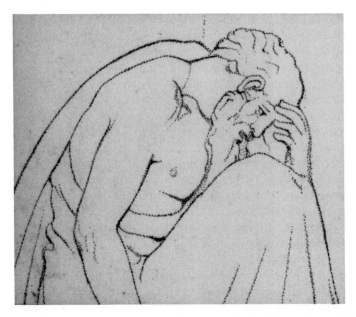

Figure 1.2   William Blake after John Flaxman. *Hesiod* illustrations (1817),
detail of plate 14. Etching/engraving in stippled lines (Essick collection).

notable exception. Blake's Hesiod plates, executed between 1814
and 1817, show a combination of continuous outline and lines composed of dots, with the latter in the majority. If we magnify individual lines (Figure 1.2), we can perceive the minute subdivisions
out of which an indefinite illusion of a line has been constructed.
As noted earlier, the 'Chaining of Orc' – hardly a commercial
endeavour – reveals a similar dissolution of a pictorial image into
dots. As these particles emerge above the threshold of vision, they
become intermeasurable with stipple, mezzotint, aquatint and
Newton's fluxions of an atom.

If I am even half right about all this, how can we account for the
divergence of general concept and artistic performance? Viscomi
hints at an answer with his distinction I quoted earlier about the
inherent Aristotelian bias of graphic execution and the Platonistic
tendencies of verbal theorizing. And if, as Viscomi also claims,
Blake's printmaking styles and variants between impressions are
'less symbolic' (176) than English professors would prefer, then
graphic media – in their production as well as in their interpretation – would seem resistant to the binary logic of the sort that sets

line and tone in opposition, and to the generalizing, abstracting and transcendentalizing momentum intrinsic to language. To revise my favourite aphorism in Eaves's *Counter-Arts Conspiracy*, there are no burins in theorizing discourse.

While in pursuit of differences, I have been implying some new continuities. Blake's divergence from the tastes of his age and from the larger history of printmaking is not as extreme as his aesthetic statements would suggest. Further, rigid distinctions between his commercial work – often characterized as an economically necessary evil – and his most singular productions as a printmaker tends to collapse as we look more closely at both. Even the tendency for Blake's theory and practice to diverge would seem to be part of a larger pattern in the history of eighteenth-century British art. As writers on the arts, particularly those supportive of principles promoted by the Royal Academy, tried to convert picture making from a craft into one of the liberal arts, dependent less on manual skill than historical knowledge, the visual became textual – at least in theory. The actual objects produced by artists, and the tastes creating and created by the market for them, resisted such high-mindedness. John Barrell has aptly characterized this split as a central problem in the art-historical debates of the last decade:

> Perhaps the main issue at stake was how to explain the apparent mismatch between the theories of painting most influential on 18th-century connoisseurs and critics, committed to the promotion of a public art of manly virtue and idealised forms, and the predominantly private, informal, even (as the century got older) feminised works which actually got produced.[24]

If we follow Blake's lead and equate 'manly' with 'linear' and 'feminised' with 'tonal', Barrell's overview would be a fine summary of my argument here.

Let me conclude with a brief epilogue, one that returns to my titular subject. Too often, the perspective of the collector or bibliographer appears to be anti-iconographic, against interpretation and against theory. It is certainly true that Viscomi's *Blake and the Idea of the Book* restricts a few approaches, such as those based on the assumption that every pictorial variant in the illuminated books is loaded with iconographic intention. But while some doors are closed, others are opened, as I have tried to indicate in this essay. More important than a shift in specific interpretations is the way

attention to connoisseurship and bibliography can increase the
range of what constitutes meaning or value. Collectors often
respond to the qualities of a work of art that seem most resistant to
verbal manipulation and thus are generally absent from interpretive discourse – or even from the theorizing of the artist. Are such
responses insignificant? In both the aesthetic and the semiotic
realms, leading theoreticians have proposed that the objective presence of a work of art or a sign finds its cultural function through a
process whereby the object is supplemented by its users to compen-
sate for a lack, in the object as such, and to integrate it into the
interconnections constituting the discourses that make us human.[25]
Such conjunctions and resonances between the worlds of the connoisseur and the critical theorist point us towards the largest semiotic and hermeneutic issues at stake when we participate in the
production of meaning.

Notes

1. For a recent and philosophically clever study of this manoeuvre, see
   Stanley Stewart, 'A Critique of Pure "Situating"', *New Literary History*
   25 (1994) pp. 1–19.
2. See Essick in the Bibliography.
3. E. D. Hirsch, Jr, has constructed a distinction between 'meaning'
   and 'significance' similar (but not strictly identical) to my point here.
   While Hirsch discriminates a stable, 'original' or even 'anachronistic'
   meaning from 'meaning-as-related-to-something-else' or 'meaningful-
   ness', I merely wish to indicate a difference between value-neutral
   meaning and the imputation of value to that meaning which makes it
   (or the object representing that meaning) significant. See Hirsch,
   Validity in Interpretation (New Haven: Yale University Press, 1967)
   pp. 62–7, 140–4; *The Aims of Interpretation* (Chicago: University of
   Chicago Press, 1976) pp. 79–81.
4. Both books are cited hereafter by page number in parentheses.
5. It might be argued that certain substitutes for 'invent' (e.g., 'think of',
   'dream up') use the preposition, but these supposed synonyms make
   my point. Their emphasis on invention as a mental act distinguishes
   them from material acts of construction implicit in Viscomi's sense of
   'invention'.
6. At this juncture, Eaves is referring to Essick (1980) p. 35, and Viscomi
   (1993), no page reference specified.
7. Note the allusion to Satan, 'The God of this World', in Blake's annotations to J. T. Thornton's *The Lord's Prayer* (E668).
8. Artistic materialism has no *necessary* connection with the unity
   of invention and execution, for this supposed unity could be based on

a transcendentalized notion of execution. My point is simply that Viscomi's sense of invention and execution is influenced by his materialist orientation.

9. See for example Terry Eagleton, *The Ideology of the Aesthetic* (Oxford: Basil Blackwell, 1990).

10. Both these graphic processes were used for the production of tonal gradations. Mezzotint was particularly suitable for the reproduction of oil paintings, while aquatint could imitate the qualities of water colour and wash drawings.

11. Mitchell, 'Representation', in *Critical Terms for Literary Study*, ed. Frank Lentricchia and Thomas McLaughlin (Chicago: University of Chicago Press, 1990) p. 21.

12. For just two of Blake's many statements on the superiority of line to other means of representing a visual image, see *A Descriptive Catalogue* (1809): 'neither character nor expression can exist without firm and determinate outline' (E549) and 'The great and golden rule of art, as well as of life, is this: That the more distinct, sharp, and wiry the bounding line, the more perfect the work of art ... ' (E550). As these statements indicate, the doctrine of line has for Blake epistemological and psychological, not merely stylistic, import. See also Blake's letter of 12 April 1827 to George Cumberland, quoted later in this essay.

13. See Essick (1972) pp. 63–5, 68–70; and Essick (1980) pp. 52, 72–4, 154–5.

14. See Essick (1983a) for reproductions of the late states of 'Joseph of Arimathea Among the Rocks of Albion,' 'Albion rose', and the large 'Job' and 'Ezekiel' plates.

15. For Blake's sense of gender implications in graphic processes, see Essick (1991). For a good overview of the development of tonal graphic techniques in eighteenth-century Britain, see Richard T. Godfrey, *Printmaking in Britain* (Oxford: Phaidon, 1978) pp. 41–65.

16. 'Morning Amusement' and 'Evening Amusement' after Watteau (1782), 'Zephyrus and Flora' and 'Calisto' after Stothard (1784), and 'The Idle Laundress' and 'Industrious Cottager' after Morland (1788). These and all other reproductive prints by Blake noted in this essay are in Essick (1983a).

17. For an overview of all these unusual techniques, see the introduction to Essick and Viscomi (1993) pp. 18–19. This volume also contains good reproductions of all the *Milton* plates discussed here.

18. Essick (1983b).

19. Bentley (1977) pp. 229–30, 259.

20. On Lady Hesketh's approval of Blake's engraving of a portrait of Cowper because it had been properly 'softened', see Bentley (1969) p. 113. See Blake's letter to his brother James of 30 January 1803: 'I am sorry that I did not know the methods of publishing years ago & this is one of the numerous benefits I have obtaind by coming here [to Felpham] for I should never have known the nature of Publication unless I had known H[ayley] & his connexions & his methods of managing' (E726).

21. Caroline Watson, her possible influence on Blake's gendering of line and tone in his writings on the arts, and her role in shaping misogynistic tendencies in Blake's late poetry are discussed in Essick (1991a).

22. For reproductions and information about the 25 large prints Haughton executed after Fuseli between 1803 and 1813, see D. H. Weinglass, *Prints and Engraved Illustrations By and After Henry Fuseli: A Catalogue Raisonné* (London: Scolar Press, 1994) listing on p. 381.

23. Butlin (1994) p. 119.

24. Barrell, rev. of Ronald Paulson, *Hogarth, London Review of Books* 16, no. 7 (7 April 1994) p. 18.

25. For aesthetic 'aura', a valorized supplement brought to works of art, see Walter Benjamin, *Illuminations*, ed. Hannah Arendt, trans. Harry Zohn (New York: Schocken Books, 1969) p. 221. Jacques Derrida's fullest exploration of his concept of the *supplement* within all semiotic acts appears in *Of Grammatology*, trans. Gayatri Chakravorty Spivak (Baltimore and London: Johns Hopkins University Press, 1974) esp. pp. 141–64. For a briefer explanation, see Derrida, 'Structure, Sign, and Play in the Discourse of the Human Sciences', in *Writing and Difference*, trans. Alan Bass (Chicago: University of Chicago Press, 1978) esp. pp. 289–90.

2

In the Caves of Heaven and Hell: Swedenborg and Printmaking in Blake's *Marriage*

Joseph Viscomi

It was granted me to see from beginning to end how the last judgment was accomplished; and also how the Babylon was destroyed (Rev. 18), how those who are understood by the dragon were cast into the abyss; and how the new heaven was formed; and a new church was instituted in the heavens, which is meant by the New Jerusalem. It was granted me to see all these things with my own eyes, in order that I might be able to testify to them. This last judgment was commenced in the beginning of the year 1757, and was fully accomplished at the end of that year.

Emanuel Swedenborg, *A Treatise Concerning the Last Judgment and the Destruction of Babylon* (1758; English translation, 1788)

As a new heaven is begun, and it is now thirty-three years since its advent: the Eternal Hell revives. And lo! Swedenborg is the Angel sitting at the tomb; his writings are the linen clothes folded up.

William Blake, *The Marriage of Heaven and Hell* (1790)

The present essay is the third of three on the evolution of William Blake's *The Marriage of Heaven and Hell* (Viscomi 1997, 1998). The first argues that the *Marriage* evolved through 4–6 distinct printmaking sessions in the following plate order: 21–4; 12–13; 1–3, 5–6, 11, 6–10; 14–15, ?4; 16–20; and 25–7. From the chronology of plate production, we can infer that Blake began the *Marriage* without a completed manuscript, a hypothesis supported by the technical exigencies of illuminated printing. We can also infer that the *Marriage*'s disjointed structure resulted at least in part from its production history. While literary models, such as Menippean satire or the Higher Criticism's theory that the Old Testament was a gathering of redacted fragments, may also have influenced the structure, they appear to have come into play only after plates 21–4 were written and executed. These four plates constitute an autonomous text expressing almost exclusively Blake's criticism of Emanuel Swedenborg. The text's autonomy and the fact that its four plates were quarters cut from the same sheet of copper (the first of seven sheets eventually cut) support the hypothesis that it was written as an independent, anti-Swedenborgian pamphlet, as does the fact that plates 21–4 were first printed in black ink on a conjoined sheet of paper folded in half.[1] But instead of being issued separately, this four-plate text became the intellectual core of what became the *Marriage*, helping to generate 20 of its subsequent 23 plates.

The second essay reads plates 21–4 closely as a pamphlet to demonstrate thematic, aesthetic and rhetoric coherence. It also argues that 'The Bible of Hell', announced on plate 24 as forthcoming and thus before the other *Marriage* plates were written and executed, probably referred to the 70 proverbs of hell, or to an anticipated work (or series of pamphlets) that included them. This essay also dates Blake's interest in and disillusionment with Swedenborg, placing the latter within the context of critiques most likely known to Blake, and it identifies the primary Swedenborgian texts and themes that Blake satirizes and the audiences he addresses. Blake's decision to combine two separate projects – the anti-Swedenborgian pamphlet and the devil's Bible – to form what became the *Marriage* required writing new plates to contextualize the proverbs and connect them to what had already been written. His decision provided new opportunities to satirize Swedenborg and what he came to represent to Blake, such as organized religion, oppression, imitation, usurpation and misreading.

The present essay focuses on Blake's allusions to printmaking, their connections to Swedenborg, and the way they evolved. The plates to be examined are 10, 11, 14, 15, 16, 17 and 20. Each presents a cave, a literary and mythological symbol that has various and often contradictory referents. While it can refer to the material universe, obscurity or illusion, to sex, birth or death, in *Marriage* it is first and foremost an emblem for hell, its traditionally depicted opening. In this inverted world, hell represents creative energy and originality, subjects Blake explores and displays. Their loci are illuminated plates – the impressions we read and the copper plates from which they were printed – and enlightened minds, each symbolized by the open cave. The latter's contrary – the mind closed to all save reason and the five senses – is symbolized by a cave closed save for narrow chinks.[2] As a symbol for the illuminated plate, the cave, along with other allusions to the mechanics and materiality of the written and printed word, sets into play the self-reflexivity usually associated with formalism. When read in light of Swedenborg, however, the symbol can also be seen as part of Blake's intense expressionism.

At first glance, caves seem present only on *Marriage* plates 14, 15 and 17, and these are exclusively verbal. On plate 14, a cave signifies limited perception: 'for man has closed himself up till he sees all things thro' narrow chinks of his cavern.' On plate 15, in 'The Printing house in Hell', a cave is transformed into a book. And on plate 17, a cave opens to the immense abyss that hosts the leviathan. These references seem unrelated and too infrequent to support the claim that the cave is a major symbol in *Marriage*. A closer look at *Marriage* plates as originally designed and executed, however, reveals that the cave was a visual motif on plates 10, 11, 15 and 20 (Figures 2.1–2.3 and 2.5). The motif is clearly present in *Marriage* copies G and I, but because these were the last two copies printed (*c*. 1818 and 1827 respectively), it is thought to have been added to the impressions (Bentley 1977, p. 290). In fact, the cave forms were drawn on the copper plates themselves, as part of the original plate designs; their absence in the seven copies printed and colour printed between 1790 and 1795 (i.e., copies A–F and H, though ink traces of the cave forms are present in copy B), is due to the way Blake inked and printed illuminated plates at this time. From 1789 to 1795, Blake wiped the ink from the plate's borders, thereby concealing the plate's rectangular shape and producing impressions that appeared more page-like than print-like.[3] But deleting the borders altered those images whose forms were partly delineated by the border line. In the case of *Songs of Innocence*, it removed the streams on plates 4, 7, 8, 10, 20, 21 and 23 by erasing the bottom line that defined them; in *Marriage*, wiping the borders removed the caves on plates 10, 11, 15 and 20, because it erased the outer defining lines. When Blake began printing plate borders, streams and caves reappeared.

Plates 21–4 are quarters from the same sheet of copper (sheet I); the second sheet quartered appears to have been *The Approach*

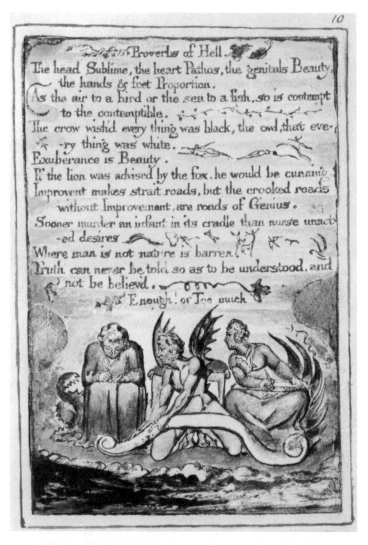

Figure 2.1 *The Marriage of Heaven and Hell* copy I, plate 10 (Reproduction by permission of the Syndics of the Fitzwilliam Museum, Cambridge).

of Doom (sheet II), which now yielded plates 12 and 13, after which there appears to have been a hiatus (see Viscomi 1997). Production resumed with three sheets of the same size (III, IV, V) quartered to provide plates for the proverbs (7–10) and their introductory

Figure 2.2   *The Marriage of Heaven and Hell* copy I, plate 11 (Reproduction by permission of the Syndics of the Fitzwilliam Museum, Cambridge).

material (5–7), the introductory material for *Marriage* (1–3), the ancient poets' episode (11), and two interrelated narratives explaining the origin, purpose and method of Blake's special mode of printmaking (14 and 15). The texts of these last two plates may have been written and executed with plates 1–3, 5–10, or they may have been written shortly afterward, along with plate 4. In either event, note that the cave motif appears with the plates cut from sheets III, IV and V, on plates 10, 11, 14 and 15, and that it continues in the next multi-plate textual unit written and executed. This unit consists of plates 16–20, cut from sheet VI (16–19) and II (20), and has caves on plates 17, 20, and, as will be argued, 16 in the form of the Giants' cell. Visually and/or verbally, then, caves are present on plates 10, 11, 14, 15, 16, 17 and 20, and they entered *Marriage* during the third stage of its production and continued through the next one or two stages.

Not coincidentally, plates 10 and 11 picture three figures on an island set within a cave open to the text (Figures 2.1 and 2.2).[4] The chronology of production, however, suggests that plate 11 was most likely composed and executed before plate 10 was executed. Because Blake worked from texts but not from models for his illuminated pages, the illustration on plate 10 was probably not sketched out when plate 11 was designed and executed (Viscomi 1993, chs. 1–4). One could argue that plate 11's text was written with the texts of plates 14 and 15, where Blake uses the cave metaphor to signify limited perception and etching a copper plate, and thus that the *design* of plate 11 was influenced by their verbal imagery. But the production record strongly suggests that textual units were executed soon after they were written, and that plates 14 and 15 were probably written after plate 11 was written and exe- cuted and were influenced by it (see below). Even if their texts did precede the design and execution of plate 11, such a sequence does not explain what the cave means on plate 11, or whether we view this scene from within a cavern, as Erdman proposes, or are outside looking into a cave (1974, p. 108). To answer these questions – and to ascertain whether the various caves cohere as a unified symbol – requires recognizing plate 11's allusions to Swedenborg and the internal–external dialectic they continue from plates 21–4 and 12–13.

'ANCIENT POETS ANIMATED ALL SENSIBLE OBJECTS'

The Memorable Fancy of plates 22–4 presents an angel and a devil debating the nature of God. To the devil, God is incarnate in 'great men' and the 'greatest man' is Christ, who was 'all virtue & acted from impulse; not from rule'. To the angel, Christ 'sanctioned ... the law of ten commandments', is an external and powerful lawmaker

and 'all other men [are] fools sinners & nothings'. Given the connotations of 'devil' and 'angel', the devil's victory challenges orthodox
morality and, more disturbingly, reveals how language affects perception and experience, a point Blake will make explicit on plate 3,
where he states that 'Good & Evil' are merely what 'the religious
call' those qualities 'springing' from 'reason' and 'energy'. In the
debate, these contraries correspond to 'rules' passively followed by
angels and 'impulses' associated with devils, yet acted upon by
Christ. The former, grounded in intellectual laziness, validates imitation and rationalizes restriction; the latter encourages originality
and freedom. That spontaneity requires more effort and courage
than imitation Blake will make explicit on plates 12–13, 11, 5–6 and
16–20; in the debate, it is implied by the angel's response to the
devil's argument: he 'embrac[ed] the flames of fire' to arise 'as
Elijah' and 'become a Devil' – and Blake's 'particular friend' (see
also Viscomi 1997, n. 24).

The angel's conversion signals the truth of the devil's position.
Plates 12–13, which show Blake learning from prophets and not,
like Swedenborg, from angels, offer another version of the same
debate and a similar conversion. Dining with the prophets Isaiah
and Ezekiel, Blake inquires about the nature of God. Again, the
issue is whether God is transcendent or incarnate, with Blake initially accusing the prophets of being like Swedenborg, 'assert[ing]
that God spoke to them', and thus potentially being a cause of
'imposition' (plate 13). Blake discredits Swedenborg's angelic
sources but believes the prophets' 'Poetic Genius', which they
identify as 'the first principle' of 'human perception', from which
'all Gods would at last be proved to originate' (plates 12–13) (see
also Viscomi 1997b). Whereas plates 21–4 differentiate Blake and
Swedenborg, associating the former with great writers and prophets and the latter with imitators and followers, plates 12–13 differentiate true prophets and followers, between those who continue
the Word and those who codify it. Blake 'confess[es his] own conviction', signalling, like the converted angel, the validity of the
prophets' positions.

Plate 11 echoes themes raised in these and the other plates composed before it. It states that the 'ancient Poets animated all sensible
objects with Gods or Geniuses … Till a system was formed, which
some took advantage of & enslav'd the vulgar by attempting to
realize or abstract the mental deities from their objects: thus began
Priesthood.' Plate 11 presents the origin of organized religion as yet

another version of the fall of man, a theme expressed also on plates 2 and 5–6. It also comments on plates 12–13 and 21–4 by explaining why belief in 'the jews code and worship[of] the jews god' – that is, accepting the angel's version of God – is the 'subjection' claimed by Isaiah and Ezekiel. The 'vulgar' were subjected or 'enslav'd' because they 'forgot that All deities reside in the human breast' (plate 11), forgot, that is, what the prophets knew, that 'all Gods would at last be proved to originate in ours & to be the tributaries of the Poetic Genius'. This belief in man's divinity, expressed earlier in Blake's *There in No Natural Religion* and *All Religions are One* (1788), echoes the devil's version of God as incarnate, a belief that Blake will restate on *Marriage* plate 16: 'God only Acts & Is. in existing beings or Men'.

While expressing the sentiments of the French Revolution, Blake's anti-clericalism follows closely Swedenborg's description of Babylon (signifying the degenerate Christian Church, but more specifically the Catholic Church), which itself follows closely Protestant ideology that casts priests as mediators, deliberately keeping the Word from the people. 'All they who make Dominion their end, and Religion as a Means conducive thereto, constitute Babylon in general.' In the 'Spiritual World', those from Babylon 'consult about various things relating to their Religion, especially how the Vulgar are to be kept in blind Obedience, and their domin-ion extended'. They keep 'the People in Ignorance' by extinguish-ing 'the Light of Heaven by forbidding the Reading of the Word'.[5] Blake gives this neat causality an infernal spin, accusing 'Priests' of *creating* the light of 'heaven' by their misreading – and forbidding the continuation of – the poetic/prophetic Word. Their attending to the external rather than the internal, to the letter rather than the spirit and source of the poetic/prophetic texts, created ritual, 'forms of worship' derived from 'poetic tales', a displacement they claimed 'that the Gods had ordered'. Foiling infinite perception, 'Priests' are to 'ancient Poets' what 'heaven' is to 'hell' (plate 6); they are derivative, an imitation, a falling away from the original – and provide the model for Urizen, 'the primeval Priest' (*Book of Urizen*, pl. 2: E70).

Swedenborg's description of Adam's Church and its fall also fig-ures into plate 11. According to Swedenborg, the 'four Churches' that preceded the New Church were those of Adam ('the Most Ancient'), Noah ('the Ancient'), the Jews ('the Israelitish') and the Apostles ('the Christian').[6] Of these, the Most Ancient was closest to

God. Its members understood the 'science of correspondences', the system of analogies that links every perceived thing and event to its spiritual counterpart and cause. Moreover, they

> had no other than internal worship, such as there is in heaven; for with them heaven so communicated with man that they made one. This communication was the perception of which so much has been said above … perceiving in all objects of sense something Divine and heavenly. … Thus it was with the man of the Most Ancient church; whatever he saw with his eyes was to him heavenly; and thus with him each and all things were as if alive. From this it is evident what the nature of his Divine worship was; that it was internal, and in no respect external.[7]

It did not remain authentic, however. According to Swedenborg, 'the representative rites of the [Most Ancient] church' were slowly 'converted into things idolatrous', and 'knowledge [of correspondence] … was gradually lost, and among the Israelitish and Jewish people entirely forgotten'.[8] 'Images representative of spiritual truths' 'became objects of worship' and 'adored as deities'.[9] The Christian Church provides only a partial correction, for it professes one God while actually praying to a 'Trinity of Divine Persons', whom Blake identifies as 'the Father [as] Destiny, the Son, a Ratio of the five senses. & the Holy-ghost, Vacuum' (plate 6).[10]

These are the 'idols' of 'priesthood', but the New Church's 'One God' is also an idol, an abstraction unaware of its origin in the 'Poetic Genius', the origin of 'all Gods'. Swedenborg's 'representative rites' did not degenerate into idolatry, but were themselves idolatrous, for as derivations of 'poetic tales', they represent the earliest misreadings of works of the imagination and the beginning of their repression. Blake examines the same history as Swedenborg, and he once again implies that Swedenborg has not gone deep enough and is part of what he criticizes, a priest complicit in the repression of poets.[11] Blake also implies that he, not Swedenborg, will restore our original, Adamic state of being.

The conflict between ancient poets and priests parallels that between devil and angel, as well as that between Blake and Swedenborg, with the latter fixated on external forms, looking outward for answers, and the former looking to the Poetic Genius within (a conflict given its most demanding expression in *Jerusalem*). In light of Blake's ongoing debate with Swedenborg, plate 11's cave appears anti-Platonic, with reality residing in and within the cave rather than outside and transcendent. The living island's deities reside in the 'human breast' and are 'mental', representing a mode of perceiving and not external objects perceived.[12] As such, a cave opening to reveal an island recalls the devil's message: 'How do you know but ev'ry Bird that cuts the airy way, / Is an immense world of delight clos'd by your senses five?'[13] In peering into the cave, readers peer into the mind of the ancient poets, glimpsing their own potential in this 'immense world of delight' (plate 7). Using hell's emblem to symbolize the creative mind reinforces the link between hell and 'Genius' made on plate 6 and, as we shall see, points to the illuminated book as the embodiment of that 'Genius'. Blake's depicting on copper the 'immense world' of the cave is his 'displaying the infinite which was hid' (plate 14), a prophetic task expressed concisely in *Jerusalem*:

> ... I rest not from my great task!
> To open the Eternal Worlds, to open the immortal Eyes
> Of Man inwards into the Worlds of Thought: into Eternity
> Ever expanding in the Bosom of God. the Human Imagination.
> (5: 17–20)

One might wish to agree with Erdman that the design places the viewer inside a cave and represents limited perception, illustrating either the 'clos'd' rather than the 'immense' part of the devil's message, or that 'man has closed himself up, till he sees all things thro' narrow chinks of his cavern' (plate 14). Caverned Man is Man as rock, with the senses figured as crevices or chinks through which he experiences the external world. As noted, however, plates 14 and 15 were executed after plate 11, though it is not clear from the production record whether their texts were written afterwards as well. The caves, trip to hell, and images of writing and etching on plates 11, 6–7 and 10 all figure prominently in the texts of plates 14 and 15 and may have given rise to them. Be that as it may, plate 11's design pictures a cavern wide open, not a narrow chink, and while the view is limited by our being outside the opening – and in a different state of mind from the one represented – the mode of perception depicted within is more likely meant as limited perception's contrary. The caves in *Marriage* come in two states, open and closed, representing either limited or, as on plate 11 and those plates dealing with creativity and illuminated printing (plates 10, 15 and 20; see below), illimitable perception.

Blake's identifying creativity with hell, and hell with open minds, inverts Swedenborg's oft-used metaphors of open and closed, light and dark. Indeed, Blake seems deliberately to invert Swedenborg's key terms about open minds: 'in Proportion as the Interiors of the Mind are open, in the same Proportion Man looks toward Heaven, but in Proportion as the Interiors are shut and the Exteriors open, in the same Proportion he looks toward Hell'.[14] In *Marriage*, the mind looking towards or from 'Heaven' as defined by the 'religious' is passive, imitative and hence closed, whereas the mind looking toward or from 'Hell' as defined by Blake is active, original and open. The one is an ascent into constriction, the other a descent into expansion.

'... AT LIBERTY WHEN OF DEVILS AND HELL'

Blake's recreational trip to hell to retrieve its proverbs not only makes the connection between creativity and hell explicit, but also reveals the angels' and priests' deepest fears. 'To Angels', the 'fires of hell' and the 'enjoyments of Genius' – that is, desire and energy – 'look like torment and insanity' (plate 6). These, Blake's first recorded uses of the words 'insanity' and 'torment', allude possibly to Swedenborg's statement that 'evils cannot otherwise be restrained and subdued' without 'torments' and 'fear of punishment', without which the 'evil would burst forth into madness and the whole world would be dispersed, as a kingdom on earth where there is no law and no punishment'.[15] By entering hell, Blake shows himself as *not* 'restrain[ing] desire' (plate 5) or 'resist[ing] his genius' (plate 13), though the visit's origin may lie in his accusing Swedenborg of never having made such a visit, of his not having 'conversed ... with Devils' (plate 22). Swedenborg's failure implied his being poorly informed and, more subtly, uninspired: a criticism now reinforced. He shares the angels' fear of hell fire, of 'Eternal Hell', whose person-ification as a naked woman lustfully and shamelessly enwrapped in flames (plate 3) links creative fires to the sensual and physical.

The physical presence of the open caves on plates 10, 15 and 20 also suggests that creativity has a material component, as does Blake's coming 'home, on the abyss of the five senses' (plate 6). At first, Blake sounds Swedenborgian, likening the body to an 'abyss', but in light of the satire, the term is positive, a synonym for hell.[16] Moreover, Blake uses the preposition 'on' instead of 'to', suggesting that the 'abyss' is a vehicle of transport and not the thing to which he returns. By coming home 'on' the body, not 'to', and by identifying the body in this way. Blake conflates the sensually material with the creative. His return 'home' actually criticizes Swedenborg. For example, Swedenborg states, 'On hearing and understanding all of these Things, my Heart exulted within me, and I went Home with Joy, and there returned to the Body, from being in the Spirit, and wrote the Things which I have seen and heard'.[17] Blake, on the other hand, does not separate vision and body; he collected/wrote the proverbs while in 'hell' and returned home with them. Instead of referring to consciousness, to a return to sensation after being asleep, 'home' more likely refers to everyday life, akin to leaving the printing studio to take out the rubbish – that is, to a cessation in the overtly artistic process (see note 25). In the immediate context of travelling, 'home' suggests England, 'where a flat sided steep frowns over the present world'. That a 'Devil' writes on the 'sides of the rock' suggests that Hell and Earth are not mutually exclusive and that Blake returns without completely leaving hell. The presence of earthly things ('Men' and 'libraries') in the sixth chamber of Hell's 'Printing house' suggests the same (see below).

Blake became increasingly sceptical about vision requiring a separation between body and spirit. To Swedenborg's claim that 'Man, in whom the spiritual Degree is open, comes into that Wisdom when he dies, and may also come into it by laying asleep the Sensations of the Body, and by Influx from above at the same Time into the Spirituals of his Mind', Blake says, 'this is while in the Body. This is to be understood as unusual in our time but common in ancient' (E606). At first, Blake tried to defend Swedenborg by accusing his followers of 'perversely understand[ing] him. as if man while in the body was only conversant with natural Substances. because themselves are mercenary & worldly & have no idea of any but worldly gain' (E606). Indeed, Blake's belief that 'Man has no body distinct from his Soul' (plate 4) made having visions outside the body 'in this age' (plate 4) impossible.[18] Blake's entering hell is entering the creative state, which for an artist must manifest itself materially, in his physical body and artwork. The open, visionary mind, in other words, is realizable in body and, as visionary art, materially realizable. This view of the oneness of spirit and body underlies Blake's insights about invention and execution (E637, 643, 657) and his idea of himself as a visionary artist. In this sense, art is vision's physical form, the marriage of heaven and hell.

The ancient poets and the prophets Isaiah and Ezekiel exemplify the visionary mind. The latter identify themselves as 'poets', affirm the Poetic Genius as an internal voice and the voice of God, refute external instruction, and make no distinction between vision and writing, or between spirit and sensual body. Isaiah says: 'I saw no God. nor heard any. in a finite organical perception: but my senses discover'd the infinite in every thing, and as I was then perswaded. & remain confirm'd; that the voice of honest indignation is the voice of God. I cared not for consequences but wrote' (plate 12). Hearing the inner voice and writing appear to be simultaneous rather than sequential acts. That, in any event, is how Blake pictures himself at work on plate 10, writing from dictation, from 'the voice of the devil' (Figure 2.1).[19]

The devil dictating the 'Proverbs of Hell' – which Blake claimed 'shew the nature of Infernal wisdom better than any description of buildings or garments' (plate 6) – is naked (as is that other paragon of inspiration, the child dictating to the Piper in the 'Introduction' to *Songs of Innocence*). Presumably, Blake means to present the Wisdom of Devils as the 'naked truth', akin to the resurrected (and linen-free and hence) naked Christ (plate 3) and Blake-as-Christ (plate 21 [see note 21]), and to contrast it with Swedenborg's *Wisdom of Angels*.[20] The dictating devil kneels between two scribes. Erdman identifies the one on the devil's left as Blake, because he and the devil are both in profile (1974, p. 107). It seems more likely that Blake is the one recording what he *hears*. In terms of *Marriage*'s composing process, Blake had heard the devil speak when witnessing him and the angel debate (plates 22–4), saw it inscribed in rock (plates 6–7), and now pictures himself creatively working from that voice. (These instances of devils speaking all precede the writing and execution of 'The Voice of the Devil' (plate 4), which, as it were, gives the devil his due.) Blake depicts himself as writing from dictation, indifferent to consequences, which not only shows him to be of the devil's party, like Milton and the prophet Elijah, who heard the lord's voice in a cave (I Kings 19: 13), but also likens him to the prophets Isaiah and Ezekiel (plates 12–13).

The illustration's ironic comment on originality also associates the devil with Poetic Genius. While Blake appears to be illustrating the line about his recording the devil's proverbs (plate 6), the proverbs are clearly his own creations, depicted as originating from an inspiriting, diabolical voice. That the voice/source is internal is implied by the manner in which Blake works, attending

exclusively to what he writes (or draws) and to no external referents, models or figures.[21] The other figure also ignores the devil, but
for very different reasons: he strains to see the first scribe's work,
altogether oblivious of its source (Figure 2.2). The former, working
from the origin, is creative, whereas the latter, imitating the form or
letter of an inspired text, exemplifies the priests' misreading and
appropriation of poets – the heart of Blake's critique of Swedenborg.

Writing from the Poetic Genius without fear of consequences,
Blake not only behaves like the prophets but also like Christ, acting
'from impulses; not from rules'. His art, the site of originality and
inspiration and not imitation, contrasts starkly with the 'systematic
reasoning' of angels (plate 21) and priestly rituals and laws. By
placing poets, prophets, Christ and now himself in the devil's
party, Blake clarifies the conflict between angels and devils as one
between Religion and Art. Picturing himself writing, Blake mirrors
the creative process embodied in the illuminated plate and book.
This connection between mind – both the artist's and the reader's –
and plate/book becomes explicit when caves reappear verbally and
visually on plates 14, 15 and 20 to represent perception, illuminated
plate and illuminated printing. And in all these cases, states of open
and closed represent Blake's hell and heaven, and reverse what
Swedenborg identifies as open sight and closed sight.

'MELTING APPARENT SURFACES AWAY' OR 'NARROW CHINKS OF HIS CAVERN'?

The texts of plates 14 and 15, which appear to have been executed
together, may also have been the first ones that Blake *wrote* after
writing and picturing writing, trips to hell, infernal messages and
ancient poets (plates 6–7, 10, 11), in which case they not only extend
or develop the preceding metaphors of book and perception but
were possibly generated by them. If invented in response to previously executed plates, as many of the latter textual units and
designs assuredly were, then they exemplify the fluidity and flexibility of Blake's composing process, which enabled execution to
generate invention quite literally, and enabled Blake to print plates
and sections of books without completing the manuscript. Even if
the texts of plates 14 and 15 were executed with the other plates
from sheets III, IV, V, they appear to have been written to develop
themes previously executed and to express Blake's awareness of his

mode of production. Blake states that he will print 'in the infernal method, by corrosives ... melting apparent surfaces away' (plate 14), which is relief-etching poetically described. A copper plate's pre-etched and etched surfaces are identified as 'the rock & the cave' (plate 15), with 'rock' recalling the medium upon which the 'mighty Devil' inscribes – graves open – (plate 6) and 'the cave' recalling the devil's cave in which Blake writes his book (plate 10), as well as the mind of the ancient poets (plate 11).

By printing 'in the infernal method', Blake intends to display 'the infinite which was hid' and 'expunge ... the notion that man has a body distinct from his soul', a notion responsible for 'man [having] closed himself up till he sees all things thro' narrow chinks of his cavern' (plate 14). By stating that 'man has closed himself up', Blake implicates man – individual and species – in his own imprisonment. Blake has it both ways: external forces restrain individuals, and individuals partake in their own restraint. Individuals have the power to open their 'doors of perception' and yet need assistance to open them – or at least to see that they are closed. Their need defines the artist's role, which is, like that of the devil and prophets – and that espoused by Swedenborg – to open the mind. Blake's means for opening the mind, the illuminated book, is also the paradigm for the open mind. Just as the illuminated plate displays the 'infinite' when its 'apparent surfaces' are melted away, so too perception: 'if the doors of perception were cleansed every thing would appear to man as it is: Infinite' (plate 14). The 'infernal method', or its manifestation, the illuminated book, here the symbol of original art, is the cleansing agent. The relation between illuminated plate and mind is thus causal as well as analogous, with the former a key to opening the latter.

Blake's metaphor for perception was well chosen. A door, which signals, like a cave, an entrance or passageway to a hidden world and can be open or closed, was also used by Swedenborg for the same purpose:

Who is not able to see that the Lord cannot enter so long as the devil is there? And he is there so long as man keeps the door closed, ... That the Lord enters when by means of man this door is opened the Lord teaches in the Apocalypse: – 'Behold, I stand at the door and knock: if any man hear My voice, and open the door, I will come in to him, and will sup with him, and he with Me'. (Revelation 3: 20).[22]

For Blake, the devil – in the form of Blake and the 'infernal method' – opens the door, and the open door reveals the devil, for it opens to hell, to desire, energy and creativity, and therein lies Christ. One does not open the door to let Christ in; one opens the door to find Christ there: 'God only Acts & Is. in existing beings or Men' (plate 16).

The causal relation between illuminated plate and reader appears also to allude to Swedenborg. As prophet/poet/printer, Blake intends to open the doors of perception – transform them into the gates of hell – through the hellish light of illuminated printing. Ironically, by aiding and abetting the reader's entrance to hell, Blake functions like Swedenborg's God: 'the internal man is not opened except by Divine Truth proceeding from the Lord, because that is the light of heaven and the life of heaven.'[23] In Blake's incarnational aesthetic, the 'Lord' or Christ symbolizes Imagination and is manifest in Blake as Blake is manifest in his book; reading/entering the illuminated book (and by extension all original, visionary works of imagination) is to participate in the body of Christ. In other words, visionary art alters perception and holds open the possibility of conversion and salvation, the subjects expressed by the illustration on plate 14.

With arms outstretched (like those of the sky-God at the bottom of plate 11), a female figure hovers over a naked and an apparently dead male body in flames. The illustration may symbolize the mistaken notion of soul separate from body, or the 'cherub with his flaming sword' guarding the 'tree of life' (plate 14; see Genesis 3: 24), in which case the supine body represents either a dormant Eden or tree of life. The image's overt sexuality, though, and its place in the chronology of production suggests that the body is the one shown on plate 21 as being resurrected. Presumably, by this time in the composition of *Marriage*, Blake knows that he will end with plates 21–4, enabling him to connect the two male figures causally. The body's transformation from supine to erect is analogous to that of the plate's, from a flat, unetched surface to a design cast in relief. In this analogy, the illustration alludes to both the 'infernal method' and to the 'hovering' devil writing on rock with 'corroding fires' (plates 6–7), with the body symbolizing a copper plate, the flames the acid ('corroding fires'), and, in place of the abstract sky-god, the hovering figure the printmaker. Hovering over the entire creation are both Blake and his reader.

Swedenborg's ideas about the Most Ancient Church and about law and restraint lying behind plates 3, 11 and 5–6 resurface on plate 14. For Swedenborg, 'Adam and his Wife…meant the most ancient Church', and 'the Garden of Eden…meant the Wisdom of the Men of that Church', and 'the Tree of Life [meant] the Lord in Man, and Man in the Lord'.[24] For Blake, Adam's return to Paradise was the restoration of the ancient poets, which required removing the 'cherub with his flaming sword…guard[ing] the tree of life'.[25] Blake again turns the tables. An angel, clearly a member of Swedenborg's camp, *prevents* the apocalypse and must, like preconceptions and the copper plate's surface, be removed, at which point 'the whole creation will be consumed and appear infinite. and holy whereas it now appears finite & corrupt' (plate 14). But Blake also states that this transformation 'will come to pass by an improvement of sensual enjoyment'. By giving two causes for altering perception, Blake appears to equate removing the angel/plate surface with improving sensual desire. Both actions are to be realized through illuminated printing.

As mentioned, Blake returns from hell 'on' and not 'to' the body, and he identifies the body as an 'abyss' in and on which the 'enjoyments of genius' take place, thereby associating hell with both the creative mind and the sensual body. Blake's celebration of the senses throughout the *Marriage* is, no doubt, directed at Swedenborg, who consistently associates the sensual with evil.

It is unlawful to inquire into the mysteries of faith by means of things of sense and knowledge, by which means his celestial quality is destroyed. A desire to investigate the mysteries of faith by means of things sensuous and known, was not only the cause of the fall or decline of the Most Ancient Church,…but it is the cause of the fall…of every church; for hence come not merely false opinions, but evils of life also.[26]

Blake argues that the contrary is the means of returning 'home', that only through an 'improvement of sensual enjoyment' does one re-enter Eden or the 'Most Ancient Church' of Adam.

'But first', before such an improvement can take place, 'the notion that man has a body distinct from his soul is to be expunged' (plate 14). The relation between perception or preconception ('notion') and experience ('sensual enjoyment') recalls the angels' inability to enter the creative fires of hell, and anticipates the Giants, harper, and leviathan episodes on plates 16–20. Logically, if the notion that body and soul are distinct obstructs perception and experience, then it

must be removed. But note that Blake proposes to cleanse the mind
of this restricting and self-fulfilling perceptual bias by *example* and
not argument. He says 'this I shall do by printing in the infernal
method, by corrosives... melting apparent surfaces away, and displaying the infinite which was hid.' He may be implying that he
will print illuminated texts specifically attacking this notion, but
here he explicitly proposes to rectify the problem by working in a
printing process whose material product exemplifies or manifests
the infinite Imagination. In this process, the relation between 'surface' and 'infinite' is not analogous to that between body and soul,
as though melting or removing the body reveals essence. That position is orthodox and Swedenborg's. The key word is 'apparent' and
not surface; remove what *appears* to be true to see what is really
true. If cleansed perception is exemplified by relief-etching,
wherein the 'infinite' revealed after etching is the design cast in
relief and embodied in paper, then, as is suggested by the caves on
plates 10 and 11, the visionary mind is materially manifest. In addition to providing an analogy for the open mind and the means to
open it, the illuminated plate manifests the apocalypse: the metal
removed, consumed, expunged, cleansed and melted away displays the 'whole creation' after it is 'consumed in fire'. Like the
devil's 'Bird', the small illuminated plate is an immense and Edenic
world of delight.

Plate 14 is about removing restraint, in the form of angelic
guards, misleading appearances, metal surfaces and false notions.
Removing the angel is removing law, usurper, governor, oppressor
and restrainer; it is to remove Edom's 'yoke' (plate 3, Genesis
27: 40) and is synonymous with Adam's return and creation's consummation. The word 'consumed' (Blake's first recorded use of the
word) appears to pun on Swedenborg's 'consummation', which
describes the end or last judgment of a Church.[27] In *Marriage*, being
'consumed' in fire represents creativity (e.g., Blake's stroll through
hell), or it represents conversion and resurrection (e.g., the angel's
embracing 'the flame of fire' and arising 'as Elijah'). Swedenborg
believed that a Church comes to its last judgment or consummation
'by various Causes, particularly by such as make what is false to
appear like what is true'.[28] True enough, but the causes that make
the false appear true, Blake asserts, are Church and State, which
pass off 'passivity' and 'reason' as good and creativity and 'energy'
as 'evil'. Hence, the true and infinite world 'now appears finite &
corrupt'.

Plate 14 enriches through graphic allusions the satire on Swedenborg begun on plates 21–4. The announcement, for example, that Blake will print to change the world not only anticipates 'The Bible of Hell' but also echoes Swedenborg:

> Since the Lord cannot manifest Himself in Person … and yet has foretold that He would come and establish a New Church, which is the New Jerusalem, it follows that this will be effected by means of a man, who is able not only to receive the doctrines of that church into his understanding, but also to publish them by the press.[29]

Again, Blake provides the contrary, identifying his press with the devil's and arguing that the Lord manifests Himself in true artists and works of art. Blake's describing the stages of infernal printing also satirizes Swedenborg, who acknowledges that 'infernal spirits' have their 'atrocious arts', the third kind of which 'relates to … communication and influx of thoughts and affections, by conversions, by inspections … ' Swedenborg, however, refuses to 'describe them specifically … because they are too bad to be told'.[30] Blake describes them on plate 15 in detail. They are dragons, vipers, eagles and lions, a motley crew perhaps meant to evoke Joseph Johnson's printing house in St Paul's Churchyard and his circle of friends. They more obviously recall the animated island of plate 11, suggesting that they are the presiding deities assigned by the poet, which in turn reinforces Blake's connection to the ancient poets and his role in returning Adam to Eden (Eaves et al. 1993, p. 215).

'DRAGONS … HOLLOWING THE CAVE'

Plate 15 continues the news from hell, picturing the 'infernal method' as eagle and viper opening a cave (Figure 2.3). That hell's symbol represents the illuminated plate continues the theme of the whole manifest in the part. It also puns on engraving itself, whose inner word 'grave' connotes an opening in the earth. Blake's method for making or hollowing caves in rock has five stages, which correspond to preparing copper plates, writing and drawing, etching, inking and printing. These stages are depicted as chambers in the printing house. Through them passes 'the rock & the cave', which, like the caverned man, will be transformed from stony to

Figure 2.3 *The Marriage of Heaven and Hell* copy I, plate 15 (Reproduction by permission of the Syndics of the Fitzwilliam Museum, Cambridge).

infinite landscape, with 'immense cliffs' and valleys, the topographical metaphors for the raised and shallow portions of the relief-etched plate.

In the first chamber is 'a Dragon-Man, clearing away the rubbish from a caves mouth; within, a number of Dragons were hollowing the cave'. The dragon's activity is not mere house-cleaning, for it refers to preparing the plate for etching by removing the greasy film from its surface so that etching ground will adhere firmly. Symbolically, clearing reveals hell's entrance, making possible all subsequent stages and events. Like cleansing 'doors of perception', melting apparent surfaces away, and removing the cherub from Eden's gates, clearing rubbish is one of infinite perception's prerequisite acts.

The 'dragon-man' revives the debate between faith in Christ (or 'firm perswasion' in 'poetic genius') and faith in the decalogue, first expressed on plates 21–4 and then on plates 12–13. Swedenborg identifies those who believe in Christ but reject the law as the 'dragons' mentioned in the Bible.

> It is said that the dragon has much power, because the salvation of man by faith alone, without the works of the law – which faith is meant by the dragon – captivates the minds of men, and then confirmations produce conviction. It captivates, because when a man hears that the damnation of the law is taken away, and that the Lord's merit is imputed to him through faith alone therein, he can indulge in the pleasures of mind and body without any fear of hell.[31]

Exactly. Fear of 'torment' closes 'immense worlds of delight', as the angel's response to hell evinces (plate 6); conversely, as evinced by Blake's infernal stroll, 'Hell' unfeared is mental and sensual pleasure. By placing the 'dragon' (his first recorded use of the word) inside the first and fundamental chamber, Blake reasserts his faith in an impulsive, rule-breaking, incarnational Christ (22–3).

Blake's dragon, representing unrestrained creative energy feared by Church and State, is pictured as a 'flying' or 'winged serpent', the traditional description of dragons. It is formed by a viper in the talons of an eagle (Figure 2.3) and designed apparently to echo the devil and his serpentine scroll (plate 10). Blake's depiction may allude to Swedenborg as well: 'Serpents in general signify the sensual things of man, and thence sensual men; and therefore the dragon which is a flying serpent signifies the sensual man, who though sensual yet flies towards heaven, in that he speaks and thinks from the Word, or from doctrine derived from the Word'.[32] The viper and eagle inhabit the second and third chambers, which in the technical analogy represent writing and etching. The former is the calligraphic line bending 'round the rock & the cave', and the latter 'caused the inside of the cave to be infinite' and 'built palaces in the immense cliffs'. As composite being, viper/eagle is the devil's 'Bird that cuts the airy way', 'an immense world of delight' (plate 7) that is the illuminated plate. And, as a conflation of writing and etching, it conflates invention and execution. As such, it represents the writing devil's mode of production, in which text was written *'with* corroding fires' (plates 6–7), as opposed to being written and then etched to make it printable. The devil's writing implement is pictured at the bottom of plate 6 as a lightening bolt inscribing an 'H' (the first letter of 'How') on the same plane as Blake's text. As a writing instrument, the bolt is like Job's 'iron pen' (19: 24). More interesting, Swedenborg states that in ancient Hebrew 'the H, which was added to the Names of Abram and Sarai, signified Infinite and Eternal'.[33] As a conflation of writing and etching, the devil's message – the proverbial writing on the wall – alludes to and diabolically inverts the 'stony law' of the 'ten commandments' (plates 27 and 23), 'written with the finger of God' (Exodus 31: 18).[34]

Blake's fourth and fifth chambers refer to inking and printing, which is the job of the pressmen, 'who apply ink upon [the type] and take off the impression'.[35] After the marriage of plate and paper, the creative process ends anticlimactically, in the form of a book closed, unread and shelved with many of its own kind: 'the metals…cast…into the expanse' in the 'fifth chamber' were 'reciev'd by Men who occupied the sixth chamber, and took the forms of books & were arranged in libraries'. The sixth chamber is outside of hell proper but is part of the creative process; its being occupied by readers suggests that they have a role in the production and completion of a work of art. As is demonstrated by the devil's presence on earth and Blake's in hell, the creative and everyday interact. Indeed, the causal relation between plate and reader is inherently interactive. Furthermore, the illuminated book, in embodying a fabulous but hidden journey, exemplifies the devil's message about seemingly common objects possibly being 'immense worlds of delight'. Its journey through hell to the surface recalls the journey of the 'just man' from garden into exile (plate 2). It more clearly recalls the *Marriage* title page (Figure 2.6), where enormous energy and desire lie hidden just below the surface, in a cavelike space framed by flames and clouds, the elements of Rintrah and relief-etching.[36] The surface is delineated by a thin line, the erasure or melting of which would reveal the 'infinite which was hid' (plate 14). The surface is a small and bland place, the 'earth' where the book is 'perceived by the minds of men, & read by them' (plate 7). The question is whether one will read it as angel or devil, in Swedenborg's 'internal sense' or Blake's 'infernal sense'.

Writing is a theme on plates 21–4, 12–13, 3, 5–7 and 11, and it is implied by the list of proverbs on plates 7–10. But only on plate 10 is it the subject of an illustration, and only on plates 14 and 15 is the purpose and technique of its dissemination explained. In these plates, Blake becomes overtly self-referential and proclaims mythical significance for his new technique and for his daily life as a printmaker. By modelling his own printing house on the one in hell, earlier associated with the sensual body and creative mind, Blake again alludes to the inseparability of execution and invention. In taking us into and through hell's 'Printing house', Blake takes us deeper into the creative process in which he and readers are engaged, transforming the 'now' of the writing devil's audience (plate 7) into the 'now' of Edom and Adam and the ancient poets (plates 3, 11), a reality always present but hidden in the 'now' of the 'just man''s exile and the dominion of the 'finite and corrupt' (plates 2 and 14). The mythopoeic and creative processes of ancient and visionary poets are manifest in and surging through the illuminated plate and the mind of its maker and reader. Indeed, plates 14 and 15 force readers to rethink the meaning of the caves encountered earlier, on plates 10 and 11, which foregrounds the figurative process, revealing the reader's role in producing the work of imagination.

'... WITH ALL THE FURY OF A SPIRITUAL EXISTENCE'

Images of hell and caves, begun on plates 6, 11 and 10, continue on plates 14 and 15; all five plates appear to have been written and executed before plates 16–20, which continue the cave imagery, were written or executed. On plate 16, the 'Giants who formed this world into its sensual existence' are identified as 'the causes of its life & the sources of all activity'. They are further identified as 'energy', 'portions of being', 'portions of existence', 'producers' and the 'prolific'. As the 'source' and 'cause' of life and its 'sensual existence', the Giants are a version of the prophets and ancient poets. Like them, their vision of and place in the world have been usurped. But unlike them, they are pictured as prisoners, huddled together inside a cave-like cell (Figure 2.4). They are shown as they

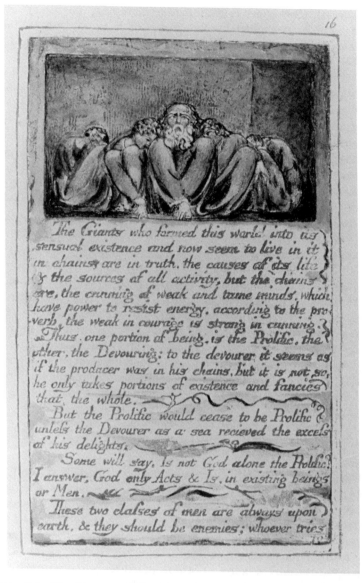

Figure 2.4 *The Marriage of Heaven and Hell* copy I, plate 16 (Reproduction by permission of the Syndics of the Fitzwilliam Museum, Cambridge).

appear to non-producers, to 'Those who restrain desire' (plate 5), just as the devil's fall is pictured as it 'appeared to Reason' (plate 5) and as illuminated printing is depicted as it appears to angels (plate 20, see below).[37] Blake calls the non-producers 'devourers', one of the 'two classes of men ... always upon earth' and whose reconciliation would 'destroy existence'. Devourers have 'weak and tame minds', the 'power to resist energy', a lack of 'courage', and an abundance of 'cunning'. The 'Giants ... now seem to live' in the devourers' 'chains', but 'it is not so', for devourers, like Swedenborg and others denying the devil's voice, 'only take portions of existence and fanc[y] that the whole'. The portion chained, in other words, is the portion they exclude and restrain in themselves and wish to restrain in others. Hence, on one level, the prisoners represent devourers' disdain for the prolific, creative mind, and, on another level, they represent the individual's repression of his or her own desires and energies. Plate 16 repeats the basic design of plate 11, with the cave at the top of the plate, only here readers peer inside the ancient poets' contrary, the cave/mind of the devourer. The very static, unanimated prisoners reminiscent of the cannibalizing Ugolino and his sons represent not only what devourers do to themselves and wish to do to others, but also what they look like to the prolific: the caverned man in need of emancipation.

Plates 10, 15 and 20 are also similarly designed, with the cave in the plate's bottom half. Indeed, plate 20 repeats the form of the two earlier caves overtly, a repetition again focusing readers' attention on what happens inside the cave and signalling that this cave also refers somehow to illuminated printing. The leviathan is the viper grown ever more dragon-like, the devil's scroll more fully animated. It is the 'infernal method' causing the 'inside of the cave to be infinite' (plates 14 and 15). It is also the serpent of Revelation 12: 9: 'And the great dragon was cast out, that old Serpent, called the Devil, and Satan ... was cast out into the earth, and his angels were cast out with him'. Swedenborg notes the same: 'Those who are understood by the dragon were cast into the abyss',[38] which has creative connotations from the devil's perspective, since the illuminated plate is itself a cast and was 'cast', like the devil, 'into the expanse' (plate 15), described here as the 'infinite Abyss'. This Abyss is 'fiery as the smoke of a burning city', where 'a cloud and fire burst and rolled thro ... blackning all beneath, so that the nether deep grew black as a sea & rolled with a terrible noise ... [of] a black tempest' (plate 18). The apocalyptic imagery recalls that of the title-plate and echoes Swedenborg's description of Babylon's destruction. 'Some endeavor[ed] to escape by Flight, some hiding themselves in Caves, some into the Cells and Vaults where their Treasures were deposited'. But after an earthquake, 'ebullition' from below, and 'strong wind from the East', everyone in the 'southern quarter' was

> cast into a Sea of black Water … afterward, there arose a Smoke from that whole Region, as from a great Fire, and at last a thick Dust … [which] signifies Damnation. At length there was seen as it were Something black flying over the whole Tract, which had the Appearance of a Dragon, a sign that the whole of that Great City, and the whole of that Tract, was made a Desert. The reason of such appearances was, because by dragons are signified the falses of that religion, and by the place of their abode is signified a desert after its overthrow, as in Jer. IX, etc.[39]

The angel, with whom Blake 'hung over this immensity' and 'beheld the infinite Abyss', perceived the leviathan as hell, the revolutionary power of artistic creation – here manifest in illuminated printing – and good reason for him to flee the scene. Overlooking the leviathan and cave, Blake sits in the roots of an oak (Figure 2.5). He hovers like the devil 'folded in black clouds' before England's cliffs (plate 6), while the illustration's tri-part structure – Blake–leviathan–cave – associates it with the other tri-part illustrations: devil–scroll–cave, woman–flames–body, and eagle–viper–cave of plates 10, 14 and 15.

The leviathan's 'infinite Abyss' was hidden by 'a church' and entered by way of a 'cavern' (plate 18), and no doubt to Blake it was 'an immense world of delight'. To the angel, however, the Abyss and everything inside it were monstrous. After removing himself from the scene, as the cherub must before Eden (plate 14), the truth of place and moment – and Blake's perception of illuminated printing – revealed itself. Blake sits 'on a pleasant bank beside a river by moonlight hearing a harper' sing about how the 'man who never alters his opinion … breeds reptiles of the mind' (plate 19; see also Revelation 15: 2). For the angel to see a harper, the poet's traditional symbol, as a leviathan plays ironically on what Swedenborg states should be the case. The outward appearance of devils 'is a fallacy; for as soon as any ray of light from heaven is let in their human forms are turned into monstrous forms, such as they are in themselves … For in

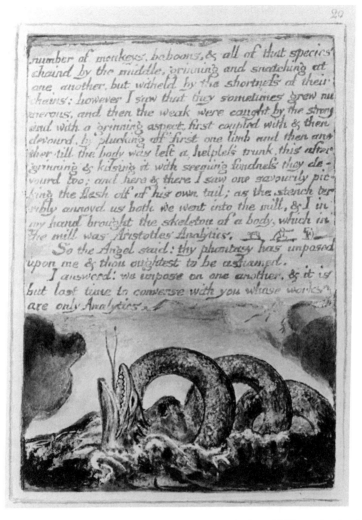

Figure 2.5 *The Marriage of Heaven and Hell* copy I, plate 20 (Reproduction by permission of the Syndics of the Fitzwilliam Museum, Cambridge).

the light of heaven everything appears as it is in itself.'[40] Blake again reverses Swedenborg, treating the angelic 'light from heaven' as a distorting force, claiming that the leviathan's form was 'owing' to the angel's 'metaphysics'. The core of that metaphysics was revealed in the angel's belief that 'God alone [is] the Prolific', and in its contrary as expressed in Blake's response: 'God only Acts & Is. in existing beings or Men'. Plates 16–20 recapitulate the debate between angel and devil, between the 'law of ten commandments' and, as represented by the leviathan's dragon-like shape, 'salvation of man by faith [in Christ] alone, without the works of the law'.

The trip to the Abyss alludes to Swedenborg's *Conjugial Love*, n. 477, in which an angel shows a young man various contrary visions to scare him onto the correct path. In mistakenly assuming that he and Blake shared the same fears, the angel revealed only his own. Blake initiates their next trip: taking the angel and, moving away from hell, they

> flew westerly thro' the night, till we were elevated above the earths shadow: then I flung myself with him directly into the body of the sun, here I clothed myself in white, & taking in my hand Swedenborgs volumes sunk from the glorious clime, and passed all the planets till we came to saturn, here I staid to rest & then leap'd into the void between saturn & the fixed stars. (plate 19)[41]

Parodying Swedenborgian space travel, Blake implies his ultimate victory, for the phrase 'clothed … in white' alludes to Revelation 3:5: 'He that overcometh, the same shall be clothed in white raiment.' As victor, Blake uses Swedenborg's writings as an anchor, to assist his entrance into the 'void', which is a vacuum or empty abyss and thus only an imitation of its model. In the 'void', Blake and angel saw 'the stable and the church', and at 'the altar … open'd the Bible, and lo! it was a deep pit', a grave-like opening leading not to an 'immense world of delight' but to a cannibalizing simian house (plate 20), whose stench – a possible allusion to the descent into Swedenborg's tomb – was overwhelming (Paley 1985, p. 25).

The chained simians appear to be a version of the chained giants. Whereas the latter reflect what devourers look like to producers, the former reflect what they look like to Blake. After catching the weak 'with a grinning aspect', the strong 'coupl[ed] with & … devour[ed]' parts of the body till it 'was left a helpless trunk', which, 'after grinning & kissing it with seeming fondness they devourd too' (plate 20). Within the devourers' exclusively rational mind lie chaos and violence.

Upon Blake's return, no writing devil awaits. Instead, Swedenborg's writings had revealed their true form, becoming in Blake's hand 'the skeleton of a body, which in the mill [became]

Aristotles Analytics', an author treated sympathetically by Swedenborg in his *Worlds in the Universe*, n. 38, of which Blake was aware (E602).[42] In Swedenborg, images are constantly changing 'by Virtue of the Influx of Light'.[43] Here, the transformation of Swedenborg's writings to 'skeleton' (presumably simian) to *Analytics* mirrors the transformation of viper/eagle to leviathan to harper.

Figure 2.6   *The Marriage of Heaven and Hell* copy I, plate 1 (Reproduction by permission of the Syndics of the Fitzwilliam Museum, Cambridge).

Blake presents his writings as a living continuation of the Word and
Swedenborg's as tied to the dead past. Moreover, 'skeleton of a
body' puns on 'skeleton', the repeatable portions in the body of
a book.[44] Blake portrays Swedenborg again as a copyist of the analytical or 'systematic reasoning' of 'Angels', though now the attack
is even nastier. Symbolically, by reducing him/his writings to bare
bones, Blake kills Swedenborg, and does so in stark contrast to his
own idealized and resurrected self pictured on plate 21. Blake's pun
prepares for another play on printing. The angel accuses Blake of having 'imposed' his 'phantasy', which, metaphorically, in the printing
sense of imposing type into pages to create books, he has, but so
has the angel, 'whose works are only Analytics'. Blake and the
angel 'impose on one another' in a sort of battle of books, which
opens Blake to accusations that his visions are owing to his metaphysics and that versions of reality are relative and equally valid –
or invalid. Or, as I argue in the second part of this study, it suggests
a hierarchy of texts, of the kind Blake clearly establishes in his
attack on Swedenborg on plate 22 and again in his defence of the
prophets and ancient poets.

CONCLUSION

Swedenborgian rhetoric, images and ideas figure consistently in
the *Marriage* and helped to generate Blake's narrative counter-
statements. If Swedenborg spoke only to angels and published
their wisdom (plate 21), then Blake would present himself as
Swedenborg's contrary, one who spoke to devils and published
their wisdom, their 'Bible of Hell'. If Swedenborg claims heaven,
angels and reason for his own, then his adversary claims hell, devils and energy, using these controlling metaphors to express their
different ideas of God, the remote and external sky-god of angels
versus the incarnate spirit of devils. In the inverted world of
Marriage, descent into hell is an ascent into eternity, and ascent into
heaven a descent into the caverned man. As a satirist, Blake intends
to sound like Swedenborg; he too announces that a new age has
begun, and agrees that a special kind of reading or perception once
ours must be restored to perceive what is hidden. The loss of this
perception, though, is not due to the devolution of the Churches,
but to mankind's forgetting that 'all deities reside in the human
breast', an act synonymous with the usurpation of the 'just man'
and 'man [having] closed himself up till he sees all things thro'

narrow chinks of his cavern' (plates 11, 2 and 14). Its restoration lies
not in Swedenborg's writings, but in opening the cave – in opening
Blake's illuminated books.

Reading *Marriage*'s textual units in the order in which they were
executed reveals thematic and visual connections not readily apparent in the book's finished order. It reveals the cave as a motif and its
role in making *Marriage* both overtly self-reflexive and expressive.
The cave symbolism, by drawing readers' attention to the book and
to the creative processes it embodies, reveals clearly that one of
Blake's major purposes in the *Marriage* is to show what opens
and closes the human mind. Blake offers 'The Bible of Hell' and
an infernal way of reading the Bible, demonstrates his reading
prowess, and takes us deep within the creative mind without losing
sight of his main object of criticism and satire. In doing so, he produced an aesthetic manifesto defining the nature of God, himself as
a prophet, and art as the marriage of heaven and hell.

Notes

1. The separate printing of plates 21–4 is referred to as *Marriage* copy K.
    See Bentley (1977) pp. 287–8.
2. For the 'cave' in the 'Printing house in Hell' as both the metal plate
    and its impression and, by extension, the illuminated book as an
    'immense world of delight', see Erdman (1974) p. 19.
3. Plate borders are the strips of metal standing in relief around the
    copper plate. They were created by strips of wax forming a dyke to
    hold acid. After the etch, the wax was removed, and the metal it pro-
    tected from the acid became part of the relief line system and helped to
    support the inking dabber. For a fuller account, see Viscomi (1993) ch. 8.
4. In copies H, I and G, the ground is framed by water.
5. Emanuel Swedenborg, *A Treatise Concerning the Last Judgment and the
    Destruction of Babylon* (London: R. Hindmarsh, 1788) nn. 54–6.
6. Emanuel Swedenborg, *True Christian Religion; Containing the Universal
    Theology of the New Church*, 2nd edition (London: R. Hindmarsh,
    1786; 3rd edn, 1795) n. 760.
7. *Arcana Coelestia*, n. 920, in *A Compendium of the Theological Writings of
    Emanuel Swedenborg*, compiled by Samuel M. Warren, 1875 (rpr. New
    York: Swedenborg Foundation, Inc., 1974). The perception of the
    Most Ancient Church was 'diminished in the succeeding churches
    and became more general' (*Arcana Coelestia*, n. 502).
8. *True Christian Religion*, n. 204.
9. *Conjugial Love*, n. 78, in *A Compendium of the Theological Writings of
    Emanuel Swedenborg*, compiled by Samuel M. Warren, 1875 (rpr. New
    York: Swedenborg Foundation, Inc., 1974).
10. *True Christian Religion*, nn. 132, 172.

11. By 1790, the Swedenborgian New Church emphasized external rituals, the decalogue and priests (Viscomi 1997b).
12. A cave enclosing mental processes puns visually on the human skull, the 'cavity of the cranium' (see 'Anatomy', sect. IV, of the Brain in the *Encyclopaedia Brittanica*, 1769). For gods in caves, see also Jacob Bryant, *A New System; or an Analysis of Antient Mythology*. 6 vols, 3rd edn. (London. J Walker, 1807), I: 269; my thanks for this reference to Denise Vultee.
13. For the source in Thomas Chatterton, see Eaves et al. (1993) p. 212, nn. 3–4. Swedenborg wrote that 'birds correspond, according to their species, to the intellectual things of both spiritual and natural mind', *A Treatise Concerning Heaven and Hell* (London: J. Phillips, 1778) n. 110.
14. *True Christian Religion*, n. 188; see also *Heaven and Hell*, nn. 250, 76. In this light, the figures on plates 21 and 24 are, ironically, open and closed. For the visual puns on Blake as Christ and Swedenborg as Nebuchadnezzar and/or King George III, see Viscomi 1997b.
15. *Heaven and Hell*, n. 581.
16. 'Abyss', from the Greek meaning 'a place of great depth', is a translation of the Hebrew word for 'deep'. In the Book of Enoch (21: 7), it refers to fiery punishment; in the New Testament to the name of Hades and the place of the dead; in Revelation, to 'the bottomless pit' (9: 1).
17. *True Christian Religion*, n. 625.
18. The words 'body' and 'soul' do not appear in the *Marriage* until plates 14 and 4, which explicitly refute the 'notion that man has a body distinct from his soul' (14) and assert that body is 'a Portion of Soul discern'd by the five Senses, the chief inlets of Soul in this age' (4). The chronology of production suggests that plates 14 and 4 were executed near one another, after the trip to hell and proverbs, with plate 14 probably written and executed before plate 4.
19. For Blake working from dictation, see *Europe* plate 3 and the letters of 25 April and 6 July 1803 (E729–30). For an incisive discussion, see Essick (1989) ch. 4.
20. See Peter Provo's *Wisdom's Dictates; or, a collection of maxims and observations concerning divine, and spiritual truths … Extracted … particularly from [the works] of Emanuel Swedenborg*, published in 1789 and sold by Hindmarsh. Provo, a Swedenborgian, celebrated restraint, submission and order as virtues.
21. For copying Imagination rather than Nature, see E547, 574 and 577.
22. *Divine Providence*, n. 233 in *A Compendium of the Theological Writings of Emanuel Swedenborg*, compiled by Samuel M. Warren, 1875 (rpr. New York: Swedenborg Foundation, Inc., 1974); see also n. 119. For the open door as metaphor for understanding, see *True Christian Religion*, n. 178. See also John 10: 9, 'I am the door: by me if any man enter in, he shall be saved, and shall go in and out, and find pasture'.
23. *Heaven and Hell*, n. 250.
24. *True Christian Religion*, n. 466.

25. An angel is stationed to guard the tree of life (Genesis 3: 24), but Ezekiel prophesizes that the 'covering cherub' will be burned up (28: 11–19) – which happens to the angel on plate 24 when he converts and becomes a devil.

26. *Arcana Coelestia*, nn. 126–7.

27. *True Christian Religion*, nn. 753–6.

28. *True Christian Religion*, n. 754.

29. *True Christian Religion*, n. 779. Blake may be satirizing Robert Hindmarsh, Swedenborg's publisher and the official printer to the Prince of Wales.

30. *Heaven and Hell*, n. 580.

31. *Apocalypse Revealed*, n. 539 in *A Compendium of the Theological Writings of Emanuel Swedenborg*, compiled by Samuel M. Warren, 1875 (rpr. New York: Swedenborg Foundation, Inc., 1974).

32. *Apocalypse Explained*, n. 714 in *A Compendium of the Theological Writings of Emanuel Swedenborg*, compiled by Samuel M. Warren, 1875 (rpr. New York: Swedenborg Foundation, Inc., 1974).

33. *True Christian Religion*, n. 278.

34. The origin of engraving was often traced to Exodus 32: 16, the 'writing of God ... engraved upon the tables' of stone (see Joseph Strutt, *A Biographical Dictionary; Containing an Historical Account of All the Engravers*, 2 vols., London, 1785, vol. 1, p. 8).

35. See the entry for 'Printing' in *Encyclopaedia Britannica*, 1769.

36. Erdman notes that the cave on plate 15 is 'indicated by cloud-rock sides and floor' (1974, p. 112). This is an apt description, for in etching, copper nitrate turns blue and, when biting much exposed metal, clouds over with orange fumes.

37. In plate 5, a naked man, a sword, a horse and possibly a chariot fall upside down from the sky into flames. Swedenborg states that the fallen are seen from heaven 'with their Feet upwards and their Heads downwards' (*True Christian Religion*, n. 613).

38. *Last Judgment*, n. 45.

39. *Last Judgment*, n. 61. The dragon is a celestial power in Eastern philosophy. In the *Marriage*, the dragon appears 'to the east, distant about three degrees' (plate 18). Blake writes that the 'philosophy of the east taught the first principles of human perception' (plate 12), while Swedenborg also identifies the East with God and clear perception (*Heaven and Hell*, nn. 141, 148, 149, 151; see also *Divine Love and Divine Wisdom*, nn. 83–167). Swedenborg also wrote that the 'natural mind' is a 'form and image of hell' and descends through 'three degrees' or levels (*Divine Love and Divine Wisdom*, nn. 273–5; see also nn. 237–9, which Blake annotated, E605–6). See also Eaves et al. (1993) p. 217, n. 23.

40. *Heaven and Hell*, n. 553.

41. According to Swedenborg, good spirits turn left to right, and bad turn right to left (*Divine Love and Divine Wisdom*, n. 270).

42. See also *True Christian Religion*, n. 696, and Paley, p. 27.

43. *True Christian Religion*, n. 187.

44.   The skeleton refers to the frame of furniture in the printing chase that forms the margins of pages and holds the forme in which the type lies. Repeated portions, like 'the headlines of a book … remained in position in the skeleton after type was distributed and subsequent pages were imposed' (*Encyclopaedia Britannica*, 1769, Printing).

3

Spectral Imposition and Visionary Imposition: Printing and Repetition in Blake

Edward Larrissy

Valuable work has been accomplished in recent years, by writers to whom I shall refer, on the topic of Blake's printing method. My intention in this chapter is to bring into relation with some of this work the figurative language and pictorial images Blake uses in the context of his own reflections on his endeavour. My findings will bring new evidence to support the conclusion, already advanced elsewhere, that Blake at first saw his own method as embodying the Sublime of Energy; and they will support the idea that in his later work some of his thoughts about printing are bound up with the idea of redemption.

I have adverted elsewhere to the implications of the words 'imposition' and 'impose', suggesting that they comprise, for Blake, the assertion of vision by means of that 'firm perswasion' which is itself an inseparable attribute of the visionary character (Larrissy 1985, p. 10). In *Historicizing Blake*, I further suggested that 'self-imposition' was an opposed category, embodying the idea of internal division and 'Self Contradiction' (Larrissy 1994, p. 70). But there is another aspect of Blake's usage of the word 'impose', related to printing, which has never been noticed. For the word 'impose' means 'to lay pages of type or stereotype plates in proper order on the bed of a press and secure them in a chase'. The word is a staple of printers' and compositors' terminology, and it would be an easy but otiose task to demonstrate that it normally receives a separate section, for which it provides the heading, in compositors' manuals: thus, in Moxon (1683–4) we have the section *'Of* Imposing'.[1]

Furthermore, at least in the days before offset (and now electronic)
printing, this usage was well enough known to the non-expert. It
still appears in recent editions of popular dictionaries such as
Chambers.

Now this usage refers to the printing of books or journals, and in
implying 'proper order', does so because it refers to the need to
print a number of pages onto the folio at once, in such a way that
the versos, rectos and juxtapositions are in the right places, so that
when the folio is folded and cut, the pages will be consecutive.
Blake is not producing a book by the conventional method, and
thus he does not produce large folded signatures. Nevertheless, it is
perhaps significant that we know from *The Ghost of Abel*, and from
J. T. Smith's *Nollekens and his Times*, that Blake would have accepted
the designation 'stereotype plates' for his own relief-etched plates;
and conventional books could indeed be produced from stereotype
plates.[2] Furthermore, Joseph Viscomi has conclusively shown that
Blake often printed in gatherings: in the case of *Innocence*, for
instance, he printed editions of the book by impressing pairs of
plates onto both sides of the folio (Viscomi 1993, pp. 112–18). For
this reason, Viscomi is content to refer to Blake's 'printing plates in
formes' (forme being the word normally used for the body of type
set up in a chase) and to his use of 'folio *imposition*' (my emphasis)
(Viscomi 1993, p. 117). In other words, Blake's invoking of 'the idea
of the book' does extend to the practical question of their printing,
and this invoking was chiefy constituted by a kind of imposition.

It is not surprising, then, to find that Blake himself employs the
word 'imposition' in the context of printing. The word first appears
in *The Marriage*, plate 12, where Blake dines with Isaiah and Ezekiel.
This is quite close to the place where the printing metaphor is made
very explicit in plate 14, in the passage about the 'infernal method'.
One may grant, of course, that the word 'impose' in this context
possesses other connotations, those of 'deceive' (a now almost
defunct sense) and 'impress'. The first connotation, when unrav-
elled, would imply that those whose visions are opposed may well
experience their opponents as deceivers: angels are likely to feel this
way permanently; devils will feel this way about angels; but among
themselves, devils will recognize that 'Opposition is true Friendship'.
The second connotation is itself congruent with a reference to printing. Both connotations would sit comfortably with a metaphor
derived from the printer's sense of the word 'impose': referring as it
does to the order in which plates are laid down, it suggests that

what is essential to Blake's vision has something to do with its being unfolded over a plurality of plates, and with juxtaposition of plates as a concomitant of that unfolding.

But there is yet another meaning with which Blake would have been familiar. Repetition and plurality may suggest the arbitrariness of the sign. This, of course, is a condition of the fallen world for Blake. Nevertheless, it is one with which he has to struggle; and he is undoubtedly aware of the semiotic debates about arbitrariness in which the word 'imposition' had a venerable place. Thus Aquinas, taking a hint from Aristotle's *De interpretatione*, refers to signification under two kinds: *impositio secundum naturam* ('imposition according to nature') and *impositio iuxta arbitrium humanae voluntatis* ('imposition according to the judgement of the human will').[3] The former is more indicative; the latter more arbitrary (*arbitrium*). Urquhart's translation of Rabelais, in the scholastic tradition, also makes use of the idea of *impositio*:

> All Speeches have had their primary Origin from the Arbitrary Institutions, Accords and Agreements of Nations in their respective Condescendments to what should be noted and betokened by them. An Articulate Voice (according to the Dialecticians) hath naturally no signification at all; for that the sence and meaning thereof did totally depend upon the good will and pleasure of the first Deviser and *Imposer* of it. (my emphasis)

And in Locke's *Essay* we are informed that 'Words ... come to be made use of by Men as the *Signs of* their *Ideas*; not by any natural connexion ... but by a voluntary Imposition, whereby such a Word is made arbitrarily the Mark of such an *Idea*' (III.ii.1). The point Blake would have accepted here, as Robert Essick's work makes clear, is the difference between an Adamic language on the one hand, and the arbitrariness of the conventions of the fallen human world on the other. (My argument does not depend on any of the possible beliefs about what Saussure intended in his own doctrine of arbitrariness.) If we bring together the associations cited so far, including that which would simply comprise the idea of 'impressing' or imposing a plate on the paper, we might suggest the following conclusion: imposition refers to Blake's sense that, by his 'infernal method', he is, with a hint of paradox, asserting a 'firm perswasion' through a medium characterized by succession, difference and juxtaposition. But in view of the fact that there is some contemporary dispute about the character of the 'difference' intended by Blake's method, it will be necessary to be fairly precise about what does and what does not seem to be supported by a parallel consideration of that method and of his language about it. Stephen Leo Carr has argued strongly for the marked significance of the facts of variation in different printings, in terms both of different ordering of plates, and, even more, of different approaches to colouring (Carr 1986, pp. 177–96). He has connected this variability to Derrida's concept of *différance*, especially in relation to the way in which that concept comprises the notion of 'iterability': the inevitable capacity of the utterance to be repeated, which entails that it is constituted by significative elements which can never be reduced to an original context (Carr 1986, p. 187). Robert Essick and Joseph Viscomi have offered disagreement with this analysis, largely on the evidence of Blake's actual production, and of its artistic context, rather than in repudiation of its theoretical treatment (Essick 1986, pp. 197–217; Viscomi 1993, pp. 163–76). Robert Essick suggests that the actual variation, though present, is not nearly as significant as the persistence and continuity, which he relates to Blake's avowal of the 'Eternal' character of his designs: 'My Designs unchangd remain' (*Notebook*, 87) (Essick 1986, p. 204). Both Essick and Viscomi refer to the prevalence of variation in the market for eighteenth-century prints, though Essick concedes that the 'degree of variation' is greater in Blake (Essick 1986, p. 202). This seems to me to be a significant concession. But what features of Blake's books are emphasized by the idea of 'imposition' as both a literal and figurative use of a printing term? The term surely has everything to do with juxtaposition of plates (several plates are printed onto one folio), and nothing intrinsically to do with variation in the order or colouring of them. And if it be said that imposition is a feature of all book-printing, it must surely be conceded that Blake is trying to derive significance from emphasizing what is involved in it in a context where he has also drawn attention to the union of word and design. In other words, what Blake is indicating as a novel and radical feature of his method is the potential for a composite art on lines the most ambitious analysis of which remains that of W. J. T. Mitchell. This, rather than anything about variability of colouring or order, is what can strictly be inferred from a consideration of the prominence of the word 'imposition' in *The Marriage*. The point remains radical enough: the 'firm perswasion' of the honest prophet is not characterized by the univocal, but by the polyphonic, and by the overcoming of barriers between genres and senses. Furthermore, while nothing can strictly be inferred about variability, Essick's concession is not only significant but surely correct: there is a high degree of variability in Blake, and while this is not referred to by the word 'imposition', it does possess an affinity with what that word is pointing to.

The infernal method is also essentially characterized by the preference of relief etching to intaglio. It seems likely to be profitable to assume that a figurative meaning, a 'spiritual sense', attaches to this choice and to its effects. I believe that there is such a figurative meaning, and that it is especially associated with another sense of 'imposition' which I earlier called 'impressing'. Now the method was in part devised in order to permit what Ackroyd calls 'painting rather than engraving the copper plate'; and this was a means towards the end of combining design and text (Ackroyd 1995, p. 112). Given that this combination (however we may wish to conceive its effects) was intended to 'expunge' the 'notion that man has a body distinct from his soul' (*MHH*, 14), we must read Blake's intention of 'melting apparent surfaces away' (including its figurative aspect) as referring not to any type of engraving, but specifically to his own method of relief etching. Two further questions follow: how much of the body is referred to in any aspect of the new method or its effects? To put it another way: we know that the sense of vision (and vision in more than a limited corporeal understanding) is invoked by the co-presence of text and design. We also know that the auditory was important to Blake, both from stories of his composing melodies for the *Songs* and from the discussion of 'cadence' and 'numbers' in the address 'To the Public' at the beginning of *Jerusalem*. To come to the point: is the sense of touch alluded to in any way? A number of critics and scholars have noticed connotations and effects which suggest that it is. Robert Essick has been the most explicit about this possibility:

> Blake's illuminated texts ask us to see the individual, ever-various shapes and textures of designs and autograph letters through an eye integrated with, and thus expanded by, the sense of touch. In this way, relief-etching is itself a stimulus to 'the improvement of sensual enjoyment' and cleansing of the senses to make them 'enlarged and numerous'. (Essick 1980, p. 12)

The reason why we may feel that the sense of touch is invoked has to do, I would claim, both with the connotations of the printing method, and with the effects procured by it. Thus Joseph Viscomi speaks of the 'infinite' being 'displayed' because it is 'made prominent, as it literally would be when the design was etched into relief' (Viscomi 1993, p. 81). And Vincent De Luca speaks of the appearance of 'a wall of words' on a large scale as figuring 'the energy of the sublime experience' (De Luca 1991, p. 93). Neither of these last two critics invokes the sense of touch, but both of them adduce the considerations which lead Essick to do so. But if the idea of touch seems controversial, it is worth recalling that Blake may be assumed to have been serious in his desire to equate body and soul in the most comprehensive way, and that in several well-known passages he refers to the body by referring to each of the senses. In fact, it seems eminently probable that Blake is specifically relating touch and sight by reference to a precisely contemporary phenomenon: the invention of relief printing for the blind. It was the Abbé Valentin Haüy who, in 1784, invented this aid in its first true form. An account of the technique was provided in his book of 1786, *Essai sur l'éducation des aveugles*. The blind Scottish poet, Thomas Blacklock, made a translation which appeared posthumously in his collected works. The technique involved the creation of books with relief text by punching relief plates into the cards which made up the pages. Despite earlier haphazard efforts at the use of relief letters, this was the first example of systematic relief printing, and was recognized as such.[4] It seems likely, then, that Blake is providing an analogue of relief printing for the blind, one that exploits the figurative senses of blindness and vision, in that it makes relief etching a means of access to imaginative vision among those who require their 'doors of perception' to be cleansed.

The wider point is scarcely controversial: namely, all that is involved in what Viscomi refers to as the design's being 'made prominent'. In view of Blake's espousal of 'Opposition', the mere fact that his method is 'a simple reversal of intaglio' (as Morton Paley puts it) is surely significant (Paley 1978, p. 14). For intaglio could scarcely be described as a method involving the sense of 'prominence'. Where Blake extrudes design and text, intaglio incises them. The figurative advantage accorded to relief etching is that, by virtue of an energetic extrusion of the sign, it is both 'honest imposition' and 'firm perswasion', and these two concepts involve what I earlier called 'impressing'. (I use the word sign as Essick does in *William Blake and the Language of* Adam, in the wide sense according to which it may refer not only to words but also to significative icons, indices and figures, and thus also to Blake's engraved plates considered in their totality as significative entities – considered, that is, in a term which has gained some currency, as 'hieroglyphs'.) The commercial version of intaglio, on the other hand, is an incision into the self, which Blake associates the absence of 'firm perswasion': with the doubt which he would later equate with self-contradiction. If this be accepted, it becomes worth enquiring as to whether or not 'self-imposition' also implies the printing metaphor. The word is to be found in *Milton*, in Palamabron's characterization of Satan:

You know Satans mildness and his self-imposition,
Seeming a brother, being a tyrant, even thinking himself a brother
While he is murdering the just...

(7:21-3: E100)

It is surely worth entertaining the hypothesis that self-imposition comprises a reference to the prevalent method of commercial engraving. Support for this idea can be found in the line at the centre of the tables of the Law, which descends onto the centre of Urizen's head on the title-page of *The Book of Urizen*, where, significantly, he is holding writing instruments. There is, then, a type of book-creation which is characterized by division of the self. The later reference to his 'book of Brass' (3:44: E72) lends credence to the idea that such creation may comprise the making of books through the agency of etched metal plates, even if we may not share the confidence of Erdman and Mitchell that all, or indeed any, of the versions of the title-page show Urizen holding a burin.[5] *The Book of Urizen* thus begins to address the topic of how what is termed the Spectre in Blake's later work is 'the ghostly double of imaginative vision, haunting and tracking it with its negative self-image' (Vine 1993, p. 46). And we can conceive how this large, general topic might already comprise the subordinate one of the spectral quality of Blake's labours as 'working engraver', labours which included the use of intaglio (Paley 1983, p. 253). This technique, which Blake, as Paley points out, reverses, is itself a 'reversal': 'the Almighty hath made me his Contrary/To be all evil, all reversed' (*J* 10: 57; E154); 'as a distorted & reversed Reflexion' (*J* 17: 42; E162). The topics of reversal and reflection are bound up with the practical task of engraving in the most essential manner. The need to reverse the design on the copper plate, like any practical task for the true craftsman, was not a matter (it should scarcely need saying) for complacent inadvertence or idle guesswork, but for explicit precept and rule. A manual which makes this very clear, since it provides many sub-heading, is Maxime Lalanne's of 1866, in which a section called 'Reversing the Design' is followed by 'Use of the Mirror'.[6] This will remind Blakeans of the piquant fact that the result of George Cumberland's engraving experiments was to produce a reversed text: he averred that his works might be read with 'the looking glass', and playfully suggested that they would be 'none to the crowd': that is, inaccessible to the *profanum vulgus*.[7] Albion, who sits in despair in the illumination to *Jerusalem*, plate 37, is unable to read the reversed mirror-writing, on the scroll to the left of the design, which would tell him the way in which Humanity escapes the power of the Spectre.

Extrusion versus incision can be seen as exuberance versus prudence and timidity. But they can also be seen as positive and negative, with the negative shadowing the positive. Thus, when Blake says to the Angel 'we impose on one another', we may read this one way as 'we print on one another', but alternatively as 'each of us prints on the parts the other leaves out' ('But thou read'st black where I read white', *EG* p. 33: 14 E524). Furthermore, if one visualizes the way in which the same shape would be treated by relief etching on the one hand and intaglio on the other, one can see how the line of intaglio might look as if it were providing an outline for the line of relief engraving. ('Reason is the bound or outward circumference of Energy', *MHH*4, E34) Translated into terms more related to printing, this perception suggests some such thought as the following: 'Your printing, which seems to provide a line for my conceptions really only offers weakness and recessiveness, where mine offers boldness and salience.'

Since printing is permitted by the possibility of repetition, what we have is two types of repetition, a positive and a negative, each the reversal of the other. The point about repetition has been put rather well by Morris Eaves: '*Printing* is a translation of one set of visual signs into another, made possible by the division of words into uniform letters, for the sake of repetition' (Eaves 1977/1986, p. 176). For Blake, printing as repetition is explicitly linked to questions about influence, originality and the redemption of time. For while we are bound to repeat in the world of time, the difference between a time that can open onto Eternity and a time that cannot conceive of such an opening is the most important difference that can be perceived. The former is a repetition that is always new, the latter the repetition of weariness and despair. But reversal itself is a form of repetition: Urizen's 'book of Brass' is a reversed repetition of illuminated engraving, which is part of what Steven Vine meant by referring to 'the ghostly double of imaginative vision'.

But it is of two forms of repetition that we are speaking, and Blake is capable of pondering on the character of what I have called redeemed repetition by means of a reference to the looking-glass effect. I am referring to *Milton*, where we are first shown a full-page illumination of 'William' facing to the right and about to receive the star of Milton into his left foot, and some pages later 'Robert', his brother, the very same image facing to the left with a star about to enter his right foot.[8] There is, as we shall see, a reference to engraving here, a clue to which is provided by Smith in *Nollekens and his Times*: 'His brother Robert stood before him and decidedly directed him to take up his method of "stereotype" printing.'[9] For if the presence of Robert raises the question of his significance, and if it is uncontroversial to think that William regarded his relief etching as bound up with his prophetic intention, we are entitled to entertain the notion that one of Robert's chief significances for William is in his directing the use of the method. In this context it is relevant to recall that in a letter of 1800 Blake professed still to write from Robert's 'Dictate' (6 May 1800, E705). All of these facts, and the connections between them, are highly significant, but lest familiarity should have staled their import it may be as well to rehearse them with due emphasis. Thus: the intrusive appearance of Robert in *Milton*, in a manner which begs comparison with 'William', itself attributes importance to him (never mind yet of what kind, though it is obviously to do with repetition); this appearance makes a third reference alongside the two quotations already cited; the importance of Robert is to do with influence, as the two quotations make clear – they lend authority to each other in this respect; one of the quotations claims that this influence was as the source of Blake's relief method; this peculiar method of relief, or 'stereotype', engraving is central to the purpose of his artistic endeavour; 'stereotype' in this period would be a word specifically chosen to evoke the special nature of Blake's engraving method. And now, with reference to the reversal of the image: where there is repetition of the same image, we are absolutely enjoined to notice whether that repetition is direct or reversed, and not indolently to ignore the fact; reversal and the looking-glass effect are central to the art of engraving, to the extent that mirrors might actually be employed; reversal and the employment of mirrors took place at the stage of transferring the original design to the plate; reversal also occurs when the plate prints on paper. The reversal, then, refers to Blake's printing from Robert's original. Blake's juxtaposition of William and Robert is a way of putting his work – absolutely including his method – under the sign of redeemed secondariness. For the two images taken together allow us to see his whole *oeuvre* either as a plate designed from Robert's original, or as a page delineated from Robert's printing plate. It does not matter which, the important point being the sense of secondariness implied by reversal. This notable case of being haunted refers to engraving as the repetition that is time redeemed, in the sense that repetition is a phenomenon of the fallen world. Robert is a creative and fraternal spirit seen in vision, and enabling vision, not a weary Spectre.

It is also relevant that both William and Robert are, in the engravings in question, wearing a kind of diaphanous boxer shorts: the famous Blake's underpants. Clearly, this is part of the large and well-rehearsed topic of vesture and integument in Blake. Its relevance in this case is in reminding us that there is no opportunity of walking naked in the fallen world: form and influence are ineluctable, both temporally as repetition, and spatially as embodiment. One must choose between two types of form and repetition: the one moulded by inspiration that seeks honest imposition, or the one that seeks to impose itself on inspiration, which 'seeming a brother [which Robert actually is], is a tyrant' – for, as Morton Paley points out, it is essential to the Spectre that its God is the Negation of Blake's 'brother and friend' (*J* 4: 18; E146) (Paley 1983, p. 245).

The possibility that repetition might be redeemed is reminiscent of the thought of Kierkegaard, who in *The Concept of Dread* describes the redemptive moment through which man is 'the same and yet not the same': 'the whole of life and existence begins afresh'.[10] This is one Protestant thinker's version of the Pauline conception, so influential on Protestantism in general, of the individual believer's transition to the new life. The classic statement of the influence of this conception on writers of the Romantic period is to be found in M. H. Abrams's *Natural Supernaturalism*, in his treatment of 'Christian History and Psycho-Biography';[11] and readers can accept the broad sense in which his ensuing references to Blake are coloured by this treatment: for instance, in the reference to Blake's 'redemptive imagination'.[12] Indeed, while the matter is not much discussed, there is nothing remotely controversial about a broad acceptance of the influence of the Pauline conception on Blake, and the contemporary emphasis on Blake's radical Protestant inheritance renders the idea more, rather than less, acceptable. In adducing the case of Kierkegaard, the purpose is to lend some precision to the specific cast Blake gives to that inheritance, in the belief that there are particular similarities. Some of these, though real enough, turn out not to be so distinctive after all. Thus, J. R. Scrimgeour had understandably compared Blake's Spectre of Urthona with Kierkegaard's demoniacally despairing individual; but there are other writers who evoke a comparison with this (Scrimgeour 1975). For instance, when discussing Carlyle in the light, among other things, of his exposition of Christian Psycho-Biography, Abrams is understandably content to compare the *Angst* of Teufelsdroeckh with that of Kierkegaard.[13] It is in the particular topic of *repetition*, I feel, that the illumination cast by a comparison with Kierkegaard yields most light for Blake studies – and yields light precisely because there are so many striking instances of the perceived difference between mechanical and redeemed repetition. The one who enters on the new life is 'the same and yet not the same'. Lorraine Clark's description of Kierkegaardian repetition does not do justice to the uncanny force of this idea: 'Repetition is ... a rupture not a continuity,' says Clark (1991, p. 104). But to all appearances it is a continuity. That is why it is called 'repetition'. As David Simpson remarks, 'Blake, like Kierkegaard, sees despair *and* joy, and a great many implications for both ... '(Simpson 1986, p. 24). Indeed; and like Kierkegaard, he is also aware of how similar in outward appearance they may seem.

One prime example of the possible similarity between the spectral and the visionary is provided by the similarity between the bard figure on the one hand, and the 'old man' figure who represents the Urizenic and may represent the spectral or Satanic. This ambiguity reveals how poetry and prophecy may congeal into scripture, and the roots of Blake's usage are to be found not merely in eighteenth-century primitivism and theories of the decline of poetry, but also, it seems, in his acquaintance with some of the central ideas of the Lurianic Kabbalah. The most relevant doctrine is that of the withdrawal of God from the universe. The doctrine of *Tsimtsum* states that this withdrawal occurred at the Fall. Simultaneously, the divine light fled from the spheres of the Tree of Life, leaving it as dead husk or bark: its own spectral double (as in

Yeats's poem 'The Two Trees', which reveals a knowledge of the same sources).[14] Since the Tree of Life also figures the world of Time in its seven lower spheres (the seven days of creation and of the week), the departure of the light evokes the idea of unredeemed temporality; mechanical repetition. And the God who could thus withdraw could be seen as having entered a malign and fallen state: as also having become a spectral double of his former self. The influence on *The Book of Urizen* is likely to have been mediated by Robert Fludd, though work is continuing on other possible sources (Raine 1968, II. p. 77).

I wish now to turn to a work which can be shown to make notable reference to the idea of the redemption of time, including the redemption of the creative efforts of Blake's whole life as an engraver, and which itself implies the idea of redemption in its very medium: I am referring to *Illustrations of the Book of Job* (1825). This work employs some striking duplications of the old man figure: God is a projection of Job's vision, and in appearance his double; the God with extended and 'creative' fingers in XIII, XIV, XV and XVII, who is associated with the recovery of Job's imagination, is all but indistinguishable from the weary and spectral God who presides over its decline; Job at the end of the series is indistinguishable from his portrayal at the beginning, except that he has exchanged book for harp: in a sense he is 'the same and yet not the same'. Yet it is made patent that this transformation is wrought in the world of time and repetition, a world that compels secondariness. This point is partly conveyed by the figure of vesture to which I referred earlier, for a notable instance of the diaphanous garment in Blake is the leotard-like one worn by Elihu in *Illustrations of the Book of Job XII*. The very moment of the awakening of vision is shown to be only possible within the forms and inheritances of time, albeit when those forms mould themselves to inspiration. This moment of vision is preceded by two designedly uncanny-looking prints: 'Then a Spirit passed before my face the hair of my flesh stood up' (IX), which shows Eliphaz's hair standing on end; and Job's Evil Dream ('With Dreams upon my bed thou scarest me', XI) It may indeed be useful to be reminded, in this context, of those various *Doppelgänger*, spectres, Brocken spectres and Life-in-Death figures of the Romantic period which can be seen as a terrible reminder that our own existence cannot be assimilated to our mundane constructions of ourselves and the world (Rose 1977). This is worth bearing in mind first, because of the sometimes comical resemblance between Job and his God, second, because any occurrence of hair standing on end in this period must be referred to the cultural context of the literature, and indeed the painting, of terror. Job is haunted by a repetition of himself, which terrifies him by reminding him of the isolation and misery he has made for himself; Eliphaz is terrified by possibilities suddenly apprehended in the shape of a figure which, though it looks superficially like the tired God he has been worshipping, is actually the true God of inspiration. Once Job has accepted this God, he is ready for positive rather than negative repetition, and thus it is that the last plate in the series looks so similar to the first, except that in the first he is reading and in the second singing to the strains of his harp: repetitions of each other which also allude to two types of repetition. As in Kierkegaard, redeemed repetition is the product of a moment of conversion: 'Each man is in his Spectre's power/Untill the arrival of that hour,/When his Humanity awake/And cast his Spectre into the lake' (*J* 37, E184) – words which, as already noted, are printed in reverse: an instance of the mirror effect facilitated by printing. This means that the Spectre repeats the wrong way, or causes mechanical repetition (the arrival of 'that hour' reminds us of the waste, sad time which precedes it). In all of this Blake reveals the profoundly Protestant character of his vision: one thinks of the bundle falling from Christian's back in *The Pilgrim's Progress*. An illuminating contrast with this Protestant character may be pointedly provided by comparing with Blake's the work of another poet-engraver whose chief themes included the topic of redemption and the repetitions of time: namely, David Jones. Jones, however, is profoundly of the Catholic tradition, and for him, the 'rehearsals' of time are essentially characterized by being 'continuings', rather than embodying any element of rupture.[15] When offered the opportunity to illustrate the suddenness of illumination, which is a venerable topos of Protestant accounts of redemption, he chooses not to take it up: Jones's illustrations to Coleridge's *Rime of the Ancient Mariner* do not include a treatment of that turning point at which the Mariner blesses the water snakes 'unaware' and the albatross falls from his neck (a notion which owes something to Bunyan, though it is given even more salience in Coleridge than that of the bundle is in *The Pilgrim's Progress*).

The use of intaglio in *Job* also suggests that thoughts such as the above are close to the heart of his intention there. For the return to incised lines is a return to more conventional methods. But, as

Morris Eaves points out, Blake here uses not the contemporary smoothness of dots and lozenges, but the firm lines and simple crosshatching of the older method he had learnt from James Basire in his youth (Eaves 1977/1986, pp. 190–1). In other words, the very method of *Job* is an example of redeemed repetition. Furthermore, since this is an example of the artist's recovery of a lost method, we might care to reflect on its appropriateness in a work where we are shown a series of quotations from Blake's earlier work. I do not mean by this chiefly the fact that Blake started making designs to the Job story quite early (*The Complaint of Job, c.* 1786), but rather that images from the earlier books reappear: Satan in II resembles the running figure at the bottom right of *The Marriage,* plate 3 and more or less repeats a figure running in flames at the top of Urizen, plate 3; God and his gestures recall Urizen; Job's Evil Dream recalls *Elohim Creating Adam*; Job playing his harp looks like the ancient bard in 'The Voice of the Ancient Bard'. Is this significant? Some critics would say no, as if to ask, 'What would you expect?' Yet I would only claim that a re-working and rediscovery is going on. These figures do not mean what they did: they have acquired new more complex significances, with associations gathered from the later stories of Albion and the Spectre, and the later themes of Vision and Forgiveness. Yet they retain reference to those distant figures conceived in the early 1790s, as if these had always contained an element of unrecognized potential, and thus they embody a repetition that is the redemption of a past story. This new discovery of significance in images of the past is itself a topic addressed in Blake's *Job*, in Illustration XX, where Job is seen pointing out to his daughters three narrative designs to be found on the walls of the room they are seated in. The precise content conveyed by two of these designs is a matter of dispute, but the one behind Job's head is almost identical with XIII, 'The Lord answering Job out of the Whirlwind', and the one on the right shows a figure almost identical in posture with 'William' and 'Robert'.

It is tempting to look for the brief formulation that would hold together in a few concise words these various related phenomena in Blake's work, and perhaps help to explain the enduring fascination of that work for our age. As it happens, there is a twentieth-century thinker who provides a suggestive and illuminating parallel with these ideas, as Carr has pointed out, namely Walter Benjamin (Carr

1986, p. 188). Blake's use of printing both as a trope and a practice of redeemed repetition suggests analogies with the theses of Benjamin's essay, 'The Work of Art in an Age of Mechanical Reproduction'. This is not, of course, to claim a literal – and certainly not an historical – relation to Benjamin's study of the effects of lithography, photography and cinema on the very concept and practice of art, but rather to assert a limited but potentially fruitful analogy. Blake's practice of issuing his books in different versions, with different order of text, different colouring, even different motifs, undermines the sense of the absolute authority of any one version. This is not the same as Benjamin's notion of the loss of aura in repetition: rather the reverse, for it is an attempt to recover aura in relation to a method which could literally decline into mechanical repetition. Yet Blake's usage alludes to the same sources: both drew in part on a Kabbalistic model of the relation between time and the eternal. Benjamin's friend and correspondent, Gershom G. Scholem, provides, in his great book, *Major Trends in Jewish Mysticism*, a succinct account of the Kabbalistic doctrines upon which both Benjamin and Blake drew. As we have seen, according to the Lurianic Kabbalah, the Fall leaves the Tree of Life and its spheres as empty husks or outlines. In the case of Benjamin this idea is a source for that of the loss of aura in repetition. The analogy is very substantial: if one were to draw up an index of subjects under which writers might be grouped together, I hazard that one would not find many apart from Blake and Benjamin who scored both for Kabbalah and Mechanical Reproduction. In this way, Benjamin can act as an illuminating lens for our age as it contemplates Blake.

There is a danger, however, with this kind of analogy, in leaping to the conclusion that Blake is some kind of meteoric portent of modernity. There is, of course, something in this, but it needs to be balanced by a sense of where Blake's sources and contexts are. The condition that enables us to think in terms of Blake's modernity lies in a unique confluence of early modern radical Protestant prophecy, artisanal predilections and contemporary revolutionary and Romantic discourses. This condition leads to an acute self-consciousness about the possibility for division and alienation in one who still longs to find an image of unity. Looking back, we can see an image of our own fragmentation and our own yearnings for origin and unity. But we submit ourselves to an illusion if we forget the extent to which Blake himself remains true to the Protestant idea of a spiritual conversion. However, this point, though it should not be controversial, is too broad and lacking in precision unless we incorporate another insight which this essay has attempted to underline: namely, that Blake's description of the moment when vision is renewed ascribes it to the intervention of a brother or a fraternal spirit. It is perhaps not surprising to find that an interrogation of Blake's way of figuring the significance of his own method finds that it is congruent with the conclusions of recent literary historians, who place Blake within the traditions of a fraternal and communitarian Protestantism.

Notes

1. Joseph Moxon, *Mechanick Exercises on the whole Art of Printing (1683–4)*, ed. Herbert Davis and Harry Carter, 2nd edn (London: Oxford University Press, 1962) p. 223.
2. J. T. Smith, *Nollekens and his Times*, 2 vols (London, 1828) II, p. 461.
3. Aristotle is presumably responding to the distinction unfolded in Plato's *Cratylus*, but unlike Plato takes the view that language is essentially composed of conventional signs. For a discussion of the whole question of the debate about convention and motivation, as it might have influenced Blake, see Essick (1989) pp. 28–103.
4. Haüy 'invented the art of printing in relief for the blind', according to *The Penny Cyclopaedia of the Society for the Diffusion of Useful Knowledge* (London, 1833–6) IV, p. 517.
5. The design is reproduced in Worrall (1995) p. 63. Worrall points out (p. 26) that the confidence about the burin once possessed by Mitchell is hard to maintain, and that Mitchell himself is now less sure. See Mitchell (1969) p. 84. Compare Erdman (1974) p. 183: Urizen is holding 'an etching needle'.
6. Maxime Lalanne, *A Treatise on Etching. Text and Plates*, trans. S. R. Koehler from the 2nd French edn (London, [1880]). First French edn, 1866.
7. For a description of Cumberland's ideas in the context of Blake's experimentation, see Lister (1975) p. 66. Michael Phillips also discusses Cumberland, placing his experiments in the context of the atmosphere of suspicion prevalent in Britain during the Terror (and also placing the local and small-scale character of Blake's production in that context) (Phillips 1994, pp. 263–97).
8. Copy C (NYPL), plates 29, 33. Repro. Essick and Viscomi (1993).
9. Smith, *Nollekens*, II, p. 461.
10. Søren Kierkegaard, *The Concept of Dread*, trans. Walter Lowrie (Princeton: Princeton University Press, 1944) 16n.
11. M. H. Abrams, *Natural Supernaturalism: Tradition and Revolution in Romantic Literature* (New York: Norton, 1971) pp. 46–56.
12. Ibid., pp. 120–1.
13. Ibid., p. 131.

14. Gershom G. Scholem, *Major Trends in Jewish Mysticism*, 2nd rev edn (New York, 1946) p. 260.
15. See Edward Larrissy, '"Deposits" and "Rehearsals": Repetition and Redemption in *The Anathemata*', in Paul Hills (ed.) *David Jones: Artist and Poet* (Aldershot: Scolar Press, 1997) pp. 132–40.

4

'Something in My Eye': Irritants in Blake's Illuminated Texts

Stephen C. Behrendt

William Blake's illuminated poems naturally invite the hard questions about the relation of visual texts and verbal texts in any illustrated book, and in his in particular. In what follows, I should like to revisit a few of the more troublesome problems that continue to face us as readers and viewers of Blake's illuminated pages, and to pose some questions about those pages and the ways in which Blake may or may not have intended us to proceed in digesting them. I say 'digesting' deliberately, for it seems to me that Blake asks us to 'consume' his texts in a manner analogous to that of John of Patmos, by means of a distinctively *physical* process through which we quite literally internalize the texts. This is 'informed consumerism' with a peculiarly Blakean twist. The account in Revelation is that the voice from heaven commanded John to 'Go and take the little book which is open in the hand of the angel which standeth upon the sea and upon the earth' (Rev. 10. 8). The result is just what the angel predicts: 'And I took the little book out of the angel's hand, and ate it up; and it was in my mouth sweet as honey: and as soon as I had eaten it my belly was bitter' (Rev. 10. 10). Significantly, the angel makes it clear what must transpire next: 'And he said unto me, Thou must prophesy again before many peoples, and nations, and tongues, and kings' (Rev. 10. 11).

Much as John was told to consume and thereby internalize the visions revealed to him in an act replete with sacramental overtones of the Eucharist, Blake asks us to treat his texts with comparable appetite and fervency, their often inherent bitterness notwithstanding. It is not amiss, I think, to suggest that for Blake the act of reading is to be regarded in fact as essentially sacramental in nature, at least when that act is performed correctly, for it is a prelude both to individual insight and to social – or community – prophecy and redemption. When done incorrectly, however, whether frivolously or with deliberate intent to misread, the sacrilegious treatment of the text is certain to produce intellectual and imaginative indigestion. This is not to imply that Blake's notion of 'reading' is ever entirely consistent, nor is it to disregard his irreverent and often deliberately perverse rendering of everything from physical and imaginative myopia to the immensely fruitful polyvalence (and polysemy) that at once tantalizes and frustrates modern poststructuralist approaches to his verbal and visual texts alike. We shall need, therefore, to proceed from the outset with some care.

But first a problem of taxonomy: what are we to call Blake's texts? This question is not so frivolous as it may at first appear, even in the wake of Joseph Viscomi's recent, thorough examination of Blake's books (Viscomi 1993). We usually call them 'illuminated texts', but every time I teach Blake's *Songs of Innocence and of Experience*, students almost without exception talk about 'the texts and the pictures'. Nor are the students alone in instinctively prioritizing the verbal text over the visual in this fashion. Writing in *Engaging English Art*, for example, Michael Cohen refers to Blake's *Songs* in terms of 'text and picture' or 'design and poem', while David Bindman, writing earlier, likewise calls the illuminated works essays in 'combining text and design'.[1] Indeed, this dichotomous and apparently mutually exclusive terminology recurs with surprising frequency in much of recent poststructuralist commentary on Blake's work.[2] Language of this sort implies that only a literary text can be a real 'text' and that the visual text is at best the weak and subservient sister art whose function is not *textually* significant and whose nature *as art* is only minimally and marginally important in the generation of meaning. Even so perennially perceptive a student of Blake as David Erdman seems to have been driving along this one-way street, if we are to take at face value his comment in *The Illuminated Blake* that 'every graphic image has its seed or root in the poetry' (Erdman 1974, p. 16). Yet as Molly Anne Rothenberg has noted recently, this sort of bifurcation blurs the distinction that exists between Blake's illuminated poems as 'works' and as 'texts', and between the opposing tendencies towards restriction and liberation, or demarcation and freedom, that customarily typify the two (Rothenburg 1993, p. 1).[3] In reminding us of the strongly performative – and therefore communitarian – nature of Blake's illuminated poems, Rothenberg helps to redirect

our attention to what is transpiring on the pages (as aesthetic entities
or 'wholes') and in the individual consciousnesses of a varied (and
varying) readership.

My quibble here is less with the terminology of Erdman, Bindman,
Cohen et al., than with the logocentric bias it betrays. Blake offered
us at least partial guidance when in his advertising prospectus
of 1793 he described the *Songs* and the early prophetic poems as
works executed 'in Illuminated Printing', each 'with [n] designs'
(E693). Blake says, 'The Illuminated Books are Printed in Colours',
but he goes no further in defining what he means by 'illuminated', either here or anywhere else in his writings. The *OED* tells
us that in eighteenth-century usage 'illumination' commonly referred
to rich adornment of the page with gold, silver or colour, and to the
use of 'tracery and miniature designs, executed in colours', as for
instance in illuminated medieval manuscripts. This more modern
and technically specific meaning of the term had in Blake's time
become concurrent with its older and clearly relevant connotations
of enlightenment and elucidation. It would seem that the 'designs'
to which Blake refers in his prospectus are therefore those substantial visual images that range in size from a quarter-page to a full
page; presumably the interlinear and minor marginal visual details
do not in themselves add up to what Blake means by 'designs',[4]
though they do come remarkably close to the 'tracery and miniature designs' to which the *OED* refers.

We can, however, say with greater certainty what Blake's interdisciplinary texts are *not*. They are not texts-with-illustrations in the
fashion of the eighteenth-century printed book adorned with
engraved full- or partial-page illustrations, books in which the
areas devoted to verbal and visual texts not only are kept separate
by physical means but also are typically executed by different
hands (the typesetter who 'sets' the author's verbal text, the illustrator who engraves a design – perhaps from a sketch supplied by
yet another hand, and the printer-bookmaker who assembles the
package under the supervision of the editor, publisher or bookseller). In producing his illuminated books Blake either saw to
every one of these tasks himself or oversaw the work that his wife
Catherine did when she worked with him to print, colour and otherwise prepare copies. In this respect, either alone or – as frequently
happened – in creative partnership with his wife, Blake was able to
maintain virtually absolute control over every aspect of the aesthetic
nature of the final interdisciplinary product.

Blake's texts are not simply verbal texts with illustrations 'to' or 'of' them, and their verbal/visual interplay is of quite a different nature from that which governs his designs for, most notably, Milton, Gray, Young, Wollstonecraft, Dante and the Bible. Nor are they the sort of text that he seems to have envisioned for *Tiriel* (c. 1788), for which work the verse and the pictures seem to have been conceived as firmly separate (and separated) components – more in the manner of the conventional eighteenth-century typeset book with full-page illustrations. Nor are they essays in the familiar form of the later eighteenth-century illustrated children's book, although Blake also tried his hand at a variant on that form (*For Children*, subsequently reworked as *For the Sexes: The Gates of Paradise*).

Blake's illuminated poems generate what is essentially a 'third text', a meta-text that partakes of both the verbal and the visual texts, but that is neither the sum of, nor identical with either of, those two texts. The verbal and visual texts stimulate different varieties of aesthetic, intellectual and affective responses which are firmly grounded in the disciplinary natures of the two media and in the tradition and 'vocabulary' (or reference-systems) particular to each. Certainly one would scarcely think of suggesting that Blake's pages are in the manner of Hogarth, whose productions are insistently and inescapably *visual* texts – pictures – no matter how much verbal material the artist introduces into them in the form of inscriptions, bits of printed matter lying about, and so forth. When we say that we 'read' a Hogarth print, we are well aware that we are using the verb 'read' in a very special way to suggest a process of perception and cognition (or recognition) that finds an analogue – and only an *analogue*, however near a one – in the largely sequential activity by which we read a conventional printed verbal text. Even the powerful *narrativity* of many of Hogarth's pictures – and certainly of sequences like his 'progresses' – is nevertheless intrinsically different from Blake's art. Perhaps the more historically apt point of contrast is furnished by the popular caricature art of Blake's time, where the striking visual textures of images by Gillray, Woodward, Rowlandson, Isaac Cruikshank and others are regularly interrupted by inscriptions, speech balloons and undemarcated lines of dialogue that seem to float in the visual space.

Pictures present us with a symbolic system of reference in which *things* and *events* are denoted by their visible *pictorial* representations. Sir Joshua Reynolds' portrait of Captain Bligh (1785),[5] for instance, imitates the form and substance of that person, and the viewer is relatively untroubled by the reduction or expansion of figure size dictated by the size of Reynolds' canvas. Bligh's contemporaries would have looked at the picture and said, yes, that is Bligh, even though to twentieth-century audiences brought up on the 1933 Nordhoff and Hall *Mutiny on the Bounty* and subsequent cinematic versions featuring Charles Laughton (1935) or Trevor Howard (1962) he may appear unexpectedly mild. In this light it is worth noting in passing that Bligh's contemporaries were right, for recent revisionist scholarship has revealed that Bligh was a thoughtful, conscientious and remarkably lenient commander whose post-mutiny commendations appear to have been appropriate and well deserved.[6] At the same time that it delivers its primary image – Captain Bligh in this instance – any picture typically manipulates the environment in which the viewer apprehends and processes that image. Reynolds accomplishes this, for instance, through the nature of the background and the selection of colours he has used for everything that is not dictated by strict (or even ostensible) pictorial/historical accuracy. Moreover, like most commissioned portraitists, Reynolds also adapts and modifies physical features in the portrait image itself, smoothing out physical roughness, silently omitting minor physical blemishes, and generally 'touching up' the image itself so as to present the sitter in the most *aesthetically* attractive fashion. Primary image and affective environment work alike upon the viewer, then, nudged along by the exertions of the painter.

A written description of Bligh, however lively, can in no way produce the immediacy of dramatic impact that the picture does, for verbal texts are unable to provide the semblance of initial simultaneity of the total image – what we see as a visual totality, *all at once*, upon first glance – that is the particular province of the visual text. With pictures, viewers typically begin with an overall impression that forms quickly upon first apprehension of the picture and gradually work their way into the image, letting their eyes explore the full image in response to the artist's prompting. Readers, on the other hand, must proceed in just the opposite fashion, putting the subject together like a jigsaw puzzle, in linear, chronological fashion, in order to construct the overall image with its attendant impressionistic, imaginative shadings. The actual process, of course – as contemporary phenomenologies of perception, cognition and interpretation quickly remind us – is a good deal more complicated, involving as it does simultaneously ongoing activities of recognizing, sorting, comparing, reconciling, rejecting, retaining and modifying data and 'meaning' literally with every piece of information that is encountered and registered. Nevertheless, there remain profound differences in the nature and the effect of the linearity involved in apprehending the content of information conveyed in each medium, differences that are a direct consequence of the nature of the individual artistic medium.

Not surprisingly, these two very different ways of presenting their materials and thus engaging their audiences indicate the extent to which the two arts are both grounded in, and directed towards, different sorts of aesthetic, intellectual and affective modes of creation and response. The really crucial difference, it seems to me, is not that of the opposition between the inherently powerful initial dramatic impact of the stunning visual image, on one hand, and the accumulative, prolonged crescendo of impact generated on the other by the verbal passage. Rather, the crux of the matter lies, I believe, in what the responding mind is asked to do in dealing with the two arts.

The visual artist controls the picture's system of references, presenting – typically – a representational image of something or someone about which (or whom) we may or may not know anything in advance. The artist also provides – and we respond to – a variously coded set of contextual indicators that might include visual conventions, specific iconography, historical or cultural references, along with what might be called 'tonal' indicators (colours, textures, 'technique' and, of course, size) that demonstrably influence our affective response to the pictorial image. If we are intended to relate Reynolds' Bligh to Neptune – or to Francis Drake or Captain Cook, for that matter – we need to work out those relations by decoding iconographic references that the artist may have embedded in the picture.

The writer, on the other hand, could simply observe that Bligh stood on the bridge 'like Drake or Cook' or 'controlled the sea like Neptune' and the intended connections are made explicitly for us, though even such explicit suggestions still prompt us to think, compare and judge the relationships proposed to us. No matter what the writer tells us about Bligh's physical appearance, however, we will not actually see him before us as we do when we look at the picture. Instead, we compose an *unverifiable* portrait out of the verbal details that come to us piecemeal as we read descriptions both of Bligh's figure and features and of his actions in a variety of situations. Very simply, it seems on the surface of the matter that the words make us work harder than the pictures do, and in quite a different way, since we are called upon to supply what appears to be a great deal more in the act of mutual creation in which we join the author.

I stress the 'seems' in this formulation deliberately, for the difference is more one of medium – of the physical materials and sense involved – than of real degree. As the eighteenth century well appreciated (one need only recall Addison's remarks on the Pleasures of the Imagination), sight – and therefore visual experience – was understood to be paramount in aesthetic experience. Verbal language is symbolic language in a way that visual materials are not, and while visual sophistication and cultivation may enable one to 'see' more that the uninitiated do, the 'learning curve' for verbal language and sophistication is both steeper and much less intuitive. The 'word-picture' needs to be decoded by visualizing it, transferring it from one medium (and the sense that anchors it) to another in a way that the 'visual picture' does not. As G. F. W. Hegel observed in *The Philosophy of Fine Art* (1820–35), this very feature – the enhanced partnership between audience and artist which is mediated by and through *language* – characterizes the highest form of Romantic art. In this rarefied aesthetic environment the sensuousness of the art is achieved specifically by the mutual intellectual and imaginative (or aesthetic) activity of reader and author, rather than because of any directly physical aspect of the materials of the artistic medium (e.g., physical colour, visual arrangement, etc.).

Given one of Blake's illuminated pages, like *Europe*, plate 9, for instance, one almost without exception first 'sees' the visual text and – unavoidably – formulates an initial response to that visual statement. I choose this page deliberately, since it effectively demonstrates one of the most characteristic and challenging intellectual 'problems' we face in dealing with Blake's illuminated poems. This lovely, graceful, visual image portrays a pair of figures whose apparent function it is to blight the crops, an act that is in fact recounted not in *Europe* at all but rather in the poem that preceded it, *America*. The visual image is an intellectual and aesthetic trap for the unwary: its seductively attractive visual aspect disguises what subsequent investigation reveals as evil, as menace, as a force of destruction.

Is a page of this sort primarily a verbal or a visual text? That seems to me just one of the many *wrong questions* that critical commentary often permits to distract us from the real matter at hand in

Blake's art. These heterogeneous pages, with their decidedly differing and often contradictory aesthetic and intellectual demands, constitute deliberately interdisciplinary physical representations intended to put us in touch with a body of meaning, or signification, of which each text – taken both separately and in tandem – is at best merely an approximation, an analogue. Robert Essick is certainly on the right track when he observes that Blake seems in his art to be aiming at creating a 'hermeneutic community whose members share a common language' (Essick 1989, p. 223). But that community – and its language – is only partly physical, and it is only partly subject to or restricted by the limitations of the verbal and visual media that seek to convey what they in fact cannot contain.

Blake offered a useful guide when he wrote in *A Vision of the Last Judgment* of the obligations that rest on the cooperating (and thus collaborating) ideal viewer:

> If the Spectator could Enter into these Images in his Imagination[,] approaching them on the Fiery Chariot of his Contemplative Thought[;] if he could Enter into Noahs Rainbow or into his bosom or could make a Friend & Companion of one of these Images of wonder which always intreats him to leave mortal things as he must know[;] then would he arise from his Grave[,] then would he meet the Lord in the Air & then he would be happy. (E560)

An act of perception of this sort sets up a different dynamic than does the standard gallery picture (such as the Bligh mentioned above), for it requires that the viewer be both participant and co-creator. It also dictates that the communication that is the object of *both* parties (artist and viewer) is of a sort that transcends the limitations of the physical medium and approaches a sort of telepathic communication that transpires 'in the air', where the viewer leaves the 'grave' of vegetable, human sensory activity and enters directly into the world of pure vision, pure Idea, which transcendent activity the artist endeavors to mediate (and, to be sure, also to *manipulate*) through the materials and the nuances of his art. For as Viscomi observes, for Blake 'the drawn line is analogous to the word of God; the inspired line is itself inspiring [*sic*] and true art is by nature sublime' (and hence capable of producing the sort of 'transport' we have come to associate with eighteenth-century notions of the Sublime) (Viscomi 1993, p. 42).

It is worth remembering that Blake alludes in this passage to the chariot of fire that bears Elijah into heaven, away from the earth-bound Elisha, to whom the prophet's mantle subsequently descends. Blake sees the appropriate consumption of his works (and we may safely add the verbal and the illuminated to the purely visual) in very much the same terms, as the passing of the prophetic mantle, together with the visionary in-sight that necessarily attends the accession to prophetic vision. Indeed, in some ways we are perhaps even better guided by the quatrain from *Jerusalem*, plate 77:

> I give you the end of a golden string,
>   Only wind it into a ball:
> It will lead you in at Heavens gate,
>   Built in Jerusalems wall.
>
>   (E231)

I think it is significant that Blake so specifically stipulates that it is 'Contemplative Thought' that is the actual vehicle (the 'Fiery Chariot') for transcendence. Immediate sensory apprehension is to lead, in other words, to re-reading and to contemplation as the reader/viewer gradually uncovers – with the artist's assistance – layer after layer of signification and is gradually consumed, paradoxically, by what she or he is consuming.

One often hears that the verbal texts of various of the *Songs of Innocence and of Experience* appear to exploit ostensible emotional and intellectual differences, or distances, that exist between the 'naive' speakers of *Innocence* or the cynical speakers of *Experience* and the knowledgeable, intellectually mature *reader* of those texts. Analogous suggestions have been made about the verbal texts of the longer narrative poems as well. Much less consideration seems to have been given, however, to whether the *visual* texts of Blake's illuminated poems engage in any of the same deadly earnest playfulness with the viewer. Commentators may *describe* the formal visual aspects of 'The Lamb' or 'The Tyger', for instance; they may note that the asymmetrical tiger is anything but fearful or that the pastoral scene depicted on the plate of 'The Lamb' is edenic. But despite some early and passing inquiry into the functional relation of verbal and visual components, it has taken until fairly recent years for Blake scholarship to yield really detailed and systematic examination of the nature of the intellectual and aesthetic manipulations the illuminations invite us – even compel us – to pursue as part of the act of reading.

In 'The Tyger', for instance, are we asking anything like the right question when we debate (as many have) the relative realism or ferocity of the tiger? That is, we may well submit that the earnestly playful Blake offers us a visual image that shatters our expectations of a standard zoo tiger. But would we be thinking about a zoo tiger in any case? Certainly it would require an impossibly naive reader to read the verbal text in that fashion. Then why should we expect otherwise in the *visual* text? Nor does it help, for that matter, to call to mind the supposedly simplified visual vocabulary of the traditional children's book, for the child is in any event more likely than the rationalizing adult to accept that Blake's odd-looking creature actually *is* a tiger. One need only think of the imaginative paradigm behind the immensely popular American comic strip, *Calvin and Hobbes*. That is, the child is both more credulous and more imaginatively generous *by nature* than is the reasoning, Urizenic adult who can see only what is 'there'. Is the *image* of Blake's tiger, perhaps, itself a physical representation of the consequences (or the workings) of the same failed *vision* that struggles to see aright the tiger of the verbal text? If so, might we then attribute to the design (and by extension to the 'painter' – NOT necessarily Blake himself but some persona of an 'illustrator') the same sort of bound and faulty vision that informs the verbal texts (and by extension their speakers – *also* NOT Blake but rather personae who inhabit Experience)? Notice the number of plates in *Experience*, especially ('Earth's Answer' or 'A Poison Tree', for example), whose bleak designs begin to make greater sense when we consider them in this way. Much the same can be said about *Innocence*, for that matter, but with a nod instead to the positive, fertile, energetic vision the designs share with the verbal texts (e.g., 'Night' or 'Spring').

Suppose we come at the matter from still another angle and consider what happens when we regard the visual image of the entire illuminated *page* of 'The Tyger' to be the text – the 'third text' or meta-text I mentioned earlier. Suppose, too, that we nevertheless view the page with the conditioned, traditionalist eyes whose powers of observation are rooted in our *expectations* rather than in the truths that the page attempts to disclose. Given the page's small scale, the reader/viewer necessarily sees top and bottom more or less at once, picture and title serving in this relatively instantaneous apprehension reinforce one another. Or so it seems. The title encourages us to identify as a tiger that creature which we might otherwise puzzle over. What the eye first 'sees' on and in this page is this double reference, verbal and visual, tied together by the heavy tree-trunk on the right whose upper and lower lines, like its attenuated bare branches, extend out to title and picture.

Within this engineered but nevertheless problematic bracketing of equivalency the reader next begins seriously to 'enter into' the poem's verbal text. As we proceed through the verses of 'The Tyger' – continuously building and modifying 'meaning' by interconnected processes of comparing, choosing, deleting, retaining and reformulating – the words come to seem less and less applicable to either our preconception of a tiger (which the title asks us to call up) or the beast represented by and in the image at the bottom of the page. Lies abound. The page is too well lit to square with 'the forests of the *night*', and in most copies the tiger's colours cannot honestly be called 'bright'. Most significantly, neither the beast *nor the illuminated page* is symmetrical: indeed the whole notion of 'fearful symmetry' is almost laughable, given the insistent asymmetry of the page and the absurdly mild aspect of the tiger.

When we approach this page 'on the Fiery Chariot of [our] Contemplative Thought' (VLJ E560) – when we follow that initial reading with one or more increasingly sophisticated and self-reflexive rereadings (each of which proceeds in light of – *illuminated* by – all the previous readings and the various responses and insights those readings have generated) – we begin to recognize how the intellectual and aesthetic complexity of the text-as-a-whole is generated in significant measure by the interaction among the expected and the unexpected, the conventional and the unconventional. This sophisticated, studious variety of reading, rereading *and contemplation* is, of course, that which historically attended the study of the medieval illuminated manuscript, in which verbal and visual texts likewise worked in mutual cooperation, even when it might appear otherwise at first glance. With 'The Tyger', for instance, contemplation may reveal more than just the implied reference to 'The Lamb': it suggest a revisionist view of Creation and indeed of the Creator. And yet the connection with Creation (via Genesis) is apparently an indirect one, for while lions are mentioned in some form or other in the Bible some 154 times, no tiger is mentioned at all. Contemplation may, as others have remarked, suggest to the perceptive reader another more immediate and strictly socio-political connection: the French Revolution. And to that viewer familiar with the caricature print (and it is instructive to remember that such viewers were legion in Blake's time) the tiger's face might seem to suggest the profile of the oft-caricatured George III, as he appears for instance in the widely-known caricature prints that James Gillray published during precisely this period: e.g., *Anti-Saccharrites* (27 March 1792), *A Connoisseur examining a Cooper* (18 June 1792), or *Temperance enjoying a Frugal Meal* (28 July 1792), all of which present the king's face in profile, as does the image on 'The Tyger'. A visual suggestion of this sort would create several delicious ironies: one would expect the emblematic British lion, rather than the tiger, for instance, and it would take some stretch of the imagination to see in George III the characteristics of either fearsomeness or symmetry. Like the king who had suffered his first bout of mental impairment only a few years earlier, both the visual text and the rhetorical structure of the verbal text are 'unbalanced'. On the other hand, is it possible that we are being led by the author who engages in extensive wordplay throughout the *Songs* towards an alternative reading of 'fearful' in which the tiger, its awesome vigour notwithstanding, is in fact fearful of what lurks to the left of the tiger's startled eyes – *something that is off the page*?

But what is off the page? Given how we customarily interpret directionality on a map, the tiger looks west, which locates the threat not in France, to the east, but rather in the west and therefore presumably the New World and America, which Blake had during the period of *Songs of Experience* in fact celebrated in the poem of that name. Indeed, the tiger's startled expression is strikingly similar to those of the figures in a separate print from about this time, *'Our End Is Come', or A Scene in the Last Judgment: the Accusers of Theft, Adultery, Murder* (1793).[7] The title phrase, 'Our End Is Come', recalls a reference in *America* to the end of the twelve-year rule of 'Angels & weak men' (16: 19 E57) that is overthrown with the outbreak of the French Revolution in 1789. But 1793 (the publication date on the title page of *America* and the year of Louis XVI's execution) is exactly twelve years after the formal conclusion in 1781 of the war with the American colonies. This dating identifies 1781–93 as that period that intervened between contemporary England's two wars against the forces of liberty and equality and gives the reference particular force when we see it as specifically and deliberately *British* in signification. Martin Butlin notes that the second state of this colour-printed line engraving bears the inscription 'When the senses are shaken and the Soul is driven to madness.

Page 56' (a reference to p. 56 of the *Poetical Sketches* where in 'King Edward the Fourth' 'The Kings and Nobles of the Land' are held responsible for war) (Butlin 1981, p. 143). If we care in this case to draw the connections that lie at the intersection of Blake's illuminated page and its historical context, multiple possibilities present themselves to the contemplative mind – as they always do in Blake's finest performances. Working with the date of 1789, one may reasonably see a connection among '*Our End Is Come*' and its inscription, the face of the tiger and its westward gaze, and the first onset of George III's madness in 1788–9. This interpretation would make doubly ironic the tiger's *westward* gaze, for it is in reality from the direction of the east, from France, that the new threat to hereditary monarchy arises while his back is turned. Tying the reference to 1793 rather than 1789, on the other hand, introduces along with the different time-frame also the immediate scare to the royal beast represented in the execution of Louis XVI.

None of this is to take the easy way out and suggest that Blake's texts are simply – even randomly – indeterminate, or that they shirk the responsibility we typically place upon the author/artist (and certainly upon the 'illustrator') to be reliable and reasonably direct. Rather, Blake characteristically invokes and manipulates our expectations about determinacy (of word, of image, of 'meaning') to force us to recognize and appreciate the multiplicity of *potential* signification that resides in seemingly every word, every line, every suggestion. As he put it in *A Vision of the Last Judgment*, 'not a line is drawn without intention & that most discriminate & particular ... as Poetry admits not a Letter that is Insignificant so Painting admits not a Grain of Sand or a Blade of Grass "Insignificant"' (E560). *In*determinacy is not the point, then, nor is the accidental ambiguity that stems from mere carelessness; the point lies instead that unconventional sort of determinacy that rests upon the intellectual and imaginative compact that Blake takes for granted between himself and his responsive, contemplative reader, a compact mediated physically by the illuminated pages. This compact, as Joseph Viscomi (most recently) has noted, is founded upon Blake's conviction that line (rather than colour or other tonal effects) is 'the foundation of art', because 'the line that discriminates and particularizes is the line that finds and fixes form in the initial chaos of lines, marks, and blurs' (Viscomi 1993, p. 167). This is why the many apparent 'variations' among copies of the illuminated works – especially variations in printing characteristics – are not the calculated and ideologically meaningful differences for which some critics have taken them,[8] but are, rather, essentially 'accidentals' resulting from the mechanical process of producing the copy: they do not in this respect 'deviate' from the 'line' (of vision) the artist placed on the original plate to indicate 'real' (or Eternal) signification.

We are all familiar with the elaborate intertextuality of Blake's works, illuminated and otherwise. And, of course, the whole nature of *allusions* is to suggest to the audience something quite specific, *but which is not physically present in the text*. In terms of the larger process of reading and interpretation generally, allusions always lead us off the page or outside the picture frame, in other words, to other texts we must consult in order more fully to apprehend 'meaning'. Typically, these other texts are not immediately at hand, and so their perusal is frequently accomplished *in absentia* by a specific, directed act of imagination – of memory stimulated by the present textual marker which inevitably shapes and colours both what is remembered and *how* it is remembered – how its meaning is reconfigured by the present context in which it is (probably imperfectly) remembered. Like any complex artist, Blake works the veins of allusion for all they are worth, typically loading his texts so heavily with apparent intertextual references that it falls to us to determine which are genuine allusions – which ones, that is, are real and which are spurious; which are deliberate and therefore meaningful and which are accidental and therefore simply distracting or possibly downright misleading. Do we need to know who those figures are atop the first page of the Preludium to *America*? Are we helped or hindered by recognizing in the female figure a typical eighteenth-century variant of the figure of Eve at the Expulsion? Does making *that* connection force us to cast her male partner as Adam, even though if we consult Blake's own mythology the adult male would seem to be not Adam but Los, and the figure manacled to the ground Orc? And what of that latter figure, who recalls also Prometheus, the crucified Jesus, and (given the currency of Salomon Gessner's *Death of Abel*) the figure of Abel as well, with perhaps the young Isaac thrown in, too?[9]

Through their configuration in the visual text these figures are telling a story, to be sure, and we are able to read in the vocabulary of their body language a considerable tale. But, as in Picasso's enigmatic *Tragedy* of 1903, we have insufficient information (or too much!) to enable us fully and consistently to interpret the scene.[10] Moreover, the story being told by Blake's images is not at all the one being told by the verbal text on this page, which seems to be occupied with something quite other. It is instances of intellectual impasse like these that suggest that mere reconciliation – mere simple solution – is not what Blake is aiming for after all. Why, after all, do we feel culturally compelled to bring apparent inconsistency into enforced (and generally both artificial and restrictive) consistency? Later in the century Ruskin (for one) will argue in _The Stones of Venice_ (1851–3) that one of the sources of the vitality of Gothic art is its _in_consistency, its 'savageness', its lack of symmetry and the other niceties of polite 'finish'. Blake's frequent championing of 'Gothic form' should make us all the more uneasy about attempting to formalize, normalize and systematize.

Let us pursue this matter a bit further in the first two plates of _Europe_, which force us to create images and physical, spatial dimensions _outside_ and _beyond_ the two-dimensional space of the illuminated page. The frontispiece invites us to decide whether the round figure behind the Ancient of Days is a flat disk or a spherical object which has to be rendered _physically_ flat because of the two-dimensionality of visual art in a book. The colour tonalities and shading in various versions of the design do little to suggest roundness, even when they do reflect visual texture.[11] Then, too, there is the invisible but implied figure that is being drawn by the extended compass. However the Ancient manipulates that instrument, the _line_ it inscribes will have to extend into a third dimension to which the medium is incapable of lending physical form. That is, the drawn circle extends both towards us and away from us, perpendicular to the flat plane of the two-dimensional page. Likewise, on the title-page part of the serpent's body extends off the page, to the right, which forces the reader to 'create' a segment of now invisible body to make whole the body that is interrupted by the _physical_ barrier of the margin. Innumerable analogies exist in eighteenth-century printed texts (verbal and visual) in which letters are left out of words (or entire words are replaced by dashes, asterisks, etc.) and lines are left out of pictures, or silhouettes are 'created' by the edges of other objects, as in the many French royalist prints from the Revolutionary era that disclose the silhouettes of Louis XVI, Marie Antoinette and their children.[12]

Part of the later eighteenth-century aesthetic agenda involved violating (and thereby gradually undermining) the ostensible barriers separating artists from their audiences. Not an innovation at all

(Joshua Reynolds' early self-portrait from the late 1740s,[13] in which the artist shades his eyes against the light streaming in from the space occupied by the viewer, offers a splendid example, for instance), this engineered interaction with the audience is very much a part of eighteenth-century English nationalism in the arts including, later, the caricature print. It served to foster the audience's identification both with the particular artist (and his or, occasionally, her) distinctive Englishness and with the increasingly British-oriented subject matter, both of which were building to a crescendo of myth in the overarching image of heterogeneous 'British' (as opposed to the stricter and more specifically insular 'English') nationhood that would become ubiquitous in political discourse by the beginning of the nineteenth century.[14]

But Blake's interest in this nationalistic swell was a radical, revolutionary one that coincided in many respects with the antiquarian interests of an eighteenth-century England that celebrated the ancient bard (as in Gray's popular poem), the indigenous cultural heritage (Percy's *Reliques of Ancient Poetry*) and the architectural ruin.[15] In this, Blake was at once forward-looking, even revolutionary, in his view of the world that seemed to be opening up to his contemporaries, and at the same time reactionary in very much the sense of many Radicals of the 1790s who sought to channel this nationalistic fervour into a recovery of the cherished ideals of a chivalric England long past. Blake's campaign against worldly materialism – and against the seductive appeal of the material world in general – was intended not to reconcile us to the natural world, or it to us, but rather to draw us away from it and towards the imaginative and spiritual world of Eternity, itself a comparatively reactionary concept that likewise hearkened back to earlier times. Blake directed his art towards engendering in his audience the sort of accession to vision that had been Elisha's part. In this sense Blake's is a deliberately and radically iconoclastic *political* art in its distrust of – indeed its attack upon – the easy, conditioned 'answers' to complex problems that are the stock-in-trade of all Establishments bent upon maintaining control not just of individuals but indeed of all the artifacts and institutions of national culture. Blake's texts foster independence of mind and vision precisely because they deny us the comfort and intellectual leisure offered by determinacy. The more I return to Blake's illuminated poems, the more compelling is the evidence I find there of Blake's particular challenge to our expectations as readers. In the subversive, oppositional intent of his art generally lies much of the aesthetic and intellectual 'agenda' that is tangibly represented in the meta-text that emerges from Blake's illuminated pages.

Notes

1. Michael Cohen, *Engaging English Art: Entering the Work in Two Centuries of English Painting and Poetry* (Tuscaloosa: University of Alabama Press, 1987), pp. 65, 76; Bindman (1977) p. 43.
2. See the following essays in the following collections: Hilton and Vogler (1986), Miller, Bracher and Ault (1987). More helpful – and probably more faithful historically and intellectually to Blake's aesthetic in the context of his times – is the notion of the sort of 'composite' art discussed some time ago by W. J. T. Mitchell (1978) and, still earlier, the encompassing tradition of the 'sister arts' invoked by Jean Hagstrum (1964). I have discussed this matter in some detail, in a somewhat different context, in Behrendt (1992) esp. Chapters 1 and 2.
3. Rothenberg here draws the distinction which Roland Barthes examines most specifically in 'From Work to Text', in *Textual Strategies: Perspectives in Post-Structuralist Criticism*, ed. Josué V. Harari (Ithaca: Cornell University Press, 1979) pp. 72–81.
4. Comparing Blake's counts of the 'designs' with the numbers of pages containing such large-scale visual images appears to corroborate this claim.
5. Joshua Reynolds, *Captain William Bligh*, 1785 (Worcester (MA) Art Museum).
6. See, most recently, Greg Dening, *Mr. Bligh's Bad Language: Passion, Power and Theatre on the Bounty* (Cambridge: Cambridge University Press, 1992); and Gavin Kennedy, *Captain Bligh: the Man and His Mutinies* (London: Cardinal, 1990).
7. Butlin (1981, plates 333 and 383; catalogue 262.2 and 285), *c.* 1794–5. The figures had already appeared in one of Blake's drawings for *Tiriel* (*c.* 1789).
8. See McGann (1981), Carr (1986), Crehan (1984), Eaves (1977 and 1992).
9. For that matter, Blake used a close variant of this figure when he illustrated one of the tortures practised by natives in Surinam, in one of his illustrations to J. G. Stedman's *Narrative* (1796).
10. Pablo Picasso, *The Tragedy*, 1903 (National Gallery of Art, Washington, D. C. Chester Dale Collection).
11. But, then, Ruskin observed that 'Illumination admits no shadows, but only gradations of pure colour'; *OED*: 'illumination'. The best discussion of the particulars of the various copies of *Europe* is Dörrbecker (1995, pp. 161–216). His assessment of the consequences for this image of Blake's colour selection parallels my much briefer observations here about how the choice of colours – as well as the

depth and intensity of those colours – creates effects of contrast and shading, as for instance with the sun, which is sometimes a yellow tone (Copies A, C, E, F and K) and sometimes red (Copies B, D and G), while the margins of the clouds may be rendered in red (A, B, F) or brown (G).

12. Two splendid representative examples: Jacques Marchand's *Saule pleureur [Weeping Willow]* (*c.* 1793), which shows a single, large willow tree with the silhouettes of Louis XVI and Marie Antoinette flanking the tree's trunk and delineated by the lines of that trunk; and Pierre-Jean-Joseph-Denis Crussaire's *L'Urne mystérieuse [The Mysterious Urn]* (*c.* 1793), which shows a woman beside an urn overshadowed by another willow with, in this instance, the silhouettes of not just the king and queen but also their children defined by the sides of the urn (in the case of the royal parents) and the breaks in the tree's foliage (the children). These engravings are reproduced in *French Caricature and the French Revolution, 1789–1799* (Los Angeles: Grunewald Center for the Graphic Arts, Wight Art Gallery, UCLA, 1988); see catalogue entries 93 and 94, p. 197.

13. Joshua Reynolds, *Self-Portrait Shading the Eyes*, late 1740s (National Portrait Gallery, London). Blake engages in this sort of transgressive activity himself, as for instance in *An Island in the Moon*, where the narrator announces: 'Then Mr. Inflammable Gass ran & shovd his head into the first & set his hair all in a flame & ran about the room – No No he did not I was only making a fool of you' (E453).

14. On the history of British nationalism in the eighteenth and early nineteenth centuries, see especially Gerald Newman, *The Rise of English Nationalism: a Cultural History, 1740–1830* (New York: St. Martin's Press, 1987), and Linda Colley, *Britons: Forging the Nation, 1707–1837* (New Haven: Yale University Press, 1992).

15. For a detailed discussion of this cultural phenomenon, see Anne Janowitz, *England's Ruins: Poetic Purpose and the National Landscape* (Oxford: Basil Blackwell, 1990).

5

What has *Songs* to do with Hymns?

Nelson Hilton

In September 1794, a reader identified only by the letter 'E' contacted *The Gentleman's Magazine* with news of a distressing discovery. 'Two or three years ago,' E relates, 'I applied to [Joseph] Johnson in St. Paul's Churchyard, for a couple of these little books of Divine Songs by Dr. Watts, which we have all learned by heart in our younger years.'[1] But, continues this correspondent, 'After I had brought them home, a friend, who remembered better than myself the studies of infancy, took them up, and observed, upon reading some of the Hymns, that they were not the same as they used to be.' The acquisition of 'another copy in the original dress' makes clear what has occurred: 'we found that Johnson's copy was completely travestied, every scrap of Trinitarianism, every intimation of the eternity of hell-torments, &c. carefully rooted out, and its place supplied by something undoubtedly more *liberal* and more *rational*.' The account cites 'The Cradle Hymn' in particular as one of the songs which the new edition has '*reformed*' (ibid.). What, one wonders, would that correspondent – or Johnson himself – have made of that little book of Songs by the publisher's sometime author and engraver William Blake with 'A Cradle Song' reconfigured seemingly so irrationally as to intimate the mother's concern lest conjugal 'sweet moans' wake her babe?[2] Yet if 'E' is correct and 'all learned by heart' such works, then the little Blake boy also must have had in *his* 'studies of infancy' some of those verses that served to initiate many a life-long involvement with hymns. Thirty years ago John Holloway concluded that, in terms of their metrical and stanzaic variety, Blake's lyrics 'make as clear a parallel with eighteenth-century hymns, as they make a contrast with eighteenth-century lyric' (1968, p. 37), and one can imagine the poet's sensitivity, more radical and idiosyncratic than any of Johnson's liberal coterie, to the resounding ideological power not just in hymns for

96

children but in that extensive body of work which makes the hymn one of the greatest, if least appreciated, legacies of eighteenth-century English literature.

While the history of eighteenth-century hymnody, like that of most significant cultural practices, presents in its particulars a variety and complexity which mock summary, five figures with whom any account must reckon are Isaac Watts, already mentioned, who decisively augmented the existing psalmody with hymn singing at the beginning of the century; John Wesley and his brother Charles Wesley, who created an enthusiastic Methodist hymnody to reach the unchurched; and John Newton and William Cowper, whose *Olney Hymns* became a manual of 'evangelical doctrine and an instrument of spiritual discipline' for the revival within the Church of England.[3]

Deliberately setting out to redress the lack of Gospel content in congregational devotion, the Dissenter Watts published his *Hymns and Spiritual Songs* in 1707, and then in 1715 his version of the Psalms, to respond to those who resisted such innovation. He professed to 'sink' his style to the 'meanest capacity' of all Protestant believers, and succeeded so well that Donald Davie finds 'quite clearly *prima facie* evidence for supposing that Watts's *Hymns and Psalms*... has been more influential than any of the works of its century that we think of as most popular.'[4] But even Watts's best known hymn, 'When I survey the wondrous cross', illustrates the pre-eminent role of cultural sensibility in hymnody with the tension over and then general omission of its fourth stanza, which begins 'His dying crimson, like a robe, / Spreads o'er his body on the tree'[5] – the same cultural development has estranged us from Blake's 'mysterious tree' and 'robes of blood'. Voicing his Calvinist theology, Watts reiterates the despicability of mortal passions even as he favours the metaphor of erotic passion for the love between Jesus and the individual Christian.[6] Yet his stated desire that hymns should ' "compose our Spirits to seriousness, and allure us to a sweet Retirement within our selves"' inaugurates the hymn's 'transition from unflinching eschatology to sentimental education'.[7] Watts is also crucially significant for his *Divine and Moral Songs Attempted in easy Language, for the Use of Children* (1715), revisions to which so distressed the writer to the *Gentleman's Magazine* eighty years later. John Bunyan's 1686 *A Book for Boys and Girls* had anticipated this particular specialized genre, but the huge impact of Watts was responsible for popularizing the form during the subsequent century.

A growing body of scholarship relates this sub-genre specifically to *Songs of Innocence* (Pinto 1957; Holloway 1968; Smith 1991), and Nick Shrimpton goes so far as to write of Blake's 'decision to write children's hymns' in order to participate in 'the most prolific and controversial literary form of the decade' (Shrimpton 1976, p. 22). I question, however, his characterization of 'To Tirzah' as 'the single exception' to his thesis (Shrimpton 1976, p. 28), and will argue that the one plate added to the collected *Songs of Innocence and of Experience* possesses conclusive as well as exceptional importance, particularly if, as Joseph Viscomi as recently argued, it was added only a year or two after the first collected *Songs* (Viscomi 1993, pp. 239, 299).

The hymns of Charles and John Wesley, respectively the poet and the 'pope' (as detractors called him) of a movement born in song in the 1740s, introduce 'a change of atmosphere, a heightening of emotion, a novelty of theme, a new manner of expression' (Benson, 247), and a Lutheran theology of unlimited atonement which offers salvation to all. The new poetic of Charles Wesley appears in his frequent abandoning of the traditional 'common', 'long', and 'short' measures on which Watts relied, and one student claims that '[w]hen the development of hymn meters is seen in historical sequence, it is apparent that Blake', who owned at least one Methodist hymn-book (Bentley, 1995, pp. 324–5),' is closer to Wesley than to any other poet' (England, 1966, p. 48). The contamination of the world does not preoccupy the Wesleys, who see themselves as focusing instead, in the resonant words of John Wesley's preface to the great 1780 Methodist hymnal, on 'the experience of real Christians'.[8] The Wesleyan 'Hymn of Experience', as the hymn-historian Louis Benson terms it repeatedly, becomes the predominating theme of Revival Hymnody, and the point of these songs can be emphasized by recalling an earlier meaning of 'experience' as 'A state of mind or feeling forming part of the inner religious life; the mental history (of a person) with regard to religious emotion'.[9] But full of the spontaneous overflow of powerful feelings as the Wesley hymns may appear to be, Marshall and Todd conclude that 'while the *religion* of the Wesley brothers was highly emotional, the *hymn* was calculated and controlled, an evangelical tool, precisely used to encourage the people to express those emotions that led to, then testified to, conversion'.[10]

For the works of John Newton, Blake had only to look over the stock of Johnson's bookshop to find, among others, the epistolary

Cardiphonia: or The utterance of the heart, Thoughts upon the African slave trade, and, already in an eighth edition by 1792, Newton's *Authentic Narrative of some remarkable and interesting particulars* which detailed the life behind his familiar hymn, 'Amazing Grace'. Sailor, deserter, prisoner, slave-trader, convert, autodidact, the Calvinist Newton received the curacy of Olney in 1764, and then from 1780 to his death in 1807 lived in the centre of the Evangelical movement as rector of St Mary Woolnoth, half a mile from Johnson's St Paul's Churchyard address. After a coincidental meeting with him in 1767, the precariously stable Cowper moved directly to Olney to reside adjacent to Newton. They began collaborating on a hymn book in 1771 at Newton's suggestion, and Cowper's family later held the effort responsible for the poet's mental breakdown (as they reported in 1801 to William Hayley, Blake's patron and Cowper's biographer). The *Olney Hymns* appeared in 1779, with several hundred hymns by Newton and 66 hymns by Cowper, including the glories of 'God moves in a mysterious way', the last hymn Cowper wrote, though some readers have felt none the less that the collection conveys morbid self-accusation, self-contempt, dejection and, finally, doubt. When Cowper asks 'Then tell me, gracious God, is mine / A contrite heart or no?',[11] one may sense already the divided soul that appeared in vision to Blake to beseech a 'refuge from unbelief' (E663).

One other body of hymn requires notice here, for E. P. Thompson's *Witness Against the Beast* (1993) has recently urged the case for the influence of a tiny religious sect on Blake in his childhood, and a reading of the *Divine Songs of the Muggletonians*[12] finds even more material than Thompson chose to cite. It is indeed uncanny to come upon the repeated imagery of a divine 'Tyger'-like 'burning glory bright' and 'bright burning glory' (nos 185 and 183) and to have God say that '"You, reason has subjected / Now to a moral death"' (no. 16, st. 8), or – as if anticipating Urizen – that 'Your reason and you are accurst too' (no. 18, st. 2).[13] The Muggletonians eschewed formal religious service, and striking lines dated 1763 read:

> No more of your canting and preaching, no more,
> With eternal forms which have charm'd me before,
> Your vain supplications and crocodile tears,
> Nor your cries to the Lord you have made without ears;
> Your fetters I drop, from your thraldom I'm free,
> Hypocritical priests, now your falsehood I see.[14]

Instances of hymnal idiom with Blake are numerous. For example, Watts's fellow hymnist Philip Doddridge favours the phrases
'supreme delight' and 'endless night', which later appear in Blake,
and declares that

> No more the awful cherubs guard
> The tree of life with flaming sword
> To drive afar man's trembling race[15]

anticipatory, perhaps, of Blake's 'cherub with his flaming sword ...
hereby commanded to leave his guard at [the] Tree of Life'
(*Marriage of Heaven and Hell*, plate 14). Doddridge's first hymn has
its singer 'trace the desart with delight', while in Blake's 'The Little
Girl Lost', Lyca's parents 'trac'd the desart ways'.[16] And we see
more clearly the 'Son-follower' aspect of the aspiring 'Sun-flower'
of Blake's poem through Doddridge's lines on

> ... joys that cannot die,
> Which God laid up in store,
> Treasure beyond the changing sky,
> Brighter than golden ore.
>
> To that my rising heart aspires,
> Secure to find its rest ...
>   (no. 209.9–14)

The long-received close reference of Blake's 'A Cradle Song' to
Watts's 'Cradle Hymn' has been invoked already, but I add here
proleptically that the nearly identical dimensions of the respective
impressions indicate to G. E. Bentley, Jr that Blake etched 'To
Tirzah' on the verso of the first plate of 'A Cradle Song' – thus
bonding back-to-back the two 'songs' which present a mother shed-
ding tears (of a sort) over her child (see Bentley, 1977, p. 382). To a
similar closeness of 'The Lamb' in *Songs of Innocence* and Charles
Wesley's 'Gentle Jesus, meek and mild' in the Methodist *Hymns for
Children* (Glen, 1983, pp. 23–5) one might add the conclusion of the
'Introduction' to *Songs of Experience*, where the setting given Earth
'till the break of day' echoes Wesley's well-known 'Wrestling Jacob',
whose protagonist means to strive for vision 'till the Break of Day'
(the Genesis source has 'breaking of the day', 32: 24). And 'The
Shepherd' of *Innocence* who 'shall follow his sheep *all the day* / And

his *tongue shall be filled with praise*' might seem to evoke Wesley's query, also from the general Methodist hymnal, 'O when shall my *tongue be filled with* thy *praise,* / While *all the day* long I publish thy grace?' (192.5–6, emphases added).

Evident familiarity with such idiom helps to explain how it is that Blake stands as the only major Romantic poet to have authored a hymn of any renown, 'posthumously endowed' though it may be.[17] The four quatrains in long measure beginning 'And did those feet...' which make up the prefatory stanzas of Blake's *Milton, a Poem* have been called 'the perfect Methodist hymn' (Gaunt, 1956, p. 52) – and at least one popular Wesleyan hymn has also a 'Chariot of Fire'.[18] But we might note that the four stanzas also in long measure of 'To Tirzah' can be sung just as easily to Sir Hubert Parry's setting of the *Milton* poem, popularly titled 'Jerusalem' and first performed in 1916 (see Rogal 1993). Moreover, 'To Tirzah' offers additional hymnic markers in the form of the Biblical refrain, 'Then what have I to do with thee?', and the inescapable scriptural associations of its title.[19] While hardly intended for congregational use, and far from doctrinal correctness, 'To Tirzah' deserves to be considered as a song of the experience of hymns: a hymn on hymn-singing to point up the inno- cent and experienced Psalms of Blake's 'Bible of Hell' and found most frequently, like many a doxology, towards the conclusion of the *Songs*.

The contrast and similarity of 'To Tirzah' with the prefatory lyric of *Milton* continue a juxtaposition of two feminine names which Blake found in one place in the Authorized Version, the erroneous translation of Song of Songs 6: 4: 'Thou art beautiful, O my love, as Tirzah, comely as Jerusalem.' Without dwelling on the exegesis of the passage, the translation appears to be based on the mistaking a form of the Hebrew verb *tirseh*, 'thou art pleasing', for the name of one-time capital of the Northern Kingdom (thus, a contrary to Jerusalem) mentioned infrequently in Joshua and Kings.[20] Blake's interest in Hebrew may permit us to imagine a hymn addressed 'To Tirzah' as 'To Delight', that sometimes ambivalent Blakean emo- tion. The name Tirzah also appears several times, usually last, in a listing of the five daughters of Zelophehad whose collective peti- tion for inheritance after the death of their father 'in the wilderness' (Num. 27: 3) 'decided women's rights in property among the Jews'.[21] Given five daughters, some critics have proposed an allu- sion to the five senses, so that, with only the four senses of smell, sight, audition and taste directly referenced in her poem, Tirzah might be identified with the unnamed fifth, the delightful sense of touch.

It is a truth widely acknowledged that the ideology of hymns does not privilege the physical and sexual experience of the body, however much communal hymn singing can itself offer physical if not sexual engagement. 'Our flesh and sense must be denied,' writes Watts, for 'Flesh is a dangerous foe to grace, / Where it prevails and rules' (Bk. 1, 132.10; Bk. 2, 161.9–10). Through Watts's hymn, the singer asks God not to permit him or her 'to be / A stranger to myself and thee':

> Why should my Passions mix with Earth,
> And thus debase my heavenly Birth!
> Why should I cleave to things below,
> And let my God, my Saviour, go!
> Call me away from Flesh and Sense;
> One Sovereign Word can draw me thence …
>
> (Bk. 2, 122.5–10)

Rejecting anything under the sun that strives with the Lord to share her or his heart, the Methodist Hymnal scripts the wish that the Lord (not Tirz*ah*!) will 'Ah! tear it thence, and reign alone' – since 'Then shall my heart from earth be free' (335.19–23). Another Methodist hymn asks for Jesus's 'powerful death' to come into the singer's being, and

> Slay the old Adam with thy breath,
>   The man of sin consume.
>
> Withhold whate'er my flesh requires,
>   Poison my pleasant food,
> Spoil my delights, my vain desires,
>   My all of creature-good

– in short, to do whatever it takes to 'Tear, tear this pride away' and 'all my nature slay' (352.5–12, 18, 20). The *Olney Hymns* sounds a similarly ascetic note in this stanza of Cowper's:

> I was a grovelling creature once,
>   And basely cleaved to earth;
> I wanted spirit to renounce
>   The clod that gave me birth.
>
> (III.52.1–4)

and the same rhyming connection between '[body ... made of the] earth' and '[sinner ... from my] birth' appears in Wesley, *Hymns for Children, C*,[22] and Doddridge: 'What then are we, the sons of earth,/ That draw pollution from our birth?' (no. 165.5–8).

Here one could consider, with E. P. Thompson's *The Making of the English Working Class*, the 'obsessional' Methodist teaching 'as to the sinfulness of sexuality, and as to the extreme sinfulness of the sexual organs' and 'the identification of Satan with the phallus',[23] a projection which Blake illustrates on several occasions (as in the design accompanying 'To the Accuser Who is the God of this World'). The wish of 'To Tirzah''s speaker 'To rise from Generation free', must in part be taken with reference to that word's active sense as exemplified by Hume when he writes that '[t]here is in all men, both male and female, a desire and power of generation more active than is ever universally exerted'.[24] The speaker of 'To Tirzah' is, at any rate, preoccupied through the second stanza with 'The Sexes': if not their 'desire and power', then the story of how they were generated or 'sprung from Shame & Pride', then 'blow'd', that is, blossomed, pollinated – 'generated' – 'in the morn', and 'in evening died'. At this point in the speaker's capsule narrative one might think to invoke the usual account of Original Sin and the consequence that 'thou shalt surely die', 'invariably thou shalt dye' (Gen. 2: 17, *Paradise Lost* 8.330), but if 'Shame & Pride' preceded and engendered 'The Sexes' then the standard paradigm becomes rather less familiar, and the meaning of 'sexes' itself unclear.

Firmer Christian ground concludes the story of the 'sexes' as 'Mercy changd Death into Sleep', with the result that – or, alternatively, 'for which cause' – 'The Sexes rose' not free from Generation, but 'to work & weep' (note that three copies of *Songs of Experience* place this story of 'The Sexes rose' next to 'The Sick Rose'). 'Death is a sleep', wrote the Methodist hymnist John Cennick in verses appropriated by Joseph Hart in 1762: 'the grave a bed; / With Jesus I shall rise'.[25] 'Sleep' or not, 'Death' looms as another compelling concern for a speaker preoccupied with the claims of 'Mortal Birth', 'my Mortal part', 'Mortal Life' (1, 9, 14) and a tongue already closed 'in senseless clay'. This concern is ostensibly obviated by the poem's penultimate line, though that line's repetition and the poem's very existence betray the speaker's assurance: 'The Death of Jesus set me free.' The simple past tense declares an opportunity which existed only in the past – a grammatical particular which

contrasts pointedly with twenty-eight instances of 'set me free' in
the Wesley hymns, every one of which is marked as future, imperative, infinitive, present perfect or conditional. This closed grammar
matches the speaker's blank belief in 'The Death of Jesus', a specific
formulation perhaps found only once elsewhere, in a short Wesley
hymn on Mark 15: 10 which begins, 'Envy, when time began, / The
death of Jesus was, / From earth's foundations slain / It nail'd Him
to the cross'. 'Forbid it, Lord, that I should boast / Save in the
Death of *Christ* my God,' writes Watts in his familiar hymn.[26] So too
for Wesley,

> This, only this is all my plea:
>   I the chief of sinners am,
> But Jesus died for me.
>   (111.6–8)

Or, in the words of another Wesley hymn, you have only to 'Believe
in him that died for thee!', and 'sure as he hath died / Thy debt is
paid, thy soul is free' (35.13–15). And the parishioners of Olney
were only the first of many to sing of the bosom glowing 'with
heav'nly zeal, / To worship him who died for me' (Bk. 2, 38.19–20).
Sin, the hymns agree, is that from which the death of Jesus sets us
free. In the words of a Watts hymn which 'To Tirzah' also echoes
and contrasts in other ways:

> Mighty Redeemer, set me free
>   From my whole state of sin;
> O make my soul alive to thee,
>   Create new powers within.
>
> Renew mine *eyes, and* form mine *ears,*
>   And *mould my heart* afresh;
> Give me new passions, joys and fears,
>   And turn the stone to flesh.[27]

Newton has the congregation at Olney sing 'Farewell world', since
'Jesus died to set me free / From the law, and sin, and thee!'
(56.20–4), while Cowper grimly has 'Hope' bid them wait with
patience 'Till death shall set me free from sin, / Free from the only
thing I hate' (Bk. 3, 64.7–8). But Blake's poem makes strange the

familiar cultural narrative concerning sin by its disjunction between 'Generation', from which the speaker still wishes to rise free, and the implied condition of sin, from which the speaker claims emphatically to be free.

A song which sighs not 'Ah! Sun-flower' but 'To Tir*zah*' and which features both weeping on the part of the sexes and 'false self-decieving tears' attributed to the mother solicits attention to its lachrymation. Elsewhere Blake writes of 'intreating *Tears* & Sighs / O...', describes how 'in ghastly *fears* / *Ah* she doth depart', and shows a schoolboy in 'sighing and *dismay*. / *Ah!*...' (E483, 467, 31, emphases added), and others in the late eighteenth century have 'pray'rs and *tears*. Ah!' or 'eyes in *tears* – Ah!';[28] a crucial passage in *The Four Zoas*, Night 8, associates 'singing in tears' and 'Tirzah' in the space of three lines (105.29, 27, E378). Cherished by the 'age of sensibility', tears – frequently with accompanying sighs – signify feeling in the diffuse collective response to a perceived depersonal-izing ethos of the Enlightenment, and the hymns of the Methodist and Evangelical Revivals, as crucial expressions of that cultural movement, are filled with tears they celebrate and strive to occasion. Watts's 'acutely self-conscious' believer requests, 'Dissolve my Heart in Thankfulness, / And melt my Eyes to Tears' – though 'drops of grief can ne'er repay / The debt of love'.[29] Such scripted words were evidently not without effect, as one finds Doddridge reporting to Watts in April 1731, how, upon the singing of one of Watts's hymns, he 'had the satisfaction to observe tears in the eyes of several of the people'.[30] Joseph Hart's 1759 *Hymns...with the Author's experience* addresses Jesus with the thought that 'Though Thou from the curse hast freed us', may the cost never be forgotten 'Till we, viewing Whom we piercéd, / Melt in penitential tears';[31] and Anne Steele, leading hymnist of the Calvinistic Particular Baptists, regrets

> How oft my mournful thoughts complain,
>   And melt in flowing *tears*!
> My weak resistance, *ah*, how vain!
>   How strong my foes and fears?[32]

Almost any few pages of an eighteenth-century hymnal will offer further examples.

That the popular 1780 Methodist Hymnal should include a section 'For Mourners...Convinced of Backsliding' (Pt. 3, Sect. 4, with thirteen hymns), indicates, however, the always-present possibility of spurious repentance. Writing of the great preacher Whitefield, said to bring listeners to tears even with his sonorous enunciation of the word 'Mesopotamia', a colleague reported: 'I hardly ever knew him to go through a sermon without weeping more or less, and I truly believe his were the tears of sincerity.'[33] This account, however, clearly supposes that some religious tears might be less than sincere, even hypocritical or, to use the word which seems to favour a religious context, 'self-deceiving'.[34] In Blake's poem, the sincerity of the speaker's cruel attribution of 'false self-decieving tears' is compromised at least by our sense that such knowledge comes from personal experience: as Blake writes in *Jerusalem*, 'Foote in calling Whitefield, Hypocrite: was himself one' (plate 52). In calling Tirzah false, the speaker alerts us to the possibility of the speaker's own self-deception – and, like Los in *Milton*, what can readers do? how can we judge? when Satan's self believes that he is not oppressing? – or deceiving? (*Milton* 7.39–40).

While 'To Tirzah' evokes comparison with hymns in some formal respects and, I suggest, dramatizes the psychology of a hymn-singing upholder of 'the patriarchal religion' (*Jerusalem* 27), the poem itself could never be mistaken for an English hymn, most obviously in its direct, intimate address to 'Thou Mother of my Mortal Part'. The Protestant abjection of the Virgin Mother seems to have extended to a ban on almost any mention of women in hymns through the eighteenth century. Watts at one point lets slip a feminine pronoun for 'Faith' (Bk. 1, 140.17), but in another hymn, more tellingly, dwells on the treacherous female arts of 'Sin' and the guilt of Eve (Bk. 2, 150.5–16); Wesley's few 'Hymns for Girls' display a patriarchalism offensive if not incredible today.[35] One of Cowper's hymns asks 'Can a woman's tender care / Cease towards the child she bare?', and its plain answer, 'Yes, she may forgetful be' (118.12–14), glosses the melodramatic 'No no never can it be' with which the speaker of Blake's 'On Another's Sorrow' denies the possibility of maternal neglect. In another hymn collection the speaker has a vision of the cross and 'no more at *Mary* wonder[s] / Dropping Tears upon the grave', and Hart in several places compares the love of Jesus to that of a mother for her child.[36]

There was, however, one older hymn surviving in the cultural archive – appearing several times in eighteenth-century broadsides and wellknown at least in Scotland – which could have prompted Blake to supply a maternal dimension to the Song of Songs' coupling of Tirzah and Jerusalem. It is one of the very few hymns deeply involved with a 'her':

> O Mother dear, Jerusalem,
>> When shall I come to thee?
> When shall my sorrows have an end?
>> Thy joys when shall I see?

The most popular form of this hymn today opts for Jerusalem as 'the happy home' and comes from a version probably by the well-known early nineteenth-century hymnist James Montgomery; first published three years before the date of Blake's *Milton* in an 1801 *Collection of above Six Hundred Hymns designed as a New Supplement to Dr. Watts's Psalms & Hymns*, it opens:

> Jerusalem! my happy home,
>> Name ever dear to me!
> When shall my labours have an end
>> In joy, and peace, and thee?

The question the speaker of 'To Tirzah' twice addresses to the cruel mother and which contains his or her only subjective appearance, 'Then what have I to do with thee?' (4, 16), echoes, among other pertinent Biblical possibilities, Jesus' apparently rude words to *his* mother when she mentioned the lack of wine at the marriage in Cana: 'Woman, what have I to do with thee? mine hour is not yet come' (John 2: 4 – the Authorized Version's problematic translation of the Greek formula *ti emoi kai soi* ['what's that to me and to you?']). The speaker of 'To Tirzah' asserts that the death of Jesus sets the speaker free of *mater*-reality, but to the speaker's mother ritually repeats the words of him who died. Accusing the mother of moulding speaker's parts with cruelty even as speaker abuses her cruelly, speaker alleges that speaker's tongue or taste-sense is closed 'in senseless clay', so forcing the reader to call into question speaker's own speech – are these like words of 'The Dead' who figure in Blake's longer poems? is there *sensible* clay? is 'The Death of Jesus' a 'Sleep' to the speaker? Three stanzas of Hart's hymn 'Of Sanctification' capture the orthodox issue at stake:

> 3. Experience likewise tells us this;
>> Before the Saviour's Blood

> Has wash'd us clean, and made our Peace,
>   We can do nothing good.
> 4. But here, my Friends, the Danger lies;
>   Errors of diff'rent Kind
> Will still creep in, which Dev'ls devise
>   To cheat the human Mind.
> 5. 'I want no Work within, (says one)
>   "Tis all in the Christ the Head.'
> Thus careless he goes blindly on,
>   And trusts a Faith that's dead.
>   (no. 11, pp. 12–13)

Similarly self-deceived, the speaker of 'To Tirzah' seems to be a prototype of Blake's 'Moral Christian' (E877) who has yet to experience
what Los later calls 'anguish of regeneration' (*Jerusalem* 7.61).

   The one published hymnal use of 'What have I to do with thee' of
which I am aware occurs in Newton's 'Olney Hymn' on 'The Legion
Dispossessed'; significantly enough, it quotes a very different Biblical
instance of the formulaic phrase (Mk 5: 7, Lk 8: 28) as Legion recalls
how, 'Fill'd with madness, sin and woe', he was found by Jesus:

>   Yet in this forlorn condition,
>   When he came to set me free,
>   I reply'd to my Physician,
>   'What have I to do with thee?'

The healed Legion wonders why he should remain below, but
learns from the Lord that 'Love … will sweeten labours', and, in
phrasing which also anticipates 'The Little Black Boy' put on earth
'a little space', that he is to 'wait for heaven a little space' while he
tells 'friends and neighbours, / What [Jesus's] love has done for
[him]' (Bk. 1, 92). Mary Wollstonecraft, in *The Wrongs of Woman: or,
Maria*, published posthumously in 1798, also draws on the formula's association with emotional unbalance in striking fashion.
Fleeing at last from the private madhouse to which the patriarchy
confined her, Maria, a new woman taken in adultery, is seized by
'[a] being, with a visage that would have suited one possessed by
a devil' who, appropriately, 'crossed the path'.[37] Hardly can she ask
if the form is 'made of flesh and blood' when '"Woman", interrupted a sepulchral voice, "what have I to do with thee?" – Still
he grasped her hand, muttering a curse'. Wollstonecraft proposes,

at last, a response to this question, as Maria exclaims '"No, no; you have nothing to do with me,"' and with 'supernatural force' breaks from 'the being' (who casts 'a stone' after her in 'hellish sport'). Finally, recalling the etymological association of Tirzah with 'delight' and pleasure, consider the Anacreonic ode titled 'Enjoyment' in the translation by Frances Fawkes published in 1760 and again, more widely, in 1789 and 1795, and about as far from the ethos of hymnody as one could get:

> SINCE I'm born a mortal man,
> And my being's but a span,
> 'Tis a march that I must make;
> 'Tis a journey I must take:
> What is past I know too well;
> What is future who can tell?
> Teazing care, then *set me free*,
> *What have I to do with thee?*
> Ere I die, for die I must,
> Ere this body turns to dust,
> Every moment I'll employ
> In sweet revelry and joy,
> Laugh and sing, and dance and play,
> With Lyaeus young and gay.[38]

Much, to be sure, has been written which construes 'To Tirzah', like almost any hymn, as a rejection of the physical body and 'lustful joy' of generation (*Visions of the Daughters of Albion* 7.6). But, as D. G. Gillham taught many years ago, the *Songs* are dramatic poems whose speakers are not to be identified with the author; furthermore, Viscomi's new dating of 'To Tirzah' would in any event give next to no time for some massive shift in Blake's psychology to ground 'the ruthless rejection of his former self' argued by E. D. Hirsch (1964, p. 156); and, finally, even in later works Blake celebrates

> … holy Generation [*Image*] of regeneration!
> O point of mutual forgiveness between Enemies!
> Birthplace of the Lamb of God incomprehensible!
> The Dead despise & scorn thee, & Cast thee out as accursed:
> Seeing the Lamb of God in thy gardens & thy palaces:
> Where they desire to place the Abomination of Desolation.
> (*Jerusalem* [*J*] 7.65–70)

The last phrase is crucial, for Blake uses it to refer to 'Rahab or Mystery Babylon' (*J* 75.18–19) and to 'State Religion which is the Source of all Cruelty' ('Annotations to Watson', E618), and this 'Religion of Chastity' (*J* 69.34), 'Sexual Religion' (*J* 30[44].11), 'Religion of Generation' (*J* 7.63), or 'Natural Religion' originates the cruelty in which Tirzah most delights. A remarkable passage in *Milton*, plate 19[21], goes so far as to make explicit the connection of these concerns with 'To Tirzah', and seems to gloss retrospectively that poem's title in the mocking by Rahab and Tirzah of 'the Lamb of God' (emphasis added):

His Images are born for War! For Sacrifice *to Tirzah!*
To Natural Religion! to Tirzah the Daughter of Rahab the Holy ...

A poem to 'delight' or enjoyment thus becomes also 'To Natural Religion', showing again, as David Erdman writes of 'The Everlasting Gospel' with an appropriate pun, that 'entangled cross-purposes are not uncharacteristic for Blake' (Erdman 1965, p. 341). The 'Moral Christian' who hymns the 'False Christ' of the churches and of Tirzah has yet to accept and revel in the 'earthly parentage which is the essence of Blake's Jesus' (Helms, 1980, p. 144) and the scandalous idea of incarnation which led some Renaissance artists to celebrate the erection of Jesus even at death – as may Blake in the strange illustration of 'To Tirzah'.[39]

If we see the *Songs* as staging states of individual consciousness in minute, particular, overdetermined knots of language, image and perception, and showing, as the last book of *Olney Hymns* only claims to do, 'the progress and changes of the spiritual life', then 'To Tirzah' offers a unique perspective as at once the *terminus ad quem* of the collection and the jumping off point for the longer poems. In the midst of ever widening secularization, an increasingly distant aspect of Blake's collection is its concern with the powerful cultural innovation which served to hem in rather than sing out 'Human Imagination / Which is the Divine Body of the Lord Jesus' (*Milton* 3.3–4).

Notes

1. *The Gentleman's Magazine*, September 1794 (64.9), p. 805.
2. Sweet moans, dovelike sighs,
    Chase not slumber from thy eyes.

> Sweet moans, sweeter smiles,
> All the dovelike moans beguiles.
> (E12: 13–16)

Blake repeatedly characterizes 'joy', 'delight', 'bliss', and, once, their occasioning 'sexual garments' as 'sweet' (recall also the 'sweet moan' of Keats's 'Belle Dame').

3.   Louis F. Benson, *The English Hymn: Its Development and Use in Worship* (New York: George H. Doran, Co., 1915) p. 338.

4.   Donald Davie, *A Gathered Church: The Literature of the English Dissenting Interest, 1700–1930* (London: Routledge and Kegan Paul, 1978) pp. 33–4; see also Benson (1915) p. 125.

5.   Isaac Watts, *Hymns and Spiritual Songs*, 1707, rpt. (Exeter: C. Norris, 1815), Bk. 3, 7.17–18.

6.   Madeleine Forall Marshall and Janet Todd, *English Congregational Hymns in the Eighteenth Century* (Lexington: University Press of Kentucky, 1982) pp. 53–4.

7.   Lionel Adey, *Hymns and the Christian 'Myth'* (Vancouver: University of British Columbia Press, 1986) p. 154.

8.   John Wesley and Charles Wesley, *A Collection of Hymns for the use of the People called Methodists*, 1780, rpt. *The Works of John Wesley*, vol. 7, eds. Franz Hildebrandt and Oliver A. Beckerlegge, W. James Dale (Oxford: Clarendon Press, 1983) p. 3.

9.   *OED s.v.* 4b and cf. Hart's title, below (note 24).

10. Marshall and Todd (1982) p. 87.

11. John Newton and William Cowper, *Olney Hymns*, 1779, rpt. in vol. 3 of *The Works of John Newton* (London, 1826; facs. rpt., Edinburgh: The Banner of Truth Trust, 1988), Bk. I, 64.3–4.

12. [Joseph Frost, and Isaac, eds.], *Divine Songs of the Muggletonians, In Grateful Praise to the Only True God, the Lord Jesus Christ* (London, 1829 – the texts, however, date mostly from the seventeenth and eighteenth centuries).

13. Nos 185, 183; 16; 18; with regard to 'The Tyger', however, Holloway finds it 'impossible not to believe' that Blake had in mind a Watts's hymn which states that 'God is a bright and burning fire' and continues, 'his eye / Burns with immoral jealousy' (Holloway 1968, pp. 46–7).

14. No. 55, st. 4, p. 158, by Henry Bonel; Thompson quotes other verses from this song (1993, p. 75).

15. Philip Doddridge, *The Works of the Rev. P. Doddridge*. 6 vols., vol. 3 [includes *Hymns*] (Leeds: Edward Baines, 1803) nos 294, 374; 329; 284-13-15.

16. Doddridge 1.9–10, see also 'desart' in 19.11; 30.23; 310.4; Blake's is the only instance of the phrase 'trac[e]['d][ed] the desart' recorded in the Chadwyck-Healey Literary Databases. Flawed as it is in some editorial choices – and terribly weak on hymns (e.g. no Doddridge) – this archive and search engine provides a remarkable new research tool.

17. Donald Davie, *The Eighteenth-Century Hymn in England* (Cambridge: Cambridge University Press, 1993) p. 157.

18.   Charles Wesley, *Representative Verse of Charles Wesley*, selected and edited with an introduction by Frank Baker (New York: Abingdon Press, 1962) 73.35; Martin Madan, rev., edn, *A Collection of Psalms and Hymns, Extracted from various Authors*, 3rd edn (London, 1764) no. 209.

19.   I have yet to meet 'Tirzah' in a hymn, though Charles Wesley does invoke 'Rahab's Pride' in Blake-like fashion (*Representative Verse* 11.9–13).

20.   See Marvin H. Pope, trans., comm., *Song of Songs*, The Anchor Bible (New York: Doubleday, 1977) pp. 558–60; and Spector, 1990.

21.   James Hastings, *A Dictionary of the Bible*, vol. 4 (Edinburgh: Clark, 1902) *s.v.*

22.   Quoted Holloway (1968) p. 49; and Shrimpton (1976) p. 24.

23.   E. P. Thompson, *The Making of the English Working Class*, A Vintage Giant (New York: Knopf and Random House, 1963) pp. 366 fn., 370; 370, cf. 40 (to which Davie offers 'strenuous protest' [*Gathered Church*, pp. 45–7]).

24.   *Political Discourses*, 1752 (*OED s.v.* 'generation').

25.   Joseph Hart, *Hymns, &c. Composed On Various Subjects*, The Third Edition, with the Author's Experience, and the Supplement (London, 1763) *incipit* 'Christians, dismiss your fear ...'

26.   'When I survey the wondrous cross'; see Marshall and Todd (1982) p. 45.

27.   Bk. II, 130.17–24, emphases added; according to the Chadwyck-Healey Literary Databases, 'To Tirzah' offers the first appearance of the phrase 'mould my heart' after its inaugural formulation by Watts.

28.   These (Richard Grover, 'The Athenaid' [1787], and John Frederick Bryand, 'Benevolence' [1787], emphases added) and more in the Chadwyck-Healey Database.

29.   Marshall and Todd (1982) p. 54; Watts, Bk. 2, 9.19–22.

30.   Benson (1915) p. 125.

31.   'Great High-Priest, we view Thee stooping', 11, 15–16.

32.   In Richard Arnold, ed., *English Hymns of the Eighteenth Century: An Anthology* (New York: Peter Lang, 1991) p. 321, emphases added.

33.   Quoted in William Edward Hartpole Lecky, *A History of England in the Eighteenth Century*, vol. 2 (New York: Appleton, 1891) p. 621.

34.   See *OED*, *s.v.*; according to the Chadwyck-Healey Database, the Wesleys use the expression 'self-deceiving' six times more frequently than any other of its authors.

35.   Charles Wesley, *Hymns for children, and persons of riper years*, 4th edn (London, 1784).

36.   Henry Peckwell, ed., *A Collection of Psalms and Hymns* (London, n.d. [1775?]) 32.9–10; Hart, 69, p. 92; Supplement 15, p. 163.

37.   Mary Wollstonecraft, *Mary* and *The Wrongs of Woman*, 1798, eds. James Kinsley and Gary Kelly, The World's Classics (Oxford: Oxford University Press, 1980) p. 190.

38. Francis Fawkes, *The Works of Anacreaon. Translated from the Greek,* 1760, rpt. in Robert Anderson, ed., *The Works of the British Poets,* vol. 13 (London, 1795) p. 171.

39. See Leo Steinberg, *The Sexuality of Christ in Renaissance Art and in Modern Oblivion,* second edition, revised and expanded (Chicago: University of Chicago Press, 1996); and Hilton (1990) and http://www.english.uga.edu/wblake/SIE/52/hilton.html

6

Calling into Existence:
The Book of Urizen
Angela Esterhammer

According to Blake's *Europe*, as history moved towards the crisis of
the French Revolution, God became a 'tyrant crown'd' (*Eur.* 10.23,
E63). One of the ways this paradigm shift – from God to crowned
tyrant – manifests itself, both in the history of the late eighteenth
century and in Blake's prophetic books, is through the altering role
and power of speech acts. God is presented in the first chapter of
the Bible as the ideal user of language that is action, or of what
twentieth-century philosophers and linguists have called performative utterance: God spoke and it was so.[1] By contrast, the words of
the 'tyrant crown'd' also issue in immediate action, but it is because
he has authority over his subjects, not over the matter of the universe; because he can compel behaviour, not because he can bring
about the absolute unity of signifier and signified; because he has
assumed or been granted a kind of authority that is only conferred
in the first place through political or institutional pronouncements,
not because he is the Logos itself. This essay is an attempt to trace
the devolution of performative language from the God of Genesis
to the tyrant in *The Book of Urizen*. To put it differently, I would like
to consider the way utterances are seen as creating a phenomenal
world in the one case, but a world of political relations and social
distinctions in the other. This will entail a reading of *The Book of
Urizen* in light of its two great precursor texts on language and
world-creation, Genesis and *Paradise Lost*, which provided Blake
with illustrations and analyses of the creative power of utterance,
but also with a view of language as an instrument that works
within a social and political context. In addition, scholarship current in Blake's time on the language of the Bible, ranging from the
'high-cultural' lectures of Robert Lowth to the popular political
writings of Thomas Paine, parallels Blake's recognition that the 'transcendent' language of God in the Bible, along with the language of

the Bible itself, can or must be re-evaluated within a sociopolitical context. That this contextualization of utterance accounts for its ability to call a new world-order into existence, but also ties its creative power inextricably to division, restriction, and imposition, is the dilemma Blake dramatizes in *The Book of Urizen*.

The influence of biblical scholarship and theories of language of Blake's work has already been explored by Leslie Tannenbaum, Jerome McGann and Robert Essick. According to Tannenbaum, the two different versions of the myth of creation in Genesis that were being identified by some biblical scholars beginning in the seventeenth century are reproduced in *The Book of Urizen*. Tannenbaum traces the distinction between Urizen and Los to scholarship on the 'Genesis tradition' that distinguished between a more abstract and a more anthropomorphic conception of God in the Pentateuch, so that the abstract creation brought about by Urizen corresponds to the 'Elohist' (E) narrative in Genesis 1, and the anthropomorphized creative activity of Los corresponds to the 'Yahwist' or 'Jahwist' (J) narrative in Genesis 2–3 (Tannenbaum 1982, pp. 203–7). McGann and Essick (1990, pp. 141–4; 1991, p. 209) are persuaded by Tannenbaum's alignment of Urizen with Elohim and Los with Yahweh, but prefer to trace Blake's awareness of different manuscript traditions in Genesis to a different source – if not directly to the German Higher Criticism, which was being founded during Blake's lifetime, then to the radical Catholic priest Alexander Geddes, who conducted much of the current German scholarship into England while proposing alternative theories of his own regarding the origin and transmission of the biblical text.

All this is illuminating – but only up to a point, since neither Genesis nor *The Book of Urizen* allows for unfluctuating distinctions. In *The Book of Urizen*, even more than in Blake's other narratives, characters share among themselves a number of archetypal roles – those of the Elohim, Yahweh, Adam, Eve and Moses, at a bare minimum. Even while Los is performing his 'anthropomorphic' creation of a Urizenic body, he is doing so in the manner of the 'abstract' Elohim of Genesis 1 by echoing the six days of creation. Later in *The Book of Urizen*, as Tannenbaum notes, Urizen himself assumes Yahweh's role in Genesis 2 by planting a garden of fruits (*BofU* 20.41, E81). Moreover, a strict identification of Urizen with the Elohim, and Los with Yahweh, neglects the role and power of divine utterance in Genesis and Blake's response to it. The creative words of the Elohim in Genesis 1 provide what one might call the ideal model of performative utterance, and they are cited as the supreme example of the sublime power of language by scholars from Longinus of Lowth. By contrast, Yahweh in Genesis 2 and 3 is responsible for autocratic and restrictive speech acts such as the prohibition and the sentence of judgement on Adam and Eve.[2] On this basis at least, one would expect the arbitrary and judgemental Yahweh to be the target of Blake's severer critique, not the creative, life-affirming Elohim.

The comments of the eighteenth-century scholar Robert Lowth in his *De sacra Poesi Hebraeorum* (1753; English translation published in 1787 as *Lectures on the Sacred Poetry of the Hebrews*) illustrate the significance of Genesis 1 for the biblical criticism of Blake's time, while reaffirming the link between sublimity and power in the creative utterances of Genesis 1. Lowth identifies his definition of the sublime with that of Longinus, and goes on to cite the same primary example of sublimity as Longinus did, namely Genesis 1: 3: 'And God said, Let there be light, and there was light.' The force of this verse, Lowth contends, cannot be explained through long exegesis; rather, its force 'seems to proceed from the proper action and energy of the mind itself.'[3] That is to say, in accounting for the expression of God's verbal creativity Lowth rejects the role of descriptive or referential language – the thought, he says, cannot be explained in words – and points instead to the primal action that the words perform. Their effectiveness within the narrative as the world-creating utterance of God is echoed by their effectiveness within the experience of reading, where they present God to the reader in an unparaphrasable conceptual act.

This verse, and the sublime itself, are for Lowth a primary aspect of the mode of language which he calls by the Hebrew term *mashal*, and which forms one of the major organizing principles of his lectures on the Bible. *Mashal* refers to both features of style and authorial voice, but its usual translation, 'parable', does not capture the full range of meaning. Lowth's investigation into the meaning of *mashal* entails an excursus on the history of poetry, from which he concludes that the Hebrews, like other ancient peoples, used poetic expression not only for the figurative compositions that moderns call poetry, but for a variety of social and political purposes – 'as the recorder of events, the preceptor of morals, the historian of the past, and prophet of the future'.[4] Thus the role of *mashal* originally, and still in the Hebrew Bible, is to convey institutional authority, the authority that we would now associate with the educational system, with organized religion, and with the public records office.

Lowth's etymological footnote on the term *mashal* makes the association with authority and power even stronger. He points out that *mashal*, besides evoking a range of meanings relating to verbal expression, all centring on parables or comparisons, carries the alternative definition 'rule', 'be eminent', 'possess dominion and authority'. The two meanings are linked by the concept of *representation:* just as the image of vehicle stands for the tenor in a parabolic expression, so the steward or deputy (*Ha-mashel*) stands for the authority of his master.[5] 'Whence', Lowth's note continues, 'there is evidently a relation between the two interpretations of this root, consisting in this circumstance, that both the parabolical image, and the steward or deputy, are representative.' The very stylistic feature which makes it possible to describe a composition as *mashal* – that is, the use of figure or parable – is the feature which links the term to the concept of power or delegated authority.

As often as they affirm the social authority conveyed by Hebrew poetry, Lowth's *Lectures* also stress its sheer active or performative force: poetry in the Hebrew Bible makes 'a ... forcible impression upon the mind' and directs the audience's perceptions, it expresses 'energy and enthusiasm', it 'strikes and overpowers the mind'.[6] In a related vein, the whole of Lowth's eighteenth lecture argues that prophecy and poetry are virtually indistinguishable in the Hebrew scriptures, and indeed in other ancient texts and traditions. Much more than modern readers realize, according to Lowth, the poetical compositions of the ancient Hebrews are to be taken as words with power, that not only convey divinely inspired prophecy but also impress wisdom, faith, and morality on the minds of present and future listeners or readers.

This current of biblical scholarship, then, one almost certainly known of Blake,[7] attributes several types of power to biblical language. Lowth analyses the poetry of the Hebrew Bible as *mashal*, a mode of language 'expressive of power, or supreme authority',[8] which manifests itself in the sub-class of expression called the sublime, which is represented, in turn, by Genesis 1: 3, where God begins calling the world into existence. *Calling into existence* is indeed quite a literal description of what is going on in this narrative. In Genesis 1, the verb *kara*, which the Authorized Version translates 'call' in the sense of 'name' (as in 'God called the light Day'), actually means something more like 'call out'.[9] In other words, God is represented as calling out, or proclaiming, the names of his creations when they appear before him as phenomenal manifestations of his utterance. When Blake rewrites creation in *The Book of Urizen*, however, he focuses on the politicized authority that Lowth also regarded as an intrinsic feature of biblical language. The result is a text in which utterance – not only Urizen's but also the Eternals' and the narrator's – indeed has performative force, but this power carries negative connotations of imposition and even violence. To call, as I will argue later, is to label or stereotype – perhaps even, at least figuratively, to kill. As presented in *The Book of Urizen*, performative language is less reminiscent of creation by the word than of an alternative originary proclamation: the decree of God the Father in Book 5 of Milton's *Paradise Lost*.

Despite all that has been written on the relationship of *The Book of Urizen* to *Paradise Lost*, one passage which still needs to be brought to bear on Blake's text is God's exaltation of the Son, the event that leads directly to War in Heaven. This episode corresponds to Urizen's separation from the company of the Eternals inasmuch as it is, according to Milton's version of sacred history, the initial change in eternal existence from which all other changes follow. Even Blake's 'Preludium' gains new resonances when read in the context of this passage from *Paradise Lost*, which begins with Adam's comment to Raphael that he is delighted to hear him speak and his request that the angel go on to relate the entire history of creation. When Raphael briefly hesitates to '*unfold* / The secrets of another World', both because it is too hard to 'relate / To human sense th' invisible exploits / Of warring Spirits' and because it may be 'Not lawful to reveal' those secrets,[10] we have a possible explanation as to why Blake needs to reassure the Eternals who have called him:

> Eternals I hear your call gladly,
> Dictate swift winged words, & fear not
> To unfold your dark visions of torment.
> (*BofU* 2.5–7, E70)

The story Raphael tells is full of authoritative speech acts, beginning with and centring on the Father's exaltation – indeed, his creation – of the Son through a classic performative utterance:

> This day I have begot whom I declare
> My only Son, and on this holy Hill

> Him have anointed, whom ye now behold
> At my right hand; your Head I him appoint;
> And by my Self have sworn to him shall bow
> All knees in Heav'n, and shall confess him Lord:
> Under his great Vice-gerent Reign abide
> United as one individual Soul
> For ever happy: him who disobeys
> Mee disobeys, breaks union, and that day
> Cast out from God and blessed vision, falls
> Into utter darkness, deep ingulft, his place
> Ordain'd without redemption, without end.
> (*PL* 5.603–15)

The cause of the ensuing War in Heaven might well be identified as Satan's obsession with this authoriative verbal act. Trying to persuade his followers to rebel, Satan insistently refers to God's speech acts: his new laws, his new commands, his decree, declaration, proclamation, edict, and the new name of 'King anointed' that he has granted the Son (*PL* 5.772–802). Satan's oration climaxes with a challenge which implies that God does not have the authority to impose new laws, since these would contravene a previous speech act that granted dominion (in the form of 'Imperial Titles') to the angels:

> Who ... can introduce
> Law and Edict on us, who without law
> Err not? much less for this to be our Lord,
> And look for adoration to th' abuse
> Of those Imperial Titles which assert
> Our being ordain'd to govern, not to serve?
> (*PL* 5.794–802)

In calling the angles those 'who without law / Err not', Satan vaunts their virtue and accuses God of tyranny in presuming to impose unnecessary restraints. Milton, by contrast, surely means readers to hear the irony in Satan's claim that he does not err, spoken even as he is committing the ultimate error of rebellion against the Father. Satan's performance, in fact, confirms the import of his words: because God *has* pronounced a decree condemning those who refuse to worship the Son to utter darkness, Satan's words now *count* as a crime deserving of damnation. Since a law has been

introduced, Satan's transgression of it ironically confirms the truth
of his statement that error is inconceivable without law, because,
transgression is only defined – that is, created – by legislation.[11]

Both conceptually and in terms of the chronology of *Paradise Lost*,
then, the legislative word of God and the resulting transgression
of Satan precede God's use of performative utterance to create
the world. In Blake's poem, the legislating word has completely
usurped the world-creating word; or rather, as with so many events
in Blake's poetry, the two are superimposed on one another so that
the creation of any world other than a politicized and legislated one
becomes inconceivable. Urizen's speech in Chapter II of *The Book of
Urizen* represents, in one sense, his Satanic rebellion against the
community of the Eternals:

> 7. Lo! I unfold my darkness: and on
> This rock, place with strong hand the Book
> Of eternal brass, written in may solitude.
>
> 8. Laws of peace, of love, of unity:
> Of pity, compassion, forgiveness.
> Let each chuse one habitation:
> His ancient infinite mansion:
> One command, one joy, one desire,
> One curse, one weight, one measure
> One King, one God, one Law.
>   (*BofU* 4.31–40, E72)

If Urizen's speech corresponds to Satan's response, the parallel to
God's original act of naming 'whom I declare my only Son' would
seem, intriguingly, to be the initial name-giving utterance of the
Eternals: 'It is Urizen.' At the same time, Urizen's speech itself
echoes the language of God's decree. W. J. T. Mitchell has noted
that Urizen's words parody the insistence of Milton's God (and of
St Paul in Ephesians 4: 3–6) on union and 'one law' (Mitchell 1978,
p. 125). God's speech and Urizen's are similar, too, in their performative rhetoric: Urizen's 'Lo! I unfold my darkness' grammatically
parallels God's 'your Head I him appoint.' In both cases, the first-
person speaker performs the action (of unfolding or appointing) by
and in uttering the words. God makes his proclamation from atop a
flaming mountain which 'Brightness had made invisible' (*PL* 5.599),
and according to Milton's doctrine it is only through the Son that

the Father can be seen. Similarly, Urizen's speech seems to render him visible. After he finishes speaking, the Eternals and the reader see him for the first time:

> 1. The voice ended, they saw his pale visage
> Emerge from the darkness; his hand
> On the rock of eternity unclasping
> The Book of brass.
>
> (*BofU* 4.41–4, E72)

Urizen's words call into visible existence the act they announced ten lines earlier. 'Lo! I unfold my darkness: and on / This rock, place with strong hand the Book / Of eternal brass' (*BofU* 4.31–3, E72). More generally, the heavy emphasis on the 'unseen' and 'unknown' at the beginning of *The Book of Urizen* implies that the role of language in this text is to make things visible, indeed to bring them into existence. The subject of the poem is a negativity – a 'shadow' or 'void' – and the act of naming 'Urizen' is the act of naming a gap or negativity in existence (in contrast to Genesis 1, where God names positive creations). Yet the purpose of the text is to 'unfold … dark *visions* of torment', and the unusually heavy use of illustration in this illuminated book certainly suggests that the audience is to see something. The paradox of an 'unseen' event that must nevertheless be seen puts the emphasis not only on Blake's designs but on the performative aspect of language, as the site in which the 'unseen' and 'unknown' become available to sight and knowledge.

More subtle indications of the constitutive power of words emerge when acts or conditions first announced by Urizen's speech appear as part of the poem's 'reality'. The 'Seven deadly Sins of the soul' are first written in Urizen's book, then proclaimed in his utterance (*BofU* 4.30, E72); finally, they appear visibly in response to his speech: 'All the seven deadly sins of the soul / In living creations appear'd / In the flames of eternal fury' (*BofU* 4.49–5.2, E72). The flames surrounding them are also a product of Urizen's words, his challenge to his audience: 'Why will you die O Eternals? / Why live in unquenchable burnings?' (*BofU* 4.12–13, E72). Most critics would agree that the idea that the Eternals inhabit a fiery hell is a product of Urizenic delusion; but what is also significant here is that this delusion only becomes part of the reality of the poem *once Urizen utters it*.

Some of these resonances are reinforced by Blake's variant ordering of the plates in *The Book of Urizen*. In all the copies that contain
Urizen's speech (i.e., plate 4), it is followed by a full-page design
(plate 12 in Copies A and C, plate 14 in Copy B; both plates are
illustrations of a male figure, who is most likely Urizen himself).
The reader thus encounters, in sequence, Urizen's speech and its
aftermath up to the line 'All the seven deadly sins of the soul', then
a full-page vision of Urizen, then the completion of the sentence: 'In
living creations appear'd.' The hiatus in the sentence and the inter-
vening design emphasize the idea that creations appear in response
to Urizen's utterance. Yet plate 4 is missing entirely in Copies D–G,
so that these versions of the text lack Urizen's speech, the only
extended utterance in *The Book of Urizen*. Perhaps it is not too disingenuous to suggest that the absence of Urizen's speech from some
versions highlights its performative force in those versions where
it is present: the copies that contain plate 4 are, by contrast, focused
even more strongly on Urizen's interpolated speech act and its
spectacular effects.

It is not Urizen's voice alone that has the ability to shape reality.
When, at the sight of the sleeping Urizen, the Eternals utter, 'What
is this? Death / Urizen is a clod of clay' (*BofU* 6.9–10, E74), Death,
as a concept and a state, immediately comes into existence. When
the narrative voice refers to Urizen a few lines further on as 'cold,
featureless, flesh of *clay*' (*BofU* 7.5, E74; my italics), it seems as
if the Eternals' utterance has had the perhaps unimentional effect
of making clay a part of what Urizen is. *The Book of Urizen* adds
another dimension to our awareness of what is going on in figural
language: figures repeatedly take on literal existence, in ways that
both Marc Rosenberg (1970) and Robert Essick have analysed (Essick
1990, pp. 155, 224–31).[12] 'Urizen is a clod of clay' sounds like a
metaphoric way of describing his lack of emotion or expression; it
is only when a voice other than the Eternals' testifies that Urizen is
indeed 'flesh of clay' that readers may begin to wonder what effect
metaphors have in imposing attributes or associations on their subjects. To put this a different way: fictional-world semantics draws a
distinction between characters' utterances and the utterances of a
third-person narrator, since it is a commonplace of reading that we
accord a higher degree of authority and truth-value to the latter and
allow the narrator's utterances to authenticate aspects of the fictional
world.[13] Yet it seems to be a crucial feature of Blake's poetry that
this distinction is constantly elided, so that characters' utterances

shape and influence the narrator's utterance – while the very viola-
tion of the distinction constantly reminds us that it is there in the
first place.

On some level, then, virtually all the voices in *The Book of Urizen*
have the power to call things into existence in the manner of the
Elohim – but this is because their utterances also carry the politicized authority of Yahweh. Once Urizen is identified by the utterance 'It is Urizen', the narrative voice confirms his new name
in Miltonic phrases like 'Urizen, so nam'd / That solitary one in
Immensity' (*BofU* 3.52–3, E71) and 'Urizen (so his eternal name)'
(*BofU* 10.11, E75). Once again it is in Book 5 of *Paradise Lost*, which
has so much to do with the loss and acquisition of names, that
Milton must remind his reader repeatedly that the names of his
fallen angels are not the names they bore before their fall. Blake
parodies these verses in his contrary insistence that the names
he uses *are* eternal ones. His inversion of the Miltonic line '*Satan*,
so call him now, his former name / Is heard no more in Heav'n'
(*PL* 5.658–9) implies that Urizen could have had no other name
before the Eternals imposed one on him, since names are antithetical to the state before the Creation-Fall. Indeed, the adjective 'eternal', for Blake, often seems to be less an adjective of quantity than
of quality; that is, it refers less to temporal duration than to the
effectiveness of the utterance which brings about the condition
described as eternal. Thus the 'eternal' quality of Urizen's name
may be a measure of the successful performative effect of the utterance, 'It is Urizen.'

The act of name-giving becomes increasingly frequent towards
the end of *The Book of Urizen*, beginning in Chapter V after the first
female is created, and continuing as the narrative moves into the
realm of human rather than cosmic history. At the sight of the 'first
female form now separate', the Eternals 'call'd her Pity, and fled'
(*BofU* 18.15–19.1, E78). The line is most obviously an echo of the
words of Sin in *Paradise Lost* as she gives her account of how Satan
conceived rebellion against God's decree. As she emerged from the
head of Satan, Sin recalls, the angels 'recoil'd afraid / At first, and
call'd me *Sin*' (*PL* 2.759–60). More precisely, Blake's line is a conflation of the angles' naming of Sin with Sin's naming of Death a few
lines further on: 'I fled, and cri'd out *Death*' (*PL* 2.787). The separation of Los into male and female, in other words, is the equivalent of
the birth of both Sin and Death in Milton's world. On the level of language, it appears that naming, for the Eternals, is a way of making

something into an object and distancing that object from themselves. Their intention is all too clearly articulated in their immediate command that Los and Enitharmon be veiled and confined 'that Eternals may no more behold them' (*BofU* 19.4, E78). Yet this move is already implicit in their naming of the female form: 'They call'd her Pity' is the verbal equivalent of '[they] fled'. Rather than bringing the named object into relation with the naming subject, as is the case in both creation myths in Genesis, naming in *The Book of Urizen* is akin to the labelling of groups or individuals by society in such a way as to exclude them from the homogeneous majority.

The historical and geographical names at the end of *The Book of Urizen* confirm the role of naming in the establishment of sociopolitical reality. Telling readers that the sons of Urizen built cities in a place 'now call'd / Africa: its name was then Egypt' (*BofU* 28.9–10, E83), Blake now seems to be admitting that names are not 'eternal', but change as states and conditions change. Significantly, though, 'Africa' and 'Egypt' are both names imposed by human societies at different historical junctures. 'Egypt', as Blake implies, is the older, probably indigenous name, while 'Africa' was imposed by the Romans when they captured Carthage in the second century BC and established a new province on the southern continent. Whether or not Blake knew the precise origin of the names, it is clear from his use of 'Africa' in *The Song of Los* and the 'Preludium' to *America*, and from the awareness of the slavery issue that underlies *Visions of the Daughters of Albion*, that he associates Africa with oppression by the imperial powers of Europe. For both eighteenth- and twentieth-century readers, the two names function within different language games: 'Africa' is more meaningful in specifying geographical location and connoting oppression by modern imperial powers, 'Egypt' in understanding the significance of the place in terms of biblical history and typology.

When, on the other hand, the children of Urizen 'called it Egypt, & left it' in the penultimate line of the poem (*BofU* 28.22, E83), the biblical overtones of their act of naming render it an act of condemnation and rejection. Spiritually or metaphorically, Egypt designates an alien and oppressive environment; to call a place Egypt is to identify it as a place hostile to the namer. That the exact referent of the name remains ambiguous exposes, in turn, the fictionality of history. 'Egypt' can designate any number of physical or spiritual states, depending on the speaker's perspective, in the same manner as the signifiers 'Satan' and 'Messiah' in Blake's famous misreading of *Paradise Lost* in *The Marriage of Heaven and Hell* ('The history of this is written in Paradise Lost. & the Governor or Reason is call'd Messiah ... But in the Book of Job Miltons Messiah is call'd Satan' [*MHH* 5, E34]). If Blake's parody of a sacred book is about the laying down of the law, it also demonstrates how the history of origins can be adopted, or co-opted, by different parties. The drama of naming and utterance in *The Book of Urizen* works out the darker implications of biblical scholarship such as Lowth's which identifies the force and energy of biblical language with divine authority, and moreover understands that authority as operating within a socio-political context.

* * *

The significance of all of this for reading Blake's work in general, I would suggest, is threefold. First, his poetry often makes more sense *as narrative* when we consider the extent to which characters' utterances interact with and impose on the utterances of the narrative voice. The names, terms and designations used by characters can and do assume the status of reality – even, if they are persuasive enough, 'eternal' reality – at least until corrected, altered or undermined by the words of another character.[14] This observation is akin to the well-known Blakean principle of perspectivism. Readers of Blake already know that what they are 'seeing' at any given time is likely to be the (distorted) view of a conflicted character. But – in keeping with the dominant role of discourse, dialogue, invocation, call and response, declaration, and other forms of public speech throughout Blake's work – what needs to be emphasized is the extent to which it is specifically *through utterance* that characters impose their viewpoints.

As a corollary: the authority of characters in Blake's poetry is proportional to the ability of their utterances to determine others' perceptions as well as the course of the narrative. A brief example is provided by the language of the Priest in 'A Little Boy Lost', from *Songs of Experience*. In this poem, the Priest's declaration from the 'altar high' drowns out the voices of some individuals ('The weeping child could not be heard') and renders the cries of others impotent ('The weeping parents wept in vain'). The priestly definitions of words like 'fiend', 'reason', and 'holy' prevail. Most insidiously, the language of the Priest is not restricted to his actual speech in the fourth stanza, but penetrates into the rest of the poem, as when the scene of the boy's martyrdom is called 'holy' in the final stanza:

> And burn'd him in *a holy place,*
> Where many had been burn'd before:
> The weeping parents wept in vain.
> Are such things done on Albions shore.
>   (E29; my italics)

The Priest's language has even influenced the title of the poem, and thus coloured the reader's understanding of the narrative from the beginning. Whereas the little boy in the corresponding poem from *Songs of Innocence* is lost in a literal sense (at least, he and the other characters and the reader tend to agree on the sense in which he is 'lost'), this boy's lostness is not only a metaphorical but an ideological condition: he is 'lost' in a way that the Church alone defines.

Secondly, Blake's awareness of the performative dimension of language determines the form of his own prophetic rhetoric. The climactic utterance at the end of *A Song of Liberty*, as critics have realized, is an explicit declaration, which (as John Searle would say)[15] is meant to fit the words to the world at the same time as it fits the world to the words: 'Empire is no more! and now the lion & wolf shall cease.' But the imperatives of the concluding 'Chorus' need to be read in the same performative mode:

> Let the Priests of the Raven of dawn, no longer in deadly black, with hoarse note curse the sons of joy. Nor his accepted brethren whom, tyrant, he calls free; lay the bound or build the roof. Nor pale religious letchery call that virginity, that wishes but acts not!
> For every thing that lives is Holy. (E45)

Blake rejects the authority of Church and State to perform speech acts, like cursing and calling (that is, naming), which impose on their objects. Instead, he arrogates to himself the power of calling religious and secular authorities by new names – 'Priests of the Raven of dawn', 'tyrant', 'pale religious letchery' – thus undermining their attempts to declare who is free or to define what virginity is. In rebaptizing the objects of the Priests' curse as 'sons of joy', and redefining 'virginity' as that which 'wishes but acts not', Blake flouts the apparent authority of societal institutions. In so far as he forms part of the community which must ratify the Priests' speech acts, he withholds his acceptance of the conventions that would give authority to their words and so renders their performative utterances unsuccessful. Of course, Blake's utterances are in turn subject to ratification by like-minded readers and vulnerable to rejection by hostile ones; they are liable to exercise their own oppression or to be superseded by the utterances of others.

Thirdly and finally, these experiments with the performativity of language represent a mythological slant on what might be called the 1790s version, or perversion, of the creative language of the Elohim. A number of historians, philosophers and literary critics have explored the revolution in language that accompanied political revolution in the late eighteenth century.[16] The wide range of phenomena contributing to this revolution in language include the proliferation of radical books and pamphlets; sensational trials and other media events turning crucially on linguistic points, such as the trial of Horne Tooke in 1777; the debate among Burke, Paine and others over the meaning of the word 'constitution'; and the manipulation of titles and terminology by both sides in the Revolution and in the revolution debate. What these events and efforts have in common is a growing awareness that words are not descriptive but constitutive of social and political reality.

The specific aspect of this paradigm shift which is relevant to Blake's work is evident in another of the texts of 1794, Thomas Paine's *The Age of Reason*. Throughout his book, Paine insists on the right and ability of individual language users to question and redefine the ideologically charged names assigned by institutions. His attack on Christianity entails changing the meaning of the key terms of religious belief, usually to a meaning he claims is more ancient and original than the current one. The word 'prophet' must give up its contemporary meaning of 'predictor of the future' and take on what Paine claims is its original Hebrew meaning of 'poet', and 'the word of God' ceases to refer to the Christian Bible and becomes attached instead to the physical creation. Paine's obvious presupposition is that words have been and are being appropriated by his opponents as part of their oppressive designs. Here, as in his other books, Paine frequently presses home his point about the constructed nature of language by demystifying the act of naming and detaching words from their assumed significance. Thus we read of 'the book *called* the Bible', 'what *is called* the christian system of faith', 'those who *are called* Reformers', and 'what *is called* the Mosaic account of the creation'.[17]

Some of Paine's arguments are not much different from those of the biblical scholars he would seem to be attacking; his identification of 'prophet' with 'poet', for instance, parallels Lowth's argument exactly. Paine's awareness of the performative power of religious language and rhetoric is shared even by arch-enemies such as Bishop Richard Watson, whose response to *The Age of Reason* in *An Apology for the Bible* (1796) was famously annotated by Blake. In the course of the debate between Watson and Paine, and Blake's critical remarks on both, all three writers accuse the other two of misappropriating the power of language itself. Watson calls attention to and critiques Paine's effort to rename theological concepts, sneering at 'what you are pleased to call moral evidence' and suggesting disingenuously that 'you do not perfectly comprehend what is meant by the expression, the word of God'.[18] He separates the factual content of Paine's book from its accusatory force when he charges Paine with making points through inflammatory rhetoric rather than accurate argumentation: 'your abuse of holy men and holy things will be remembered, when your arguments against them are refuted and forgotten.'[19] Blake critiques Watson on the same basis on which Watson critiques Paine, when both of them pretend to affirm objective facts while actually affirming subjective opinions. They frame statements that, as speech-act theorists would point out, emphasize the performative rather than the constative dimension of utterance.[20] '*I hold it to be* a certain fact ... ,' Watson writes, to Blake's annoyance (E619), while Paine, more deliberately, emphasizes throughout his book the need to set reasoned, individual belief (including statements of the form 'I believe ...') ahead of established 'facts' or creeds. This type of writing, Watson tells Paine, 'proves the sincerity of your declaration of your opinion; but the opinion, notwithstanding the oath, may be either true of false'.[21] 'Presumption is no Proof,' Blake similarly tells Watson (E619). Both correctly perceive that the writer's assertion of belief or opinion, like that of speakers in *The Book of Urizen*, is a linguistic act that may be judged by its success or failure in achieving authority, but that evades the category of constative truth.

Blake accuses both Paine and Bishop Watson, but the Bishop more severely, of confusing Christianity with 'State Religion'. His charge relates to the way Paine and Christian theologians both sought to identify and highlight the sociopolitical authority of the Bible and biblical language, although theologians like Watson (and Lowth) affirm this quality, while Paine questions the authority traditionally ascribed to inspiration and revelation. Throughout *The Age of Reason*, Paine insists that if the Bible is to have performative force at all, it must be of the kind that can be comprehended and regulated by sociopolitical institutions such as the court system. In other words, he treats biblical texts as legal documents, insisting that they meet the standards of evidence set by contemporary courts. In doing so Paine is not being particularly iconoclastic, but rather aligning himself with contemporary theologians themselves; historicization of biblical evidence characterized not only Deist arguments but also the emerging school of Higher Criticism. But Paine extends this demystification also to the prime example of performative language in the Bible, creation by the word, which he exposes as a magic trick:

> it is a puerile and pitiful idea, to suppose the Almighty to say, 'Let there be light.' It is the imperative manner of speaking that a conjuror uses when he says to his cups and balls, Presto, be gone...Longinus calls this expression the sublime; and by the same rule the conjuror is sublime too; for the manner of speaking is expressively and grammatically the same.[22]

Paine's ridicule of the creative language of Genesis 1, by setting it in a trivializing, secular context, is a far cry from Bishop Lowth's reverent treatment of the same passage. Yet both are relevant to Blake's revision of creation and the language of creation because both, in different ways, seek to analyse the working of divine and human language in light of this example, and to define the type of authority on which it depends. Between the two lies the language of Blake, calling political and poetic consciousness into simultaneous existence.

Notes

1. To provide a focus for the aspects of language being discussed in this essay, I have used terminology that derives from the 'classic' formulation of speech-act theory by J. L. Austin in *How to Do Things with Words*, ed. J. O. Urmson and Marina Sbisà, 2nd edn (Cambridge, MA: Harvard University Press, 1975), and John R. Searle in *Speech Acts: An Essay in the Philosophy of Language* (Cambridge: Cambridge University Press, 1969) and *Expression and Meaning: Studies in the Theory of Speech Acts* (Cambridge: Cambridge University Press, 1979). Austin's and Searle's contention that utterances do not just refer to or describe the

world but alter or act on it – a quality that they called 'performative' or 'illocutionary' force – and their attempts to account for illocutionary force and classify its forms, have been adopted and adapted in various branches of philosophy, linguistics, legal theory, anthropology, and literary criticism. (For an overview of the reception of speech-act philosophy by literary theorists up to the early 1990s, see Chapter 1 of Esterhammer, *Creating States*.) I have deliberately not emphasized contemporary models or presented them in detail here because the present essay is intended primarily as an exploration of ideas about language and action that appear in late eighteenth-century texts, not as the application of a modern theoretical paradigm to these texts. In particular, the branch of literary theory that derives from Jacques Derrida's and Paul de Man's deconstructive interpretations of the performative (in *Limited Inc*, trans. Samuel Weber and Jeffrey Mehlman, ed. Gerald Graff [Evanston: Northwestern University Press, 1990] and in *Allegories of Reading: Figural Language in Rousseau, Nietzsche, Rilke, and Proust* [New Haven: Yale University Press, 1979], respectively), along with the most recent applications of the performative to gender studies and cultural critique (especially in the work of Judith Butler and Eve Kosofsky Sedgwick), is bracketed off here as a quite different understanding of the performative than that which I attempt to relate to eighteenth-century reflections on language and creation. While Butler stresses that in her 'poststructuralist rewriting of discursive performativity', the performative is to be understood 'not as the act by which a subject brings into being what she/he names, but rather, as that reiterative power of discourse to produce the phenomena that it regulates and constrains' (*Bodies that Matter: On the Discursive Limits of 'Sex'* [New York: Routledge, 1993], 12, 2), the writers discussed in the present essay (Blake, Lowth, Paine) *did* regard utterance in terms of a subject-centred act of bringing into being what one names. They also, I will argue, intuited a discrepancy between transcendent, ideal or phenomenal creativity and oppressive, divisive, sociopolitical effectiveness. One might say that poststructuralist scholarship 'resolves' this tension by regarding the performative as inevitably iterative (i.e., non-transcendent and non-original) and inevitably politicized; in this context, it would be hard to speak of an 'ideal' performative. But in eighteenth-century texts a view of speech acts as ideally creative coexists with a view of them as institutionally or politically determined, in an interesting tension that seems indicative of a paradigm shift running through literature, philosophy and political thought. For that matter, the concept of a transcendent, non-political performative still coexists in a confused and unsystematic manner with the concept of a sociopolitical performative in the first explorations of speech acts undertaken by Austin and Searle (see, for example, Searle's bipartite definition of declarations as either 'institutional' *or* 'supernatural' in his influential essay 'A Taxonomy of Illocutionary Acts' [*Expression and Meaning* 18]).

2.   For a more detailed analysis of the speech acts in Genesis 1–3, see Esterhammer (1994, pp. 42–64).

3.   Robert Lowth, *Lectures on the Sacred Poetry of the Hebrews*, 2 vols, trans. G. Gregory (1787; rpt New York: Garland, 1971) 1: p. 350.

4.   Lowth, 1: p. 97.

5.   Lowth, 1: p. 77.

6.   Lowth, 1: pp. 80, 306, 307.

7.   Although, as Christopher Heppner has recently noted, 'a full account of Blake's relation to this important book [Lowth's *Lectures*] has yet to be written' (284n), scholars concerned with Blake's interpretation of the Bible (including Tannenbaum, McGann and Heppner) habitually assume Blake's familiarity with the *Lectures*. Given the general availability of Lowth's work – before being published in English in 1787, it was also printed in monthly instalments in *The Christian's Magazine* in 1767 and summarized in Hugh Blair's popular *Lectures on Rhetoric and Beles Lettres* (1783) – it is hard to imagine that a late eighteenth-century reader with a particular interest in biblical interpretation would be unacquainted with Lowth, 'the most influential biblical exegete of the period' (Villalobos 1988, p.36). Through his association with Joseph Johnson's bookshop in the 1780s and 1790s, Blake would have had a particular opportunity to read Lowth, for among the many theological works published and collected by Johnson was the 1787 translation of Lowth's *Lectures*.

8.   Lowth, 1: p. 304.

9.   Gabriel Josipovici, *The Book of God: a Response to the Bible* (New Haven: Yale University Press, 1988) p. 64.

10. John Milton, *Paradise Lost*, ed. Merritt Y. Hughes (New York: Macmillan, 1985) 5.564–70 (henceforth abbreviated as *PL*).

11. Neil Forsyth has offered the intriguing suggestion (in a paper presented at the 1995 International Milton Symposium, entitled 'Rebellion in *Paradise Lost*: Impossible Original') that not only error, but Satan himself, is created in and by God's speech. Simultaneously with God's proclamation/creation of the Son, Satan is called into existence as the one who, breaking union, is cast into utter darkness. Mary Nyquist's poststructuralist and psychoanalytical reading of the scene also elaborates on what is created through God's speech and Satan's response: a patriarchal symbolic order, and the activity of interpretation itself, as Satan's 'dynamic and dramatic opposition' turns logos into mythos ('The Father's Word/Satan's Wrath', *PMLA* 100 [1985]: p. 187).

12. Rosenberg attributes the 'literalization of figuration' to the power of imagination in Blake's poetry, while Essick (in a wonderfully subtle reading of *The Book of Urizen* in the context of eighteenth-century theories of language) explains it as Blake's awareness of how a differential and taxonomic system of language can turn abstraction into reality. My reading provides a third alternative, by emphasizing how language in a sociopolitical context can, depending on the relations of power, performatively determine the perceptions or 'reality' of others.

13. See Lubomír Doležel, 'Truth and Authenticity in Narrative', *Poetics Today* 1 (1980): p. 11.

14. Graham Pechey makes the related observation (in another analysis of the performative quality of Blake's language) that the characters created by Blake's words and myths operate on the same level as historical characters in the prophetic poems (Pechey 1982, p. 59).
15. See Searle's analysis of performatives according to 'direction of fit' between words and the world in the essay 'A Taxonomy of Illocutionary Acts'. Declarations – which, as Searle notes, generally comprise the types of utterance Austin identified as explicitly performative – are the one category of performatives in which the direction of fit goes both ways at once: 'declarations do attempt to get language to match the world. But they do not attempt to do it either by describing an existing state of affairs ... nor by trying to get someone to bring about a future state of affairs', rather, 'successful performance [of a declaration] guarantees that the propositional content corresponds to the world' (*Expression and Meaning*, 19, 17).
16. See, especially, Olivia Smith, *The Politics of Language 1791–1819* (Oxford: Clarendon, 1984), and Steven Blakemore, *Burke and the Fall of Language: The French Revolution as Linguistic Event* (Hanover, NH: University Press of New England, 1988).
17. Thomas Paine, *The Age of Reason*, in *The Writings of Thomas Paine*, ed. Moncure Daniel Conway (New York: AMS, 1967) 4.47, 58, 62, 66 (my italics).
18. R. Watson, *An Apology for the Bible, In a Series of Letters, Addressed to Thomas Paine, Author of The Age of Reason* (New York: Carlton & Porter, n.d.) pp. 15, 58.
19. Watson, p. 158.
20. The conclusion reached by Austin over the course of *How to Do Things with Words* is that all utterances are both performative and constative; consequently, the latent performative dimension of a statement can often be made explicit by re-formulating it to include a first-person subject and verb. Thus 'the cat is on the mat' is revealed to be an act of stating when reformulated as '*I state that* the cat is on the mat'. Paine, Watson and Blake all make use of explicit performatives of this sort themselves as well as calling attention to one another's use of them.
21. Watson, p. 146.
22. Paine, p. 193.

7

'Labouring at the Resolute Anvil': Blake's Response to Locke

Steve Clark

I read Burkes Treatise when very Young at the same time I read Locke on Human Understanding & Bacons Advancement of Learning on Every one of these Books I wrote my Opinions & on looking them over find that my Notes on Reynolds in this Book are exactly Similar. I felt the Same Contempt & Abhorrence then; that I do now. (E660)

'Contempt & Abhorrence' seems, to say the least, an unequivocal response to these major Enlightenment intellectuals. Such a belligerent proclamation of lifelong intransigence apparently bears out Northrop Frye's claim that whatever influence Locke had on Blake was 'clearly a negative one' (1947, p. 14). But condemnation need not necessarily entail denigration: it can instead serve as an implicit tribute to intellectual stature. In this essay, I shall attempt to redefine the relation between Blake and Locke: at the very least, the philosopher proves a worthy opponent as the most vigorous exponent of error, setting the terms of debate and providing the most visible 'body to Falshood' (*J* 12:13 E155) to struggle against. The formative influence of Locke's *Essay concerning Human Understanding*, I would suggest, continues to determine the underlying metaphorical structure of texts otherwise as generically dissimilar as prose aphorisms, *There is No Natural Religion*, satirical treatise, *The Marriage of Heaven and Hell*, burlesque cosmogony, *The Book of Urizen*, and manuscript epic, *The Four Zoas*.

From the early analysis of *There is No Natural Religion*, through to the final award of a ringside seat at the Resurrection in *Jerusalem*,

Locke's work paid the compliment of continuous attention to the point that it might almost be considered Blake's dominant preoccupation. Yet it is indicative of the degree of neglect of Locke in current Blake studies that two recent book-length treatments of the spectre, by Lorraine Clark (1991) and Steven Vine (1993) do not even bother to index him, choosing to adopt existential and psychoanalytic approaches respectively, despite the concept's explicitly Lockean derivation as a 'fortuitous concourse of memorys accumulated & lost' and as 'the Reasoning Power in Man ... / closing itself as in steel, in a Ratio / Of the Things of Memory' (*J* 29 [33]:8; 74:10–12 E229).[1]

Blake criticism has expended an inordinate amount of effort in trying to establish links with the brief efflorescence of exotic Protestant sects in the wake of the English Civil War (most recently Mee 1992; and Thompson 1993). Locke, in stark contrast, has been routinely denigrated as proponent of an emergent scientific and bourgeois worldview, towards which it is assumed that Blake's attitude must be 'of course negative' (Lincoln 1996, p. 9). Such a characterization is no longer tenable in the face of recent studies in political philosophy, which have insisted on the continued religious basis to Locke's thought and his militant activism during the upheavals of the 1680s.[2] Unlike the ultimately impotent millenialists of the Commonwealth period, Locke was a successful revolutionary. If we read the *Essay* in the context of its implicit theological imperatives, rather than as a prefiguration of a secular and materialist culture, it becomes possible to see his work not as antithetical to Blake's, but as within a common tradition of radical Protestantism, 'corrosive of religious orthodoxy and of the political power of the priesthood'.[3]

Locke continuously insists that 'Men must think and know for themselves';[4] personal examination is the hallmark of spiritual authenticity, 'For Untruth being unacceptable to the Mind of Man, there is no other defence left for Absurdity, but Obscurity' (3:10:9). Similarly, for Blake, 'Severity of judgement is a great virtue' (E585) necessary so 'That he who will not defend Truth, may be compelled to / Defend a lie, that he may be snared & caught & taken' (*M* 8:47–8 E102). Blake never ceases to appeal to the critical force of the standards which he simultaneously denounces: Bishop Watson and Dr Thornton would surely have considered his annotation of their work, with its stubborn refusal to accept that it is 'possible to Thought / A greater than itself to know', as made by 'One who sets reason up for judge / Of our most holy Mystery'.[5]

It must be conceded that the evidence is extremely slight that Blake had read Locke's *Two Treatises of Government*, only a couple of incidental references to contract theory and a recurrence of imagery of parental authority as 'Swadling Cloths'.[6] Locke's work had sufficiently widespread dissemination in the 1790s to appear in antithetical contexts: prominently cited by the defence in the Thomas Hardy treason trial, but bitterly denounced by Joseph Wright, follower of the prophet Richard Brothers.[7] For my purposes, however, it is sufficient to assume no more than Blake's detailed familiarity with the *Essay*. Frye's polemic closes with the admission that 'Locke's reputation can perhaps be left to take care of itself', and he later concedes that his 'virile contempt of slavery, his defence of toleration and even the primacy he gives to sense experience in his theory of knowledge, are all Blakean qualities' (1947, pp. 29, 187).[8] Or Lockean ones in Blake, and it is this latter possibility which I wish to explore.

'If it were not for the Poetic of Prophetic character the Philosophic & Experimental would soon be at the ratio of all things' (*NNR*, E3); but this dichotomy must be qualified by the awareness that the 'Philosophic & Experimental' must itself be regarded as an instance of the 'Poetic or Prophetic Character' (*ARO*, E1). Numerous dramatisations are offered in the prophecies of the casting of the 'mind-forg'd manacles' (E27):

Urizen lay in darkness & solitude, in chains of the mind lock'd up
Los siezd his Hammer & Tongs; he labourd at his resolute Anvil
Among indefinite Druid rocks & snows of doubt & reasoning.

Refusing all Definite Form, the Abstract Horror roofd. stony hard …
(*M* 3:6–9 E97)

The 'mind' is 'roofd. stony hard' as the direct result of a methodological decision to proceed by 'doubt & reasoning' in 'darkness & solitude'. It must be stressed that Urizen is not responsible for the 'Form' that he inhabits, and himself protests against it: 'Enraged & stifled without & within' (3:24 E97). He has been made by Los, who immediately dwindles to the image which he has constructed, and so 'became what he beheld' (3:29 E97). At the very least, the relation of Los and Urizen is one of complex interdependence: syntactically, the 'chains of the mind' qualifies both protagonists, and as many critics have observed, Urizen's actions repeatedly prefigure and foreclose those of Los.[9]

In this essay, I will begin by contesting the assumption of the
antithetical status of Locke and Blake, and instead stress continuities between their respective forms of combative individualism. I
shall then examine Blake's attempted transformations of a Lockean
vocabulary of limitation and endeavour; and conclude by examining the unexpected consolidation of his adversary's power when
the 'Industry and Labour of Thought' (4: 3: 6) is confronted by the
alternative standard of Eternity.

I

'In bare naked Perception', Locke notoriously claims, 'the Mind is,
for the most part, only passive; and what it perceives, it cannot
avoid perceiving' (2:9:1). The understanding is assumed to have an
initial passivity, because of the way the retina receives sensory data.
This apparent dependence on the external world provides the
grounds for Frye's strictures against the 'involuntary and haphazard image' of the 'guinea-sun' in favour of 'the Hallelujah-Chorus'
which 'demands an exuberantly active mind which will not be a
quiescent blank slate' (1947, pp. 23–4).[10] Support for this position
can be found in Blake famous insistence in that 'We are led to
Believe a Lie / When we see not Thro the eye' (*AI* E 492); and his
repeated gibing at 'John Lookeye' (*IM* E456).

Such an indictment, however, entirely overlooks the secondary
stage of Locke's model of perception as the mind struggles to
reconstruct a world from the piecemeal data of ideas. As he himself
acknowledges, his psychological language is composed of 'Words
taken from the Operations of sensible Things and applied to certain
Modes of Thinking' (3:1:5). Even the claim that these may be empirically verified 'when the Mind turns in upon it self, and contemplates its own Actions' (2:19:1) relies on the peculiar image of an
eye reversing on its socket. More important though is the consistent
depiction of thought as 'Actions', as a linear process occurring in
spatial dimensions almost invariably dramatized through verbs of
physical exertion, and synonymous with 'pain and endeavour'.
Locke's very syntax places all thought in bondage to 'labour' and
'succession', and insists that the self can only be constituted through
activity in time.[11]

Locke's recurrent analogy between the composition of ideas and
the materiality of physical particles has prompted much unease

among his philosophical apologists.[12] But this analytic reduction is the necessary preliminary for the 'Worksmanship of the Understanding' (3:3:12) to utilize its 'Art and Skill ... to compound and divide the Materials' (2:2:2), which provide 'the Groundwork, whereon to build all those Notions, which he shall ever have naturally in this World' (2:1:24). Blake scoffingly but accurately describes this process as 'To build a Universe with Farthing Balls' (*PA* E579). But if '[Strictly Speaking] All Knowledge is Particular' (E648) and 'To Particularize is the Alone Distinction of Merit' (E641), it is Locke and not Blake who applies this principle in a radical and thoroughgoing manner. And Blake himself gives a splendidly economical formulation of this unending process of internal reconstruction in one of the opening plates of *Milton:*

> Within labouring. beholding Without: from Particulars to Generals
> Subduing his Spectre, they Builded the Looms of Generation They
> Builded Great Golgonooza Times on Times Ages on Ages ...
> (3:37–9 E97)

This captures the Locke's sharp division between the mind 'Within' and the sensory world 'Without', with 'beholding' providing the material of 'Particulars' out of which 'Generals' can be produced. 'Labouring' assumes similar prominence in Blake's own depiction of the fallen world, which also insists on the importance of tools and craftsmanship, on the impermanence of the structures that they produce, and on the necessity of ceaseless individual effort to sustain and recreate them.[13]

This can be read as a dramatization and conscious critique of Locke, but I would stress the common origin of the Protestant individualism of both writers in Augustinian Christianity.[14] Even where, as in the passage quoted above, Los is said to be 'Subduing his Spectre', the repetition of 'they Builded' indicates that the construction of 'great Golgonooza' is at the very least a collaborative enterprise. Elsewhere in Blake, this imagery takes on an unequivocally exhortatory function:

> to Labour in Knowledge. is to Build up Jerusalem: and to Despise
> Knowledge, is to Despise Jerusalem & her Builders. (*J* pl. 77 E232)

Therefore the opposition is not, as Frye claims, between a 'quiescent blank slate' and an 'exuberantly active mind', but between

labour within severely restricted bounds and the effortless mode
of simultaneous perception implied by Blake's own doctrine of
innate principles: 'Man is Born like a Garden ready Planted &
Sown' (E656).[15]

Before looking more closely at the implications of this imperative
to 'Labour in Knowledge', I wish to examine the process by which
the 'infinite brain' contracts 'into a narrow circle' (*VDA* 2:32 E47).

II

Whereas were the Capacities of our Understandings well
considered, the Extent of our Knowledge once discovered, and
the Horizon found, which sets the Bounds between the
enlightned and dark Parts of Things; between what is, and what
is not comprehensible by us, Men would perhaps with less scru-
ple acquiesce in the avow'd Ignorance of the one, and imploy
their Thoughts and Discourse, with more Advantage and
Satisfaction in the other. (1:1:7)

The blend of scepticism and humility advocated in the introduction
to the *Essay* seems brisk and pragmatic, a substitution of secular
ignorance for sacral mystery, a manifesto for activity in the world
as far as it is knowable. Yet this is undercut by the way the
'Horizon' fuses the radius within which sensory ideas may be
received with the physical 'Bounds' of the organs of perception.
Locke's almost ingenuous disavowal of excessive ambition conceals
an edict of colossal power.[16]

Blake singles out this audacious circumscription to designate his
major protagonist: Urizen, your reason, horizon. The creative
majesty of the 'great Work master' and 'Architect divine' is most
apparent at the very moment of 'condensing the strong energies
into little compass' (*FZ* p. 24: 5 E314, p. 30: 8, 5 E319), just as the
heroic strength of the Ancient of Days is most vividly displayed in
imposing the 'bound or outward circumference' upon itself (*MHH*
pl. 4 E34). There is no condemnation of rationality *per se* in Blake:
'Reason' was 'once fairer than the light' until condemned to be
'fould in Knowledges dark Prison house' (E446). Instead, there is an
acute insight into the disproportion between its creative power and
the world that it brings into being: 'Ah how shall Urizen the King
submit to this dark mansion' (*FZ* p. 63: 24 E343).

It is the domesticity of Locke's images of constriction – the senses as 'the Windows by which light is let into this dark Room' and 'the Understanding' as 'not much unlike a Closet wholly shut from light' (2:11:17) – that makes them peculiarly effective: the cramped and demeaning depiction of the human mind is thus given an unchallengeable familiarity. This self-evidence is what Blake is concerned to refute; his repeated depiction of a grotesque fall into senses that only act as barriers, agonizing impediments, is best read not as a Gnostic repudiation of the body, but as a protest against Locke's naturalization of limits.

'Five windows light the caverned Man' (*Europe* pl. iii: 1 E60), and Blake's fascination with images of confinement deriving directly or indirectly from Locke has been well documented. His poetry takes or recreates these tropes, and dramatizes them, pursues them through into strange and unexpected configurations. Even here, the response can be extremely specific: Theotormon not only ponders 'what is a thought? & of what substance is it made?', but also probes more subtle discrepancies in Locke's account of 'where dwell the thoughts forgotten' until they 'renew again' (*VDA* 3:22–4: 11 [E47–8]). If the mind 'retains' ideas, they must be physically preserved somewhere in the brain, a supposition for which there is no evidence: if it 'revives' them, they are in effect recreated, and the original experience lost.[17] Blake by no means, as Swinburne puts it, 'believed a thing…only inasmuch as it was incapable of proof' (1980, p. 4). Plato's claim 'that Poets & Prophets do not know or Understand what they write or Utter' is denounced as 'a most Pernicious Falshood', and the cognitive status of inspiration is fiercely defended: 'pray is an inferior Kind to be called Knowing' (*VLJ* E554).

Blake's theory of imagination can be mundanely glossed as an expansion of the innate capacity to form correct intuitive judgements beyond the realm of the aesthetic onto all perceptual activity. This is no less a legitimate outgrowth of the empiricist tradition than Berkeley's idealism, and, indeed, must face the same charge of precipitating its weak grasp of the actual into outright solipsism (see Cox 1980, pp. 127–56). It does not, however, follow that Blake, despite such propositions as 'Mental Things are alone Real' and that there is no 'Existence out of Mind or Thought' (*VLJ* E565), necessarily found Berkeley 'congenial' (Frye 1947, p. 14).[18] The only direct commentary, the irritable and dogmatic annotations to *Siris*, dated 1818 by Keynes, suggests anything but a formative influence.

Blake removes the stabilizing if ungrounded postulate of a non-immanent God, thus introducing a neo-Nietzschean relativism into his theory of knowledge. He delights in the struggle for mastery between rival imaginations, mutually antagonistic perceptions of the world. This brings back much of the individualism of Locke: the ideal of autonomous imagination comes to resemble what might be dubbed an 'inner-light rationalism'.[19]

The affinity is evident in the contrast between Reynolds's *Discourses*, and the opposing 'Opinions and Determinations on Art' propounded in Blake's *A Descriptive Catalogue* (E528). In Reynolds's suave presidential addresses, reason is essentially confirmatory: it does not construct abstractions, but instead, if properly trained, allows the justness of existing general ideas to be recognized, which thereby assume a quasi-Platonic status. Blake's manifesto, though couched in a comparably public rhetoric of rational persuasion, at every point appeals to examination as a mode of personal conscience, a means of breaking consensus rather than participating in it: 'those who have been told that my Works are but an unscientific and irregular Eccentricity, a Madman's Scrawls, I demand of them to do me the justice to examine before they decide' (E527–8).[20]

In his annotations to the seventh discourse, Blake declares 'It is not in Terms that Reynolds & I disagree Two Contrary Opinions can never by any Language be made alike', and concludes that 'the Fault is not in Words. but in Things Lockes Opinions of Words & their Fallaciousness are Artful Opinions & Fallacious also' (E659). These suspicions seem amply borne out when Bishop Watson invokes Locke to disallow Paine's definition of 'conscience'. 'I believe that the Bishop laught at the Bible in his slieve & so did Locke' (E613). But the standards to which Blake appeals are precisely Lockean ones of clarity and directness, 'Downright Plain Truth' (E618). Locke tirelessly, indeed tiresomely, reiterates that Scripture is 'to be understood in the plain direct meaning of the words and phrases'; as for conscience, no tenet is more central than 'every man has the absolute and supreme power of judging for himself'.[21] Though Locke's 'Ambition … to be employed as an Under-Labourer in clearing Ground a little, and removing some of the Rubbish, that lies in the way to Knowledge' is mocked as 'a Dragon-Man, clearing away the rubbish from a caves mouth' (*MHH* pl. 15: E40: see Cooper 1988, p. 44), it is clearly Blake, rather than Reynolds, whose ethic of 'Mental Fight' (*M* 1: 13 E95) is heir to Locke's iconoclastic energy.

Both writers share an acute consciousness of words as 'the cause of imposition' (*MHH* pl. 12 E38). Locke, as well as Los, demands of his opponent that he 'put off Holiness / And put on Intellect': 'Tell him to be no more dubious: demand explicit words' (*J* 91:55–6 E252; 17:60 E162). Their diagnoses are compatible: and it is Blake's proposed remedy, to rely solely on intuitive linguistic competence for semantic arbitration, that is potentially reactionary. 'Virtue & honesty or the dictates of Conscience are of no doubtful Signification to any one' (E613) because whoever disagrees with Blake is talking about something different. The declaration, for example, that 'Natural Religion is the voice of God & not the result of reasoning on the Powers of Satan' (E614) may perhaps be stirring, but it is also arrogantly dogmatic. Locke might reasonably enquire what entitled Blake to designate this uncoopted judgement 'Natural Religion', when his own customary usage, let alone anyone else's, signified a worship of nature, a dependence on ideas received form natural objects, and a religion devoid of all transcendent premises.[22]

This is how the term is employed in *There is No Natural Religion*, which I now wish to examine in detail.

III

The centrality of *There is No Natural Religion* should not be assumed too readily. It is by no means easy to correlate the tracts with Blake's own early poetic practice, and their traditional dating and ordering has recently been forcefully challenged by their most recent editors (Eaves, Essick and Viscomi 1993, pp. 21–6). Nevertheless, they deserve attention not so much for the impressive coherence of the first series, as for the difficulties in handling the concept of eternity in the second, which will remain an area of crucial ambivalence throughout Blake's work.

The first represents a pseudo-codification, of great precision, of the position of the sensationist.[23] The status of its logical rhetoric is not merely parodic, a pretence of logic to destroy logic. Though its terse dismissiveness cannot but provoke protest, it loses none of its inexorability. Not for the first time, we shall see a consolidation which, if anything, strengthens the opposition. E. D. Hirsch argues that the Lockean, once lulled by the Argument into accepting a 'moral fitness', which cannot be derived solely 'from Education', is obliged to concede a similar extra-sensory origin to religion (1964, pp. 297–304).[24] Yet this represents an impasse rather than a refutation. The tract may expose the privative quality of natural religion under its rhetoric of benevolence, but it remains to be shown that there is any coherent alternative.

The second series treats the conclusion reached in the first as sufficient grounds for assertion of an opposed psychology.

I Mans perceptions are not bounded by organs of perception. he percieves more than sense (tho' ever so acute) can discover.

II Reason or the ratio of all we have already known. is not the same that it shall be when we know more.

[III *lacking*]. (E2)

Man has ceased to be natural man: to perceive 'more than sense' is not to perceive at all in Lockean terms. A limit which can be exceeded is no longer a limit. Where the immediate boundary had been the senses themselves, experience now becomes inclusive of but not confined by 'organs of perception'. The 'ratio' changes from a rigid standard to the self-transforming and provisional conclusions drawn from the present total of knowledge. Knowing is introduced as a conscious activity rather than the enforced reception of data; and 'when we know more' brings time into a previously categoric sequence, in a progressive rather than apocalyptic mode. The negative aspect of temporality, however, is not addressed: what our reason shall be when we have forgotten, know less.

The alternative to this open-ended expansion is characterised in the next two propositions:

IV The bounded is loathed by its possessor. The same dull round even of a univer[s]e, would soon become a mill with complicated wheels.

V If the many become the same as the few when possessed, More! More' is the cry of a mistaken soul, less than All cannot satisfy Man. (E2)

The dizzying expansion of 'even of a universe' allies planetary orbits, the cosmic predictability of the Newtonian universe, to the microcosm of the psyche: but the comparison reduces the universe to wearisome monotony rather than elevates the mind. The mill that grinds 'the many' down into 'the few' also carries an image of the blind effort of Samson in captivity, a fit emblem for Locke, self-shorn, a figure of immense though confined power, a 'possessor' who 'loathes' the 'bounded' which he himself prescribes. Yet it remains to be demonstrated that the 'cry' of this 'soul' (a suddenly imported and unsubstantiated concept) is 'mistaken'. The imperative of 'more, more' can be seen not as crudely acquisitive but as demanding more for and from the self to fulfil its arduous duty of knowing.

VI If any could desire what he is incapable of possessing, despair must be his eternal lot.

VII The desire of Man being Infinite the possession is Infinite & himself Infinite ...
Application. He who sees the Infinite in all things sees God. He who sees the Ratio only sees himself only.

The assumption that despair is man's eternal lot is not empirically refutable: the pursuit of more may be doomed to unfulfilment, and this may turn to despair; but pessimism of an argument is no proof of its falsity. Man's life may well be 'a state in which many of his faculties, can serve only for his torment, in which he is to be importuned by desires that never can be satisfied.[25] The Lockean position that one should cease desiring what one is incapable of possessing is left unscathed. Nothing is made out of despair: its full extent has not even been addressed. As Hirsch says, at this point, Blake has 'abandoned logic in favour of enthusiastic affirmation' (1964, p. 303). It is baldly asserted that because despair is not man's eternal lot (unproven), his desire must be infinite: with the corrollaries that to desire the infinite involves its possession and possessing the infinite means man himself is infinite.
   The desire of the infinite is by no means the same as desire being infinite. It opens a gap, lack, insufficiency, which Blake himself has appealed to empirically as his only argument against the purely aggregative pursuit of more: the first non-organic thought is loathing. But if desire is co-instantaneous with possession, where does dissatisfaction with 'less than All' come from? What is needed is a transition from 'when we know more' to knowing the

infinite: nothing in the argument says we can desire the infinite without knowing it first. The more positive avenue – desire presupposing
knowledge, and it therefore being a question of conceiving a more
capacious and adaptable form of knowing – is left unexplored.[26]

A similar move from a temporal state of incompletion into an
eternal present of fulfilled desire occurs in the *Marriage:*

> If the doors of perception were cleansed every thing would
> appear to man as it is, infinite.
> For man has closed himself up, till he sees all things thro' narrow
> chinks of his cavern. (*MHH* pl. 14 E39)

The force of this familiar passage, it should be stressed, lies in its
dramatization of a fallen condition: the 'narrow chinks' are themselves a reformulation of Locke's images of the senses as 'inlets',
and 'cavern' activates the Platonic resonances to the 'dark Room' of
the self. Somewhat surprisingly, however, confinement presup-
poses agency: 'closed himself up' implies an active process, supported by the volition of 'he sees'. The alternative state entirely
lacks this power of refiguration. The 'infinite', introduced by two
passive constructions, 'were cleansed' and 'would appear', is curi-
ously static, 'as it is', defined entirely in terms of the absence of present constraint. This intransitive and evacuated quality to Blake's
eternity may be brought out by comparing his 'doors of perception'
with a close analogue in Addison's discussion of 'Inlets of great
Pleasure to the Soul': 'When these everlasting Doors shall be open
to us, we may be sure that the Pleasures and Beauties of this Place
will infinitely transcend our present Hopes and Expectations'.
Blake insists on the present availability of what for Addison will
'make up out Happiness hereafter': the question remains of whether
the proposed emancipation depends on the same orthodox structure of compensatory transcendence.[27]

This may seem implausible in the light of such famous proclama-
tions as 'Good is the passive that obeys Reason [.] Evil is the active
springing from Energy. Good is Heaven. Evil is Hell' (pl. 3 E34). It
might be argued that Reason must possess a little of the 'active' in
order to make itself 'obeyed' by Good, but I wish to make a related
but separate point concerning the following plate:

> It indeed appear'd to Reason as if Desire was cast out. but the
> Devil's account is that the Messiah fell. & formed a heaven of what
> he stole from the Abyss.

This is shewn in the Gospel where he prays to the Father to send the comforter or Desire that Reason may have Ideas to build on, the Jehovah of the Bible being no other than he, who dwells in flaming fire.

Know that after Christs death, he became Jehovah.

But in Milton; the Father is Destiny, the Son, a Ratio of the five senses. & the Holyghost, Vacuum! (pl. 5–6 E34–5)

This passage has attracted multiple commentaries in terms of its scriptural, Miltonic and Behmenist contexts, but I would prefer to cite it as an instance of Blake having 'wrote in fetters' about 'Devils & Hell', and 'at liberty' about the 'restrainer or reason' (pl. 5 E34). 'Destiny', 'Ratio' & 'Vacuum' obviously present a Lockean universe as one of impoverished determinism, but there is also a more positive aspect. The crucial point is that for all their cavortings in the flames of Eternal Delight, the 'Devils party' make nothing whereas the 'Governor or Reason' responds to the Fall by forming 'a heaven of what he stole from the Abyss', and by praying for Desire in order to 'have Ideas to build on' (pl. 5 E34–5).

In *The Book of Urizen*, this becomes:

> First I fought with the fire; consumed
> Inwards, into a deep world within:
> A void immense, wild dark & deep,
> Where nothing was; Nature's wide womb [.]
>
> And self balanced stretched o'er the void
> I alone, even I! the winds merciless
> Bound; but condensing, in torrents
> They fall & fall; strong I repelled
> The vast waves, & arose on the waters
> A wide world of solid obstruction
>
> (pl. 4: 14–23 E72)

Urizen, it should be noted, only acquires an 'I' here, and has to wait until the tenth plate for a body. Prior to this, he appears as the pure impulse of 'silent activity' and 'incessant labour', that accepts the challenge of exploring the 'deep world within', and achieves a precarious mastery over the chaos of these elemental desires.[28]

The triumphant 'arose', however, inevitably recalls the opening exclamation, 'Lo, a shadow of horror is risen / In Eternity' (pl. 3: 12 E70). To the Eternals, the 'activity' of this heroic self-creation is 'unknown and horrible', and its 'enormous labours' proof of error and contamination. (pl. 3: 21–2 E71). It is too readily assumed that their perspective necessarily implies plenitude and stability. The poem devotes only four cryptic lines (pl. 3: 36–9 E71) to describing how 'eternal life sprung'. Yet critics have consistently accepted the criteria of 'all flexible senses', defined solely through the absence of 'Earth', 'Death', and 'globes of attraction', as sufficient grounds for denigrating the heroic actions of Urizen.[29] The Eternals make no attempt to enlighten his 'dark globe': instead, they dispatch Los 'to confine / The obscure separation alone', keeping themselves "wide apart" (pl. 5: 38–41 E73). A downward spiral is set in motion that dominates the remainder of the poem, and this logic of decline has an impressive coherence: the cause of Urizen's original estrangement, however, remains unexplained. Any pre-narrative of rebellion and fall remains entirely conjectural: if Urizen simply begins in the void, his actions are unequivocally admirable. Nobody else, after all, is making any kind of world.[30]

IV

In *The Four Zoas*, the problem ceases to be why Urizen left Eternity, and instead becomes what to do with him when he returns. The climactic transformation seems unequivocal enough:

> As on a Pyramid of mist his white robes scattering
> The fleecy white renewd he shook his aged mantles off
> Into the fires Then glorious bright Exulting in his joy
> He sounding rose into the heavens in naked majesty
> In radiant Youth
>
> (p. 121: 28–32 E391)

This metamorphosis, however, has only been made possible by the decision to 'cast futurity away & turn my back upon that void / Which I have made for lo futurity is in this moment' (p. 121: 20–1 E390). Yet it is precisely this concern for past and future (in the earlier drafts, it was 'remembrance' rather than 'futurity' which was rejected (E844)) that raises Urizen above the psychology of threat and retaliation that dominates the other Zoas, who have been living 'in this moment' all along.

I will restrict myself to two examples. Urizen's initial euphoria at receiving the 'Scepter' from Albion at the beginning of the second night rapidly wanes when confronted by the 'draught of Voidness' of a Lockean *tabula rasa* 'to draw existence in' (p. 23: 14–25: 1, E314–5).[31] His response to the 'Abyss', however, is not capitulation or despair but a determination to 'Build … the Mundane Shell around the Rock of Albion' (p. 24: 7–8 E314). Secondly, in the sixth night, Urizen voluntarily explores his dens 'with a Globe of fire / Lighting his dismal journey thro the pathless world of death' (p. 70: 1–2 E346).[32] Again he seeks to reconstruct rather than lament: 'Here will I fix my foot & here rebuild' (p. 73: 13–14 E350). The 'iron power' of 'Stern Urizen' (p. 25: 40–2 E317) should not be sentimentalized, but the matrix of qualifying ironies does not invalidate what is created by his 'care & power & severity' (p. 28: 24 E318):

But infinitely beautiful the wondrous work arose
In sorrow & care. a Golden World whose porches round the heavens
And pillard halls & rooms recievd the eternal wandering stars
A wondrous golden Building

> (p. 32: 7–10 E321)

The fundamental incoherence of the poem lies not in its textual complexities, but in its attempts to discredit Urizen's endeavours, as culpable, illusory and dispensable. In *The Book of Urizen* this prejudicial commentary was conveyed by the clotted adjectival overlay; in *The Four Zoas*, through reductive motivations attributed by the authorial voice. The more Urizen does, the more autonomy that he achieves, the more his efforts must be condemned as further attempts 'to measure out the immense & fix / The whole into another world better suited to obey / His will' (p. 73: 17–19 E350).[33]

Urizen initially seems to fulfil his role as the 'labourer of ages' in the final harvest, driving the 'Plow of ages' and sowing the 'Seed of Men' (p. 124: 26, 30 E394); taking his 'Sickle' so he and his 'all his joyful sons / Reapd the wide Universe & bound in Sheaves a wondrous Harvest' (p. 132: 6–7 E400); and finally employing his 'Flail' so that 'all Nations were threshed out & the stars threshd form their husks' (p. 134: 1 E402).[34] At this point, however, he disappears from the narrative: his 'Flail' is heard once more (p. 135: 8 E403); there is a passing reference to 'ornaments formd by the sons of Urizen' (p. 137: 10 E405); and the 'Corn' is 'taken out of the Stores of Urizen' (p. 138: 1 E406). In the final pages, his functions have been assumed by the unfallen form of Los: the 'Bread of Ages' is made by the 'Mills of Urthona', who is explicitly paired with Tharmas in the final reference to 'Calling the Plowman to his Labour & the Shepherd to his rest', to the conspicuous exclusion of the figure who has hitherto laboured throughout the poem (p. 138: 29 E406).

Urizen only exists through labour: in Eternity, labour is unnecessary. There would be no place for him in a pre-or post-lapsarian state which:

> Where joy sang in the trees & pleasure sported on the rivers and laughter sat beneath the Oaks & innocence sported round. (p. 72: 39–73: 1 E349–50)

Yet, 'All that is not action is not worth reading' (E544), and how much credibility does a world possess in which Urizen's endeavours are redundant?[35] The harmonious co-operation envisaged can only be sustained within a realm that offers no resistance to the instant fulfilment of desire. 'Sweet Science reigns' (p. 139: 10 E407) at the close of the poem, but there remains one discordant reference:

> And men are bound to sullen contemplations in the night
> Restless they turn on beds of sorrow. in their inmost brain
> Feeling the crushing Wheels they rise they write the bitter words
> Of Stern Philosophy & knead the bread of knowledge with
> tears & groans
>
> (p. 138: 12–15 E406)

The lines evoke Urizen's labours, whose fallen form cannot be accommodated after the apocalypse, and raise the possibility that 'Stern Philosophy' can only 'knead the bread of knowledge' through effort, difficulty and struggle.

The same problem recurs in exacerbated form in *Jerusalem*. There is no room for the 'Great Spectre Los' (95:18 E256) in the 'Life of Immortality' (99:4 E258): his passion, vigour and defiance, his Lockean and Urizenic qualities, all deny him entry. (The most striking of the many parallels is when Los's re-enacts Urizen's descent with 'his globe of fire to search the interiors of Albion's / Bosom' [45:3–4 E194].) Thus the 'imperial clemency' (Frosch 1974, p. 93) of placing 'Bacon & Newton & Locke' alongside 'Milton & Shakspear & Chaucer' on the 'innumerable Chariots of the Almighty' (98:9–10 E257) is of dubious efficacy: nothing in the 'Life of Immortality' (99:4 E258) suggests that they could subsist there in any recognizable form.

Thus Eternity must be seen as the problem in rather than the solution to Blake's thought. He propounds an infinity defined primarily through absence of 'Industry and Labour of Thought' (4:3:6) while remaining heavily indebted to its metaphoric idiom in his presentation of the fallen world. This results not in refutation but consolidation: the power of the Lockean qualities of endeavour, self-discipline and achieved mastery of a recalcitrant world are foregrounded and massively enhanced. Somewhat heretically, therefore, I will close with the suggestion that Blake's mythology is most compelling where it incorporates its apparent adversary most directly. 'Labour at the resolute Anvil' belongs to the domain of Locke, and Blake, as a 'true poet', may be said to be of Urizen's 'party without knowing it' (*MHH* pl. 5 E35).[36]

Notes

1. Nelson Hilton's chapter on 'Spectres' also omits all reference to Locke (1983, pp. 147–72). Wayne Glausser acknowledges they are 'linked to empirical reason', but does not develop this in the context of Locke's atomistic model of sensory ideas (1991, p. 82).
2. See John Dunn, *The Political Thought of John Locke: An Historical Account of the Argument of the 'Two Treatises'* (Cambridge: Cambridge University Press, 1969); and Richard Ashcraft, *Revolutionary Politics and Locke's "Two Treatises of Government"* (Princeton: Princeton University Press, 1986).
3. See John Marshall, *John Locke: Resistance, Religion, and Responsibility* (Cambridge: Cambridge University Press 1994) p. xxi.
4. John Locke, *An Essay concerning Human Understanding*, ed. P. H. Nidditch (Oxford: Clarendon, 1975; rev. 1982) 1:4:23; 3:10:9.
5. 'A Little Boy Lost' (3–4, 15–6 E28–9). For links between Blake and Deist and Enlightenment anti-clericalism, see Sandler (1972).
6. See 'Blind Mans Buff' (66–70 E421) and 'Edward III' (194–203 E413); and compare 'The Bonds of this Subjection are like the Swadling Cloths they are wrapt up in', *Two Treatises of Government* (ed.) Peter Laslett (Cambridge: Cambridge University Press, 1960; rev. 1963) 2:55 322) with 'Infant Sorrow' (5–6 E28) and 'Auguries of Innocence' (63 E491).

7. See *The Trial of Thomas Hardy for High Treason…taken down in Shorthand*, 4 vols (London 1794–5) III 243–5; and John Wright, *A Revealed Knowledge of some Things that will Speedily be Fulfilled* (London, 1794) 22. For a survey of recent debate on Locke's transatlantic influence, see Barbara Arneill, *John Locke and America: the Defence of English Colonialism* (Oxford: Clarendon, 1996) pp. 1–20.

8. Locke's denunciation of slavery did not preclude his own indirect involvement in the slave trade; see Wayne Glausser, 'Three Approaches to Locke and the Slave Trade', *JHI* 51:2 (1990) pp. 199–216.

9. W. J. T. Mitchell comments that once Los 'is enclosed in Urizen's world, he begins to act the part of Urizenic prophet' (1978, p. 121); Paul Mann observes that 'by creating the fallen world…Urizen provides for and indeed generates Los's activity: Los's antithetical posture toward Urizen is belied by the fundamentally Urizenic nature of his activity' (1986, p. 54); Steven Vine explores the doublings whereby 'Los's creative labour ineluctably repeats Urizen's troubled creation' (1993, p. 71); and Stephen Cox notes 'Los's apparently unavoidable resubstantialization of Urizen's dialectic' (1994, p. 152).

10. Peter Otto observes that Frye's vision is as solipsistic and closed to otherness as that which is ostensibly opposes (1992, p. 12).

11. See John Richetti on the 'enforcing concreteness' of 'half-dead metaphors', and the 'subsequent busyness' of the mind after the 'initial reception of simple sensations': *Philosophical Writing: Locke, Berkeley, Hume* (Cambridge: Harvard University Press, 1983) 81–2, 84; and William Walker, *Locke, Literary Criticism and Philosophy* (Cambridge: Cambridge University Press, 1994) for links between the epistemology and the political thought (pp. 45–56).

12 'In effect a sort of conceit, doing no philosophical work', according to Michael Ayers, *John Locke* 2 vols (London: Routledge, 1991), 1: 18.

13. From a multitude of examples: 'Mechanical Excellence is the Only Vehicle of Genius' (E643); 'Throughout all these Human Lands / Tools were made & Born were hands / Every Farmer Understands' (AI 64–6 E491); 'The Man who does not Labour more than the Hireling must be a poor Devil' (E641). Morris Eaves offers little evidence to support his claim that Blake was 'contemptuous towards mindless physical labour' (1992, p. 165). For a Hegelian reading of Blake's vocabulary of labour, see Punter (1977; 1981; 1982).

14. In his account of memory Augustine implores, 'Heere doe I labour, and labour in my selfe, O Lord, and am made unto my selfe, as soyle which must be cultivated with too much paynes. and travayle': *The Confessions of the Incomparable Doctour Augustine*. translated into English by Sir T. Matthew (London, 1620), 10:15 499–500. On original sin in Locke, stressing his early Calvinist background, see W. M. Spellman, *John Locke and the Problem of Depravity* (Oxford: Clarendon, 1988).

15. The entire first book of the *Essay* denounces such 'general Propositions' because they 'eased the lazy from the pains of search, and stopp'd the enquiry of the doubtful' (1:4:24). This elicits from Frye the quite stunningly disingenuous comment'. 'Locke is denying

what from Blake's point of view would be innate generalisations, and Blake does not believe in them any more than Locke does' (1947, p. 23).

16. Cathy Caruth, in *Empirical Truths and Critical Fictions: Locke, Wordsworth, Kant, Freud* (Baltimore: Johns Hopkins University Press, 1991) notes of the *Essay* that 'its apparent subject, the limitation of reason, really tells of a new and unbounded power of reason over its own territory' (p. 5).

17. Compare Thomas Reid, *Essays on the Intellectual Powers of Man* (Edinburgh: John Bell, 1785) 3:7 pp. 343–5.

18. See also Blackstone (1949, pp. 222–6, 260–3, 333–45); Raine (1968) vol. 2, pp. 131–5); and Witke (1972).

19. On the common ground between Locke's famous denunciation of the 'firmness of perswasion' of enthusiasts (4:14:12) and Blake's 'firm perswasion' which 'removed mountains' (*MHH* pl. 12 E38–9), see S. H. Clark, "The Whole Internal World his own": Locke and Metaphor Reconsidered', *JHI* 58 (1998) pp. 241–65.

20. Other examples include: 'Oil has falsely been supposed to give strength to colours: but a little consideration must shew the fallacy of this opinion' (E530); 'But one convincing proof among many others, that these assertions are true … ' (E531); 'And what connoisseurs call touch, I know by experience, must be … ' (E540); 'These experiment Pictures … ' (E548).

21. *The Reasonableness of Christianity. as delivered in the Scriptures*, in *Complete Works,* 10 vols (London: J. Johnson et al., 1801) 7: 1–158 (5): 'plain' is used over fifty times in the treatise. *Epistola de Tolerantia: A Letter on Toleration,* ed. Raymond Klibansky and trans. J. W. Gough (Oxford: Clarendon, 1968) p. 125.

22. Locke forthrightly argues against 'a supposition so derogatory' as to reduce Christ to 'nothing but the restorer and preacher of pure natural religion' (*Works* 7:5), suggesting that if Blake had read *The Reasonableness of Christianity*, he disregarded it.

23. For comparable instances of this reduction, see John W. Yolton, *Locke and French Materialism* (Oxford: Clarendon, 1991) p. 4. However, Urizen's 'self-contemplating' (pl. 3 21–2 E70) makes explicit reference to Locke's other 'fountain of knowledge', 'the internal Operations of our Minds, perceived and reflected on by our selves' (2:1:2).

24. Compare Peter Browne's argument in *The Procedure, Limits, and Extent of Human Understanding* (London: William Innys, 1728): 'The Deists and Freethinkers … rigorously confine the Understanding within the narrow bounds of direct and immediate objects of Sense and Reason … The Progress from thence into speculative Atheism is short and easy. For if all Revealed Religion is to be rejected as merely figurative, and metaphorical; then all Natural Religion is to be likewise rejected' (p. 39).

25. 'The Adventurer', no. 120 (29 December 1753), in *The Yale Edition of the Works of Samuel Johnson,* 14 vols (New Haven and London: Yale University Press, 1958–78), vol. 2, ed. W. J. Bate, John M. Bullitt and L. F. Powell (1963) pp. 469–7.

26. Viscomi's abridged version resolves the conundrum of the missing third plate by only retaining b3, b4 and b12 from the second series, but simply accentuates the conceptual break insofar as Blake's 'succinct and overt refutation' remains 'predicated on inherent human divinity' (1993, pp. 217–25).
27. *The Spectator*, ed. Donald F. Bond, 5 vols (Oxford: Clarendon, 1965) no. 580 4: 585–6.
28. Bloom comments 'by a very grim paradox, Urizen, the limiter of energy, is himself an indomitable energy' (1962, p. 165); and Cantor notes that Blake 'makes Reason energetic enough to begin its war with Energy', and that 'one often finds oneself in the logically awkward position of speaking of Reason's passions' (1984, pp. 201–2).
29. Kittel's extended study persistently contrasts 'the active mind' of Eternity which 'is autonomous and instantaneously fulfils its desires' with Urizen's 'passive mind, a mind without creative energy' (1978, pp. 114, 132). More recently, Mee sees a 'beneficent act of creativity' become an 'act of terrible destruction' (1992, p. 183); Vine equates Urizen's 'principle of poetic articulation' with a 'hubristic boast' and 'catastrophic fall' (1993, p. 67); and Esterhammer similarly glosses 'a heroic struggle to master the elements' as intrinsically inferior to the 'teleological process of ordering the cosmos' (1994, p. 153).
30. Peter Otto who concedes that a reciprocal withholding of relationship 'to blame for the Fall' (1990, p. 367) offers no explanation for Urizen's initial withdrawal.
31. Compare, 'Incessant the falling Mind labour'd / Organizing itself: till the Vacuum / Became element', in *The Book of Los* (ch. 2: 9 49–51, E92).
32. Locke famously describes reason as the 'Candle, that is set up in us' which 'shines bright enough for all our Purposes' (1:1:5; compare 4:19:8).
33. Jeanne Moskal notes 'new layers of narrative around the initial presentation of Urizen' that serve as 'accusation rather than forgiveness' (1994, pp. 58–9). This double standard reappears in critical assessments: for example, Lincoln dismisses Urizen's 'ideal creation' of the 'Golden World' as 'chaotic vision' and his 'almost tragic dignity' as the by-product of a 'poetic style ... that presents forms of error in terms of dazzling exuberance' (1996 pp. 51, 66–7; compare Cox 1992, p. 19).
34. For parallels with Thomas Spence's agrarian communism, see Lincoln (1996, pp. 188–9).
35. Compare W. J. T. Mitchell's misgivings: 'presumably the genuine apocalypse would not involve a simple return to the prelapsarian state, but rather the assimilation of what Urizen has discovered' (1978, p. 134).
36. For gender implications of this idiom, assessment of Locke's as strong precursor to eighteenth-century poetry, and discussion of the role of empiricism in *Milton*, see Clark (1994; 1997; 1998).

8

Blake and the Two Swords
Michael Ferber

For the last few years I have been reading about the Great War with France and what the English Romantic poets said about it, with the idea that I might write something on this rather neglected subject.[1] Though they may be signs of my own ignorance, I would like to begin by reporting three things that struck me while reading. The first is that the Romantic poets, with the exception of Keats, had more to say about the French War and about war in general than I had remembered. For all of them the war must have been a recurrent preoccupation during much of their lives, and for some during nearly the whole of their lives. If the English entrance into the war in 1793 brought change and subversion to the minds of all ingenuous youth, as Wordsworth claimed (*1805 Prelude* 10.231–3), the sheer length of the war brought something similar to the mind of a poet who was an ingenuous youth when the war ended: Shelley, born three days after the Brunswick manifesto stung the French into a massive mobilization, made war one of his earliest and most frequent subjects, but unlike Wordsworth, Coleridge and Southey, he became and remained a pacifist. To a greater extent than most of us realize, I think, the war made all of them the poets they were.

The second fact that struck me was how terrible the war was, even for the British, who suffered less than any other major power. The war against France, which was really one long war despite the truces, changes of government and shifting coalitions, surpassed any war before it in scale, scope and intensity, and it was not equalled until 1914. We ought to call it the First World War. Winston Churchill gave that title to the Seven Years' War (1756–63), but only because of its wide geographical extent: from Quebec, the Ohio and the Mississippi, to India, the East Indies and Senegal.[2] The geographical scope of the Great War with France was even more impressive. As Joel Barlow advises his hungry raven, who had been following Napoleon into Russia until December's weather made the corpses unchewable, 'Go where you will; Calabria, Malta, Greece,/Egypt

153

and Syria still his fame increase, / Domingo's fattened isle and India's plains / Glow deep with purple drawn from Gallic veins'.[3] To Barlow's list of frost-free battle-sites we may add Java, the Celebes and Timor; New Orleans and the American Great Lakes; South America; and the Cape of Good Hope.[4]

In its severity and duration, moreover, the French War vastly outweighed the Seven Years' War. In the slaughterbench of Central and Eastern Europe about a 100,000 men were killed every year, on the average, for over 20 years, and in 1812 alone about a million combatants died on all sides. All six major European powers took part (France, Britain, Austria, Russia, Prussia and Spain), as well as many minor powers (Denmark, Holland, Sweden, Portugal, Switzerland, Venice and the German princedoms). Russians fought in the Alps, Swedes fought in Germany.[5] In the grand armies mustered on both sides a dozen languages might be spoken and a hundred uniforms worn. In Spain, in the Tyrol and in Russia the people themselves rose, forming partisan or guerrilla units outside the regular armies. (We owe our word 'guerrilla' to the Spanish theatre of this war.) It was a 'total' war as brutal and indiscriminate, at times, as the religious wars of the seventeenth century; it has been called the first 'ideological' war, another resemblance to 1914–18, and as such it could not be brought to an end without the surrender of one side.[6]

Essays and books on the Revolutionary and Napoleonic Wars often begin – it is almost a generic requirement – by citing von Clausewitz, who pointed out the difference between the limited wars of the eighteenth century and the unlimited wars of Napoleon's time. Fought by professional armies which were led by generals who knew each other, on behalf of kings and princes who were all cousins and spoke French, with the goal of gaining this or that advantage in territory or trade, eighteenth-century wars were usually deliberately kept small in scale and confined to the warm 'season'; they consisted mainly of manoeuvring for position and avoiding decisive encounters. 'I do not favour battles', Maurice de Saxe wrote in 1732, 'particularly at the beginning of a war. I am sure a good general can make war all his life and not be compelled to fight one'.[7] There were exceptions, such as Marlborough's brilliant march to the Danube and crushing victory over the French and Bavarians at Blenheim (1704), but the exceptions were rare. That basic principles or ways of life were scarcely at stake even in such great battles is the indisputable premise of Southey's 1798 poem 'The Battle of Blenheim', where old Kaspar tells some children about the 'famous victory': 'But what they fought each other for, / I could not well make out'. The age of military restraint was to yield at the century's end to 'the nation in arms' and universal conscription, national and ideological rather than dynastic goals, strategies aimed at defeat rather than negotiating a new balance, and, of course, the breathtaking generalship and equally astonishing ambition of Napoleon Bonaparte. Von Clausewitz implicitly replies to Maurice de Saxe in his famous maxim, 'Battles decide everything', while during the war Admiral Nelson gave an opinion that would have startled the previous generation: 'What the country needs is the annihilation of the enemy'.[8]

The third idea that came home to me is that anti-war poetry is very difficult to write well, but that, in an age when poetry was widely read and held in high esteem, it was very important to try to write it. None of the poets fought in the war, except Landor in Spain – indeed almost no one with a literary education took part in it – and so the poets had to rely on second-hand reports and even more on the over-familiar conventions of war poetry, some of which had been established as far back as the *Iliad*. I am tempted to propose a variant of the Bate-Bloom thesis on the burden of the past or anxiety of influence: how do you write a fresh, effective poem about war, and especially against war? This problem might help us look at Wordsworth's poems of 1793–1800. Take the stock character of anti-war poetry, the suffering widow, a descendant of Homer's Andromache. There is no avoiding her in the pursuit of something new, for suffering widows were stock characters in real life; one of the main things war did was make widows. Pondering this fact, perhaps, Wordsworth wrote about one war widow after another, gradually learning to incorporate rounded details into their lives and circumstances and to find the poise between sentiment and detachment until cliché evaporated and something new and (we now say) distinctively Wordsworthian emerged, as in *The Ruined Cottage*.[9]

As a part of this complex one would want to take account of the ambition of all the Romantic poets to write an epic under the shadow of Milton, the Milton who forswore tedious havoc and sang the praises of passive resistance. Southey writes a *French* war epic, Landor writes the anti-Virgilian *Gebir*, Shelley writes an anti-war epic, all filled with havoc enough, while the turning point of *The Prelude* is arguably the moment that Wordsworth decides to leave the land of epic events and return to England (1805 version 10.176–201).

To a writer who opposed England's joining the French Wars, moreover, it must have been maddeningly frustrating that the only means of opposing it seemed so paltry – a mere poem, a pamphlet, maybe a sermon. Much of the desperate tone of Blake's *Jerusalem*, I think, and of Shelley's youthful poems, comes of their painful recognition that the pen or graver's burin was not a lance. 'Many fervent souls / Strike rhyme on rhyme, who would strike steel on steel / If steel had offered, in a restless heat / Of doing something' (Elizabeth Barrett Browning).[10] To compound this frustration was their understanding that as soon as a poem or article began to look effective its author might be indicted for sedition or worse.[11]

* * *

If I had more space here I would try to track Blake's early fascination with war in 'Gwin, King of Norway' and 'King Edward the Third'. In 'Gwin' there is a very bloody-minded rebellion against the tyrant king, in describing which Blake seems both to sympathize with the plebeian rebels ('The husbandman does leave his plow, / To wade thro' fields of gore' [45–6 E418]) and lament the war itself ('The stench of blood makes sick the heav'ns' [95 E420]). More complex ironies traverse 'King Edward the Third', which when finished might have been an anti-war drama but which certainly gives effective bellicose speeches to several characters. As Blake manifestly ends up a pacifist, the task here would be to show where and when he abandons his apparent endorsement of revolutionary violence. His belief that the revolutions of his day would in fact usher peace into the world informs the one book we have of 'The French Revolution', which comes to a climax with 'the removal of war', and *America: A Prophecy*, which seems to gloss over the violence of the 'warlike men' and emphasizes the effect of strikes, demonstrations of unity and defections. With *Europe: A Prophecy*, we have a more ambiguous case, where the mysterious events in Enitharmon's heaven come to an abrupt halt when Orc descends in fury to France and Los calls his sons 'to the strife of blood'.[12]

For the remainder of this essay, however, I want to turn to the later poems, all of which were composed after the war had been under way for several years and seemed only to be getting worse.

The governing concept of Blake's longer works is the distinction between spiritual and corporeal war, and the purpose of these works is to combat the tendency of his age to suppress the one and glorify the other. In the Preface to *Milton* Blake calls of his young readers to 'set your foreheads against the ignorant Hirelings!

For we have Hirelings in the Camp, the Court, & the University: who would if they could, for ever depress Mental & prolong Corporeal War. 'In the famous quatrains that follow he vows he will not 'cease from Mental Fight' until we have built the new Jerusalem (M1, E95–6). Later we hear that the 'Gods of the Kingdoms of the Earth' fight each other 'in contrarious / And cruel opposition: Element against Element, opposed in War / Not Mental, as the Wars of Eternity, but a Corporeal Strife' (M31.23–5, E130). Both *Milton* and *Jerusalem*, as well as the abandoned *Four Zoas*, are loud with strife of both sorts; the moments of peace, such as the rapt contemplations of nature in the second book of *Milton*, are so rare as to be startling.

Mental or spiritual war, of course, requires weapons. Sometimes our weapons are just our foreheads, as in the Preface to *Milton*, but in most passages where Blake contrasts the two kinds of war his own armoury consists merely of corporeal weapons redescribed as spiritual ones. The well-equipped spiritual warrior who sings about mental fight, with his spear, sword, 'Bow of burning gold', 'Arrows of desire', and 'Chariot of fire', sounds rather too much like a corporeal warrior, no more spiritual than the two legions of angels in *Paradise Lost* who slice each other in two with swords and heave heavy mountains on top of devastating artillery; only the word 'desire', and perhaps 'fire', hint that these weapons are really different, that they are made of a spiritual substance. What this material may be we learn in *Jerusalem*. There Los has been watching Hand and the other fallen sons of Albion transform spirit into bodily war: Hand 'siez'd the bars of condens'd thoughts, to forge them: / Into the sword of war: into the bow and arrow: / Into the thundering cannon and into the murdering gun'. So Los responds by contrary labours at his own forge: 'I took the sighs & tears, & bitter groans: / I lifted them into my Furnaces; to form the spiritual sword. / That lays open the hidden heart...' (J9.4–6, 17–19, E152). Later Los speaks to the recalcitrant Albion, 'Saying. Albion! Our wars are wars of life, & wounds of love, / With intellectual spears, & long winged arrows of thought' (J34.14–15, E180). The martyrdom of the 'Monk of Charlemaine', who was punished for 'condemning glorious War', generates new spiritual weapons as well:

> For a Tear is an Intellectual thing;
> And a Sigh is the Sword of an Angel King

> And the bitter groan of a Martyrs woe
> Is an Arrow from the Almighties Bow!
>   (*J*52.25–8, E202)

And indeed at the finale of *Jerusalem* the awakened Albion stretches his hand to take his fourfold bow, 'A Bow of Mercy & Loving-kindness' (*J*97.13, E256).

With just these few passages we can begin to see what spiritual warfare consists of. It is born in desire, suffering, even death; these in turn are worked on by a craftsman; he makes them into effective weapons, somehow, against those who inflict the suffering; the resulting weapons are both thoughts – an Enlightenment commonplace – and acts of Christian love and mercy; and their effect is to pierce or open the heart. Blake elaborates this process throughout his epics, and while doing so he produces several 'weapons' that are not translations of the usual corporeal ones. Before looking more closely at these, however, it will be useful to turn to the long tradition that lies behind his fundamental distinction. We might call it the tradition of 'The Two Swords', what Blake called 'the Spiritual and ... the Natural Sword' (*J*52, E200) and it is as old as Christianity, or even older.[13]

The key biblical passage lies in Paul's Epistle to the Ephesians, a part of which Blake himself cites as his epigraph to *The Four Zoas*: 'For we wrestle not against flesh and blood, but against principalities, against powers, against the rulers of the darkness of this world, against spiritual wickedness in high places' (Eph. 6.12, E300). But he omits the verses around it that have established spiritual armour as a Christian commonplace ever since: 'Put on the whole armour of God', Paul says,

> that ye may be able to stand against the wiles of the devil. Stand therefore, having your loins girt about with truth, and having on the breastplate of righteousness; And your feet shod with the preparation of the gospel of peace; Above all, taking the shield of faith, wherewith ye shall be able to quench all the fiery darts of the wicked. And take the helmet of salvation, and the sword of the Spirit, which is the word of God. (6.11–17)

That the 'gospel of peace' should be a part of this armour might have struck Blake, who could have brought out the little tremor of paradox more effectively than Paul. A somewhat more aggressive Christian appears in Paul's second letter to the Corinthians, where he says that 'the weapons of our warfare are not carnal, but mighty through God to the pulling down of strong holds' (II Cor. 10.4). Paul's equation of the sword as the word of God, as the Gospel, probably inspired the more literal-minded John of the Apocalypse to picture the Son of Man with 'a sharp two-edged sword' coming out of his mouth, 'that with it he should smite the nations' (Rev. 1.16, 19.15). John had another source in Isaiah, who spoke of a God who 'shall smite the earth with the rod of his mouth' and who 'hast made my mouth like a sharp sword' (Isaiah 1 1.4, 49.2).

An early extension of this imagery, prompted in part by allegorical readings of the many corporeal wars of the Israelites, is the notion of the Church Militant and the Army of Christ. To quote two martyrs that resemble Blake's Monk, Maximilianus told the Roman proconsul trying him for refusing conscription, 'I cannot be a solider for the world, I am a soldier for my God', while St Martin of Tours, in the same predicament, said, 'I am a soldier of Christ; I cannot fight'.[14] Among the early Church Fathers who expanded on the metaphor is Clement of Alexandria, who wrote,

> If the loud trumpet summons soldiers to war, shall not Christ with a strain of peace to the ends of the earth gather up his soldiers of peace? A bloodless army he has assembled by blood and by the word, to give to them the Kingdom of Heaven. The trumpet of Christ is his Gospel. He has sounded, we have heard. Let us then put on the armour of peace.[15]

This militant pacifism of the early Church, we know, gave way nearly entirely when the Emperor Constantine became of Christian, not the least of the reasons Blake includes him among those whose 'Roman Sword' will be defeated by the spiritual weapons of the Monk of Charlemaine; he also calls Constantine a case of 'Religion hid in War' (J76.20, E231). But pacifism never quite died out, and it flowered again among the Czech Brethren in the fifteenth century and then among Anabaptists, Mennonites, Socinians, Quakers and other sects. The great near-pacifist Erasmus made use of the 'Two Swords' in his brilliant polemics against war. Confronting the standard argument that the God of the Old Testament, the Lord of Hosts, sanctions war for a holy purpose (such as eradicating those who block the path to the Promised Land), Erasmus replied,

> If we wish to retain old titles, let Him be called the God of armies
> if you understand armies to mean virtues united together with
> good men for the destruction of vice. Let Him be the God of
> vengeance if you take vengeance to the correction of vice, and
> if you understand the bloody slaughters of men that fill the books
> of Hebrews, not as the tearing of men into pieces, but as the tear-
> ing of wicked affections out of their hearts.

In a similar allegorical vein, in another work, he wrote,

> But since Christ gave the command to put up the sword it is not
> fitting for Christians to fight, except in that noblest of all battles
> against the most hideous enemies of the Church – against love of
> money, against anger, against ambition, against the fear of death.
> These are our Philistines, our Nebuchadnezzars, our Moabites,
> and our Ammonites, and with these we must make no truce, we
> must persistently be at war, until the enemy is completely wiped
> out and peace is established ... [16]

Even a passage that might refer to literal warfare, Christ's cryptic
saying, 'I came not to send peace, but a sword' (Matt. 10: 34),
though Shelley singled this out as the one 'prediction' of Christ to
be fulfilled, was regularly assimilated to the metaphorical imagery
of Paul and John of Patmos. Calvin, for instance, states without any
question that 'the sword is the Gospel'.[17] Another passage, which
on the face of it refers to real swords, is Luke 22: 35–8, where Christ
tells his disciples, 'he that hath no sword, let him sell his garment,
and buy one', and his disciples satisfy him by saying they already
have two. Erasmus disposes of this passage with little ado: the
sword the disciples are to buy is 'not the sword which serves rob-
bers and murderers, but the sword of the spirit which penetrates
into the innermost depths of the bosom and cuts out every passion
with a single stroke, so that nothing remains in the heart but piety'.[18]

What Shelley was to call 'Quakerish and Socinian principles of
politics' were well known in England from the mid-seventeenth
century.[19] Socinus, the anti-trinitarian reformer active in Poland,
had written that 'Christians are forbidden to wage war against their
fellow men'.[20] His followers in England, who became known as
Unitarians by about 1690, were pacifistic, though not as staunchly
as the Quakers. The Quakers regularly referred to the 'carnal
sword' in contrast to the spiritual sword, starting with George Fox,

who wrote to Cromwell in 1654: 'my weapons are not carnall but spiritual!, And my Kingdome is not of this world, therefore with the carnall weapon I doe not fight, but am *om those things dead'.[21] An occasional Methodist used the same terms. When he was pressed into the army in 1744, John Nelson, stonemason, Methodist preacher and friend of John Wesley, claimed, 'I am a man averse from war, and shall not fight but under the Prince of Peace, the captain of my salvation; and the weapons he gives me are not carnal like these'.[22] If we agree with E. P. Thompson that Blake knew the Muggletonians, then it is interesting that they too (with a few exceptions) were pacifists. The phrase 'sword of steel' seems to have served Muggletonians as 'carnal sword' served the Quakers and 'corporeal war' served Blake. John Reeve, the founder of the sect, wrote in 1656: 'is there any Rules in the Letter of the New Testament to warrant any spiritual Christians to resist the Civil Magistrate with the Sword of Steel? Nay, cloth it not altogether command the contrary'?[23] A Muggletonian petition in 1803 asking exemption from military service argued that 'our consciences are too tender to make use of the sword of steel to slay the Image of God with'.[24] Blake used this phrase himself only twice, both times in his notebook poem, which was reduced and recast into 'The Grey Monk' and 'I saw a Monk of Charlemaine', from which we have already quoted: 'Roman pride is a sword of steel', he says, but, in a later stanza, 'The Tear shall melt the sword of steel' (*N*8). This poem, if we can consider it one poem, is Blake's most trenchantly pacifistic shorter work.

In all this long history of the notion of spiritual warfare – and we could cite Swedenborg, Coleridge and many others – we see plain evidence of the pervasiveness, the ineluctable presence of corporeal warfare itself.[25] It is as if the original pacifist Christians, poor, plebeian and provincial, when faced with the terrors of martyrdom, turned for compensation not only to a heavenly reward but to a metaphorical sublimation of what they most hated and feared. Even heaven is scarred by the world it transcends. And yet, since active proselytizing was enjoined on Christians, since they were not to lie low and hide their light under a bushel, what other terms were available but those of battle? It may be, as Pierre Clastres has recently said, that 'Language is the opposite of violence', but the very language of argument or debate is fraught with military metaphors.[26] The first example of Lakoff and Johnson's *Metaphors We Live by* is the concept 'Argument is War': when we 'attack' a 'position', 'demolish' or 'shoot down' an 'indefensible' argument, or 'counter' or 'parry' the 'thrust' of a 'point' so it does not 'hit the target' or 'strike home', we are paying tribute to physical force in warfare or military games. As an alternative they suggest the metaphor of the dance, whereby debaters take turns performing aesthetically pleasing statements, but we would not consider such a performance an argument at all.[27] Something like this dance, I think, appears at the end of *Jerusalem*, where spiritual warfare itself achieves new and perhaps higher dimensions: the four living creatures walk to and fro conversing and go forth and return wearied (J98.38–9, 99.2). Let us return now, however, to the struggles of Blake and of Los during the long night of Albion's sleep, and look again at their arsenal.

Besides the spiritualized versions of traditional weapons of war, such as sword and spear, mace and shield, bow and arrow, what other weapons are at hand? One is the chariot, traditional enough in both the Bible and classical epic as a fighting machine, but capable of civilian uses as well. In Shelley the ubiquitous chariots serve as 'vehicles of thought' in an almost literal sense: the swiftness of thought or spirit is conveyed by flying chariots or 'cars'. In Blake they have something of the same function but usually retain their military role at the same time. One fascinating example is the speech of 'those who disregard all Mortal Things' in *Jerusalem*. The speech consists of tiger-drawn chariot-words: '& their Words stood in Chariots in array / Curbing their Tygers with golden bits & bridles of silver & ivory' (J55.34–5, E205), and when they give their tigers the rein the words fly, or pounce, upon those who are labouring in misery at the prow. In going Homer's phrase 'winged words' one better, Blake underscores as vividly as he can the solemn importance of this speech, which tells how humans can contract into worms or expand into gods and, as gods, see that the 'Ulro Visions' of this fallen world are mere dust or chaff or dregs. The immortal ones can contract or expand space and time, choosing either to stay below and console us weeping clods or to rise 'Upon the chariots of the morning' to Eternity (J 55:36–46 E205). These chariot-words are arrayed in battle formation, ready to drive home their message, the content of which is a mirror of its form. It has to do with chariots: it is the Good News that we can fly, we can transcend the miserable verminous state of Ulro that seems so solid and inescapable.

Another object that lies between a corporeal weapon and a corporeal tool of peace is the hammer. It is ambiguous not only because any hammer can beat in a man's brains, but because hammers are used to make even more destructive weapons, such as swords. Los, of course, primarily labours as a blacksmith, and the beat of his hammer on the anvil is the pulse of life throbbing through *Jerusalem*. What is he making? At one point, as we have already seen, he says, 'I took the sighs & tears, & bitter groans: / I lifted them into my Furnaces; to form the spiritual sword.' (*J*9.17–18, E152). He goes on at length: 'I drew forth the pang / Of sorrow red hot: I workd it on my resolute anvil: / … / Loud roar my Furnaces and loud my hammer is heard: / I labour day and night, I behold the soft affections / Condense beneath my hammer into forms of cruelty' (19–27). Blake is willing to call his own spiritual weapon a form of cruelty, much like the sword that Christ said he brought; this cruelty is like the 'kindest violence' with which Los's companions intervene to save Albion against his will (*J*39.2, E186). Spiritual warfare is, after all, warfare, and not a polite academic conference or a support group for the victimized. In his obsessive, over-compensatory elaborations of the means of warfare, however, one feels the poignancy of Blake's yearning to give words the efficacy of things, to give his poor pieces of paper covered with verses and pictures the same force in the world as the men on horseback with blood-stained sabres.

'The pen is mightier than the sword', they say, but most of those who say so are writers. Hamlet may have been inspired by Rosencrantz's report that 'many wearing rapiers are afraid of goose-quills' (2.2.341), but the quill-master who created him conceded that Hamlet needed his rapier in the end. In Blake's day Mary Russell Mitford staged a dialogue called 'The Pen and the Sword' (1810) in which the pen, of course, gets the last word. Leigh Hunt was to push this theme to its allegorical limit in his anti-war poem of 1835, *Captain Sword and Captain Pen*. It is not to deny the ultimate truth of this proverb to note how feeble and wistfully self-serving it often sounds. Blake opens *The Four Zoas* with the grand and preposterous boast that the heavens have been shaken by, of all things, 'the march of long resounding strong heroic Verse / Marshalled in order for the day of Intellectual Battle' (3.2–3, E300). But it must have felt hopeless, during most of the Napoleonic Wars, to try to write poems, or engrave pictures, on behalf of peace and brotherhood. None the less the great man on horseback himself is supposed to have said, 'Four hostile newspapers are more to be feared than a thousand bayonets'.[28]

Another 'weapon', entirely civilian in its literal use, is the plough. The chariot-worded speech of the Immortals we have just discussed is addressed to labourers at the plough, and the speech itself mentions dust on the prow, sweat on a labourer's shoulder and weeping clods in the ploughed furrow. When he moved to the country in 1800, Blake seems to have been impressed with real ploughs and harrows, and they provide much of the concrete imagery for the complicated quarrel of the 'Bard's Song' of *Milton*. When Los cries, 'follow with me my Plow' (M8.20, E102), do we not hear Blake saying, 'follow with me my Graver'? For it must have occurred to him that the graver or burin acts like a little plough, and when he scratches a line on his plate he is creating a furrow from which life will spring.[29] But the plough and the ploughman have distinct Christian meanings as well, and they seem to bear on Blake's vision of spiritual warfare.

The difference between corporeal war and corporeal peace in the Bible is summed up in the most famous of all prophecies, 'and they shall beat their swords into plowshares, and their spears into pruning hooks: nation shall not lift up sword against nation, neither shall they learn war any more' (Isaiah 2:4 and Micah 4:3), and the less famous reversal, 'Beat your ploughshares into swords, and your pruning hooks into spears' (Joel 3:10). Blake makes both swords and ploughshares into weapons of spiritual warfare; he does so, however, not so much because he needs every weapon he can get in his war against corporeal war as because there is no such thing, in his view, as spiritual peace. Even in Eden or Eternity we shall be engaged in the strenuous contentions of mental fight, in what Blake calls 'the terrors of friendship' (J45.4, E194), debating with one another and keeping each other up to the mark. What would we rather do – play the harp? So Blake's plough and ploughshare alternate with the sword and other weapons for the same spiritual task.

The key text is Christ's saying 'No man, having put his hand to the plough, and looking back, is fit for the kingdom of God' (Luke 9:62). Elaborated by medieval allegorists, this saying, combined with the Parable of the Sower, yielded the idea that priests and preachers of the word of God were ploughmen while hearers of the word were the soil to be cut by the plough. St. Gregory used the phrase 'ploughshare of the tongue' (*vomer linguae*) as the means by which 'the land of the alien heart' of the unbeliever is opened to receive the word. Langland's Piers Plowman, Chaucer's Plowman, who lived 'in pees and parfit charitee', and Spenser's St George, who was brought up in 'ploughmans state' (and hence named Georgos), all establish the literal and figurative virtues of ploughing.[30] Both the sword and the ploughshare, then, cut open the human heart, penetrating it with 'compunction' and new receptivity to peace and perfect charity.

The tears, sighs and groans that are marshalled as weapons throughout Blake's later works have the human heart as their target. St Gregory's ploughshare ploughs the alien heart; Erasmus interpreted the slaughters of the Old Testament 'as the tearing of wicked affections out of their hearts'. St Paul wrote of the circumcision of the heart (Romans 2:29), and a traditional Christian symbol of contrition is the heart pierced by an arrow. The awakened Albion takes up 'A Bow of Mercy & Loving-kindness: laying / Open the hidden Heart in Wars of mutual Benevolence Wars of Love' (*J*97.13–14, E256). That which Blake, Los and Albion want most to lay open, presumably, is the heart hidden within the tyrants and warriors of the world, a heart hardened against appeals for mercy. It comes down to something quite commonplace: that the sufferings of humanity might cause a change of heart in those who inflict them. We are to look forward to the day when 'The war of swords & spears / Melted by dewy tears / Exhales on high' (*N*8, E478).

In the real world it may happen that groans and sighs directly penetrate the heart, as those of the Monk turned directly into swords and arrows. Bloody men on horseback have been known to make generous gestures of charity to an occasional widow or orphan. Such a gesture got Trajan into heaven, according to St Gregory. But in these latter days hearts have grown more hidden and hardened partly because of common battlefield sights. One such sight, indeed, is a corporeal parody of the very purpose of spiritual war, the sight of 'hearts laid open to the light, by the broad grizly sword' (*J*65.52, FZ93.16; E217, 365). So callous have we become that artists and writers must intervene, those blacksmiths of the heart, for they know how to transform the all too familiar sufferings of men and women into effective works. Los must take action as mediator, as publicist, as expert in the vagaries of human psyches, so as to prepare the hearts of his readers for the conversion that pity for suffering will bring about.

Of course, Blake failed completely in his own day, and is still failing now as regards his longer poems, to reach the hearts of readers. The exasperating difficulties of *Jerusalem* especially may be due to Blake's indecision as to whether the poem is itself a spiritual sword or is *about* the spiritual sword, whether it is an example of spiritual warfare or a commentary on it. It seems to be both, but I think an artistic work cannot easily be both; its self-consciousness impedes its evident purpose.

Though he never witnessed an actual battle, Blake seems to have been struck by a feature of battle that nearly all participants report as astonishing the first time they meet it: the sheer noise of it all. Milton called it 'the odious din of war' (*PL* 6.408). In Blake war rages and roars and grows hoarse from raging and roaring, its victims howl and lament, and loud thunders roll. These sounds he imagined. What Blake almost certainly did witness, as it was a common occurrence in the parks and courtyards of London, is military parading and manoeuvring, and there, too, the noise is striking. At the happy climax of *The French Revolution* the troops depart:

> Then the drum beats, and the steely ranks move, and
>   trumpets rejoice in the sky.
> Dark cavalry like clouds frought with thunder ascend on
>   the hills, and bright infantry, rank
> Behind rank, to the soul shaking drum and shrill fife
>   along the roads glitter like fire.
> The noise of trampling, the wind of trumpets, smote the
>   palace walls with a blast.

> > > > > > > (290–3, E299)

And whether he witnessed it or imagined it Blake pointedly contrasts the two sorts of noise characteristic of war: 'They go out to war with Strong Shouts & loud Clarions O Pity / They return with lamentations mourning & weeping' (*FZ* 93.30–1, E365).

It must have struck Blake as well that much of the noise comes from tools of art, from musical instruments; it is they that make 'the symphonies of war loud sounding', as he put it in *The Four Zoas* (50.9, E333). War perverts everything to its own purposes, including music. 'Troop by troop the beastial droves rend one another sounding loud / The instruments of sound' (*FZ* 101.47–8, E374). The 'Trumpets of hoarse war', the 'trumpet fitted to mortal battle', blare throughout the longer poems, but especially in *The Four Zoas*, where they are mentioned fifteen times, along with the drum and cymbal and shrill fife. But Blake seems to have fallen in love with the word 'clarion' while at work on *The Four Zoas*, where it occurs thirteen times, often with the epithet 'warlike' and once with 'thunderous' (101.28, E373). Perhaps he thought its noise somehow clarified the situation, as its etymology suggests.[31] In any case Blake laments that Britain's mobilization for war with France has not only conscripted its labouring youth into the army and navy but pressed even its musical instruments, such as 'the flute of summer', into military service, for 'all the arts of life they changed into the arts of death' (*FZ* 92.20–1 = *J* 65.15–16, E364, 216).[32] Joseph Joubert remarked that 'The noise of the drum drives out thought; for that very reason it is the most military of instruments', and Urizen seems to agree with him, for he formed 'harsh instruments of sound / To grate the soul into destruction or to inflame with fury / The spirits of life' (*FZ* 102.18–20, E374–5).[33]

Blake fights back. If war is noisy, very well, nothing will be noisier than Los at his forge. If military music shakes and grates the soul, Los will drown it out: 'Roaring redounding. Loud Loud Louder & Louder' (*FZ* 61.3, E341) and 'storming, loud, thunderous & mighty / The Bellows & the Hammers move compell'd by Los's hand' (*J*10.5–6, E152), who labours continually 'at the roarings of his Forge' (*J*10.62, E154). His bellows in particular, five times in *Jerusalem* called 'thundering', make a prodigious noise; Los watches 'the bellowing flames: thundering' (*J*16.10, E159).[34]

Wordsworth's Pastor in *The Excursion* asks, 'Noise is there not enough in doleful war, / But that the heaven-born poet must stand forth, / And lend the echoes of his sacred shell, / To multiply and aggravate the din?' (7.363–6). Blake's own verse seems to aggravate the 'din' of war, whereas we might have expected moments of silence, the silence of conscience or of the peace we hope for, rather in the spirit of St. Clement's 'strain of peace' I cited earlier. At the turning point of *America: a Prophecy*, Blake dramatizes the Americans' commitment to a different kind of warfare by having them 'refuse the loud alarm' of Albion's noisy Angel: 'No trumpets answer; no reply of clarions or fifes, / Silent the Colonies remain' (A10.3–4, E55).[35] This might be called the aesthetic equivalent of what has been called 'moral jujitsu' in non-violent social struggles. But Blake abandons this tactic in his later poems. Instead he creates a rival noise, a noise that he hopes will 'appal' the thunderings of the armies of Europe. He reverts to his earliest wish, in the 'Prologue' intended for 'King Edward the Fourth': 'O For a voice like thunder, and a tongue / To drown the throat of war!' (E439).

Los seems to remember that Albion is asleep and cannot be approached except through his ear, and so he strives to drown out the bellicose bellow of corporeal war lest Albion awaken only to collapse more deeply into the sleep of deathly despair. However this may be, Los's labours, and Blake's, are meant to prepare for the right moment, the moment when all this thunderous warfare will cease and a great universal conversation will ensue, where 'Visionary forms dramatic' will redound from our tongues 'in thunderous majesty' (J98.28–29, E257).

Blake's ultimate spiritual weapon, I think, and the most difficult to wield effectively, is to hold up to our imaginations the vision of a transformed world. Pity for the world as it is must lacerate our heart, but a yearning for the world as it might be must fire our souls. Whether the astonishing pages at the conclusions of *The Four Zoas* and *Jerusalem* succeed in awakening our desire is doubtful, though I think one could make a defence of them. We can see why many serious revolutionary theorists have refused to offer anything but the sketchiest outline of the future Utopia. What is certain is that Blake believed we must acquire some picture of it and some feeling for it or we will remain submissive to the tyranny of the actual.

One feature of his utopia is the return or restoration of all things, the *apocatastasis* of the Book of Acts (3: 21).[36] Not only will the suffering victims of warriors and tyrants appear again, but, Blake hints the warriors and tyrants themselves, even Satan, will enter the universal circle. Bacon and Newton and Locke will join Milton and Shakespeare and Chaucer in their chariots (J98.9, E257). And what music will accompany this grand harvest of humanity? Somehow the 'symphonies of war' will be subsumed into a new and higher melody (I would say harmony but for Blake's dislike of it) where even the infernal instruments of the hoarse noise of war are retuned and play their part. In the apocalyptic ingathering at the end of *The Four Zoas*, we hear 'loud rejoicings & triumph / Of flute & harp & drum & trumpet horn & clarion' (132.8–9, E400). This music evidently filled Blake's soul when he signed up for the duration as 'a Soldier of Christ' and it kept him at his station through twenty-three dismal years of corporeal war.[37]

Notes

1.   Since I gave this essay as a talk in 1994 Simon Bainbridge's *Napoleon and English Romanticism* has appeared (Cambridge: Cambridge University

Press, 1995). It thoroughly and insightfully discusses the figure of Napoleon in several poets and essayists, but has little on the war itself and nothing on Blake.

2. Winston S. Churchill, *A History of the English-Speaking Peoples*, Vol. 3, *The Age of Revolution* (1957; rpt. New York: Bantam, 1963), Ch. 11, 'The First World War'. One could argue, of course, that England and France were at war almost continuously from 1756 to 1815.

3. Joel Barlow, 'Advice to a Raven in Russia: December 1812' (1812).

4. In the 'Anglo-Dutch War' of 1810–14, which was an integral part of the larger war, British fleets and troops defeated the Dutch on Java, the Celebes and Timor (127 E. Longitude), while in the 'War of 1812' the British were defeated by the Americans at New Orleans (90 W. longitude).

5. See A. D. Harvey's introduction to *English Literature and the Great War with France: An Anthology and Commentary* (London: Nold Jonson, 1981) pp. 1–2.

6. Calculation have shown British casualties to have been proportional to those of World War I. See Major Greenwood, 'British Loss of Life in the Wars of 1794–1815 and in 1914–1918' (*Journal of the Royal Statistical Society* 105:1 (1942) pp. 1–11, and discussion pp. 11–16). The difference, of course, is that the earlier war's casualties were spread over twenty-three years, not four. They were also confined almost entirely to the lower orders; as Wellington famously noted, his army was composed of 'the scum of the earth'.

7. Maurice de Saxe, *Mes Rêveries*, quoted in Robert Debs Heinl, Jr., *Dictionary of Military and Naval Quotations* (Annapolis, Maryland: U.S. Naval Institute, 1966) p. 26.

8. Both quoted in Heinl (1966) pp. 26, 12.

9. I hardly need add that, after 1802, and especially after the French invasion of Spain in 1807, Wordsworth became a bitter-ender and wrote sonnets and odes praising the enemies of France and glorying in Waterloo.

10. *Aurora Leigh* (1857) 1.942–5.

11. A fourth discovery is a little embarrassing. It dawned on me that in my book on the 'social vision' of William Blake, published in 1985, I had left out the one subject that Blake was manifestly the most concerned about: war. Anyone who bought the book should get a refund. It is to make up for that omission, to some extent, that I offer this essay.

12. I argue for the non-violence of the Americans in Ferber (1990). I suggest various meanings of the events of *Europe* in Ferber (forthcoming). For an interesting recent discussion of 'Gwin' through *Europe* that brings out Blake's attraction to violence, see Keach (1992).

13. These two swords are not to be confused with the 'two swords' passage in Luke 22:36–8, which I discuss below.

14. Maximilianus (295), quoted in *Acta Manyrum* (Ratisbon 1859), in Peter Mayer (ed.), *The Pacifist Conscience* (New York: Holt, Rinehart, 1966) p. 328. St Martin (336), quoted in Peter Brock *Pacifism in Europe to 1914* (Princeton. N.J.: Princeton University Press, 1972) p. 23.

15.   Clement of Alexandria, in Roland Herbert Bainton, *Christian Attitudes toward War and Peace: A Historical Survey and Critical Re-evaluation* (New York and Nashville: Abingdon Press 1960) pp. 72–3.
16.   Erasmus, *Querela Pacis* (1517), trans. John P. Dolan, in *The Essential Erasmus* (New York: New American Library, 1964) p. 183; *Dulce Bellum Inexpertis*, form *Adagia* (1515), trans Margaret Mann Phillips, in *Erasmus on his Times* (Cambridge: Cambridge University, Press, 1967) p. 127.
17.   Shelley, 'A Refutation of Deism', in David Lee Clark (ed.), *Shelley's Prose; or, the Trumpet of a Prophecy* (Albuquerque, University of New Mexico Press, 1954) pp. 124–5. Calvin, *Harmony of the Gospels. Matthew, Mark, and Luke*, vol. 1, trans. A. W. Morrison (Grand Rapids, Mich.: Eerdmans, 1972) p. 310. And here is Rev. William Sloane Coffin, Jr in 1993, after citing the Matthew passage: 'He could only have meant the sword of truth, the only sword to heal the wound it inflicts', *A Passion for the Possible* (Louisville, Ky: Westminster/John Knox Press, 1993), pp. 16–17. Blake himself takes Christ's sword as a divider of men into two classes, as opposed to 'religion', which reconciles them (*MHH* 17, E40).
18.   *Praise of Folly*, trans. Betty Radice (London: Penguin, 1971) p. 121. I have dwelt on Erasmus in part because he was invoked by the loose-knit British opposition to the war with France. Rev. Vicesimus Knox, a schoolmaster ordained in the Church of England, published *Antipolemus; or, The Plea of Reason, Religion, and Humanity Against War. A Fragment. Translated from Erasmus and addressed to Aggressors* in 1794. A shortened version was adopted as a tract by the Society for the Promotion of Permanent and Universal Peace in 1817 and reprinted many times thereafter. The unsigned preface by Knox carries the spiritual warfare imagery of his subject to new heights: 'Then rose Erasmus, not indeed furnished with the arms of the warrior, but richly adorned with the arts of peace. He found, in his intellectual storehouse, arms sufficient to encounter this GIANT FIEND Iwarl in his castle. On the rock of religion he planted the artillery of solid arguments against it. There they stand still' (viii–ix). For a recent attempt by a Christian pacifist to cope with the "two swords" passage in Luke, see Daniel A. Dombrowski, *Christian Pacifism* (Philadelphia Temple University Press, 1991) p. 17.
19.   Letter to Elizabeth Hitchener, 26 January 1812, à propos his pamphlet *An Address to the Irish People*, in Roger Ingpen and Walter E. Peck (eds.), *The Complete Works of Percy Bysshe Shelley* (Ernest Benn: London; C. Scribner's Sons: New York, 1926–) vol. 8, p. 254.
20.   Quoted in Brock (1972) p. 137. H. John McLachlan's *Socinianism in Seventeenth-Century England* (Oxford: Oxford University Press, 1951) is the standard history of the subject, but it says very little about pacifism.
21.   Quoted in Mayer (1966) p. 90.
22.   Quoted in Peter Brock, *Freedom from War: Non-sectarian Pacifism 1814–1914* (Toronto: University of Toronto Press, 1991) p. 11.
23.   John Reeve (and Ludowick Muggleton?), *A Divine Looking-Glass* (1656) (1760 edn), p. 66, quoted in William Lamont, 'Lodowick

Muggleton and 'Immediate Notice', in Christopher Hill, Barry Reay, and William Lamont (eds.) *The World of the Muggletonians* (London: Temple Smith, 1983) p. 130.

24. Quoted in Thompson (1993) p. 90.

25. The relentless allegorizer Swedenborg took the swords, spears, and bows of the Bible to mean the combat of truth. Coleridge in 1796: 'I therefore go, and join head, heart, and hand, / Active and firm, to fight the bloodless fight / Of Science, Freedom, and the Truth in Christ'. And John Spencer Cobbold in 1797: 'Did Religion ask protection? / Of thine arms with her's above / She disdains the curst connection; / Her's the arms of peace and love'. (From a poem called 'Reason Uttering a Soliloquy over a Field of Battle').

26. Pierre Clastres, *Society against the State*, trans. R. Hurley with A. Stein (Oxford: Blackwell, 1977) p. 36.

27. George Lakoff and Mark Johnson, *Metaphors We Live By* (Chicago: University of Chicago Press, 1980), pp. 4–6. Some of the examples are my own.

28. Quoted in Heinl (1966) p. 236.

29. A list of weapons forged in Los's furnaces moves from swords; arrows; cannons; mortars, and so on, to 'The sounding flail to thresh: the winnow: to winnow kingdoms', and then to 'The water wheel & mill' (*J* 73.11–14, E228). Blake might have known the use of the Latin verb *exoro* as both 'plow up' and 'write', and perhaps Pindar's poetic phrase for poets, 'ploughmen of the Muses' (Nemean 6.32); he would certainly have known the classical tradition of ploughing as fertilizing a woman or begetting a child. The equation of ploughing to writing, however, he might have noticed in Spenser, who late in Book Six of *The Faerie Queene* remembers some unfinished narrative business: 'Now turne againe my teme, thou jolly swayne, / Backe to the furrow which I lately left. / I lately left a furrow, one or twayne, / Unplough'd, the which my courter hath not cleft' (6.9.1).

30. On Christian plough and ploughshare symbolism to Langland, see Stephen A. Barney, 'The Plowshare of the Tongue: The Progress of a Symbol from the Bible to *Piers Plowman*', *Medieval Studies* 35 (1973) 261–93. Quotations from *Canterbury Tales*, 'General Prologue' 531–2; *Faerie Queene* 1.10.66. See Frye (1947) p. 335.

31. Most of Blake's phrases for trumpet and clarion seem to be expansions of Milton's phrase 'the warlike sound / Of trumpets loud and clarions' (*PL*. 1.531–2).

32. Blake contrives to contrast two instruments in one line in the *Jerusalem* version, 'The trumpet fitted to mortal battle, & the flute of summer in Annandale' (*The Four Zoas* version omits 'mortal' and 'Annandale'), but I believe the surrounding syntax requires us to make a strong break at the comma, and to include the trumpet with the sword and chariot of the preceding line while placing the flute with the arts of life of the following.

33. *Pensées* (1842), quoted in Justin Wintle (ed.), *The Dictionary of War Quotations* (New York: Free Press, 1989) p. 68.

34. In *The Four Zoas,* for some reason, the bellows are much quieter; only once do we hear them, though 'incessant roars the bellows' (*FZ* 105.38, *J*67.52; E379, 221). Blake is obviously indulging in the pun on the verb 'bellow', meaning 'roar' (as 'Tharmas bellowed oer the ocean thundring sobbing bursting', in *FZ* 45.9, E 330), though he might not have thought it was a pun at all, for 'The Bellows are the Animal Lungs' (*M* 24.58, 53.12, E121, 202) and it is with these lungs that 'the bulls of Luvah', for example, 'bellow on burning pastures', (*FZ* 77.16, E 353). I think he is also trying to elicit a pun on the Latin *bellum,* meaning 'war'.
35. On noise and silence in *America* generally, see Erdman (1970).
36. On 'Blake's *Apocatastasis*', see Ferber (1985), chapter 8.
37. Blake calls himself 'a Soldier of Christ' in his letter to Butts 10 January 1803 (E724).

9

Blake and the Grand Masters (1791–4): Architects of Repression or Revolution?

Marsha Keith Schuchard

Among Freemasons today, who are familiar with Blake's frontispiece to *Europe* (1794), the figure called the 'Ancient of Days' is viewed as a portrayal of the Masonic Grand Architect of the Universe.[1] In Blake's own day, his placement of the Divine Architect opposite the revolutionary serpent would have suggested the troubled relationship between Freemasonry and the radical movement in England, France and Scandinavia. In November 1790, Edmund Burke published his *Reflections on the Revolution in France*, in which he warned Britons about the sinister conspiracies of foreign Illuminati, who were spreading their 'spirit of fanaticism' to English Freemasons, who 'receive from them tokens of confraternity and standards consecrated amidst their rites and mysteries'.[2] Even worse, he claimed that:

> there is a hollow murmuring under ground; a confused movement is felt, that threatens a general earthquake in the political world. Already confederacies and correspondences or the most extraordinary nature are forming, in several countries. In such a state of things we ought to hold ourselves upon our guard.[3]

From the confiscated papers of Adam Weishaupt, the founder of the Bavarian Illuminati, Burke had learned that radical political Freemasons seduced their credulous occultist brethren by revealing the arcane teachings of Robert Fludd, the Rosicrucians and Jewish Cabalists. Then the Illuminati tricked them into serving their secret agenda. Moreover, Weishaupt planned to send Illuminatist agents to lodges in England to spread the international conspiracy.[4] Because Burke himself was a Mason (belonging to the 'Jerusalem' lodge) and a liberal Whig, his charges accelerated the political polarizations within British Masonry – with radical initiates calling him a hypocritical traitor, and conservative brothers calling him a reclaimed patriot.[5]

When Thomas Paine, who was also a Mason, answered Burke's *Reflections* with *The Rights of Man* in February 1791, he did not address Burke's charges about the Illuminati – probably because he knew they were true.[6] However, Paine did write a defence of 'Druidic' Freemasonry, which he left in manuscript, and he would later be charged with Illuminatist activities.[7] Blake, who allegedly knew Paine, responded to Burke's attacks with occulted defences of radical Illuminist Masonry and coded attacks upon conservative Grand Lodge Masonry.

To decipher Blake's Masonic allusions, it is necessary to recognize the deep political polarizations that split Freemasonry within the British Isles throughout the eighteenth century. Rooted in persistent Jacobite–Hanoverian rivalries, two different systems of Masonry competed for power and campaigned for recruits. The 'Ancients' developed out of the seventeenth-century Stuart traditions of Scottish, Irish, French and Swedish Masonry, which included an interest in Cabalistic and Hermetic studies. By the last quarter of the eighteenth century, many Jacobite Masons transformed their hostility towards the Hanoverian kings of England into disgust with all kings. The 'Moderns' were a relatively late schism, provoked by the Swedish-Jacobite plots of 1715–17 and dedicated to Newtonian science and Hanoverian loyalty.[8] Through the influence of Emanuel Swedenborg – a Swedish scientist, espionage agent, and Cabalistic visionary – the Swedish-Jacobite form of Freemasonry entered the political and artistic milieu of Blake and his family. By the time Blake used a well-known Masonic emblem for *Europe* in 1794, it is probable that he was privy to many of the most complex and clandestine developments of international, revolutionary Freemasonry.

Several scholars have argued that Blake's father was a Swedenborgian or Moravian, and it is significant that both groups were considered special forms of Freemasonry in the 1750s and 1760s.[9] The name 'James Blake' also appears on the membership list of an Ancients lodge in 1757.[10] Among the artisans and shopkeepers who flocked to the Ancients, many participated in the demonstrations for John Wilkes, who was initiated by members of Burke's

'Jerusalem' lodge when they visited Wilkes in prison in 1769.[11] While Blake was an apprentice at Basire's in Great Queen Street, he was witness to the ambitious construction of Freemason's Hall directly across the street. When the Hall opened on 23 May 1776, with spectacular public parades and ceremonies, the Ancients and Moderns thought they had reached an accommodation. Dr William Dodd delivered an eloquent speech which drew on Jewish traditions of Solomon's Temple, the original model for 'our mystical fabric', while later Masons took 'their ideas of symmetry from the human form divine', which they 'adopted as their model and prototype'.[12] Dodd's speech was followed by a performance of 'Solomon's Temple, an Oratorio', in which Uriel, Angel of the Sun, recited:

> The Lord Supreme, Grand Master of the Skies!
> Who bid creation from a chaos rise,
> Truths of Architecture engrav'd
> On Adam's Heart.[13]

However, the American Revolution revived the old polarization, for the Ancients tended to support the American rebels and the Moderns the government. From 1777 on, the Modern Grand Lodge mounted a campaign of persecution and disenfranchisement against the Ancient Masons – who, however, attracted a much larger membership in the Americas and Europe. After Blake witnessed the Gordon Riots in 1780, he may have heard the accusations that the Ancient Freemasons and their American brothers had manipulated Lord George Gordon and sustained the riots, in order to prevent the recruitment of Catholic Highlanders to fight against the Americans.[14] By the time Blake began his artistic career in the early 1780s many of his friends had joined Ancient lodges that maintained links with radical lodges in America, France and Sweden.[15] The name William Blake occurs frequently in lodge lists of the 1780s, but unfortunately no further identification is given. As I have argued elsewhere, the Swedenborg society which he attended in 1788–90 was founded in 1776 by foreign Freemasons who maintained a secret interior order (the Masonic Universal Society) for the more radical and theosophical devotees of Swedenborg (Schuchard 1992).

Given this background of rival Masonic systems – the more liberal, mystical Ancients versus the more conservative, deistic Moderns – the reasons for Blake's ambivalent, even contradictory, allusions to

Freemasonry become clear. By focusing on his access to or awareness of three Grand Masters of Masonry – the British Prince of Wales, the French Duke of Orleans and the Swedish Duke of Soudermania – we can trace his reactions to the struggle between internationalist Illuminism and nationalist chauvinism revealed in their Masonic careers.

From the time of *An Island in the Moon* (1785–6?), Blake envied those artists like Cosway and Loutherbourg who received the lavish patronage of the Prince of Wales. Long alienated from his stingy and repressive parents, the Prince delighted in defying his royal father by consorting with foreign libertines, radicals and occultists (Schuchard [in DiSalvo and Rosso] 1998). His paternal uncles, the Dukes of Cumberland and Gloucester, shared his hatred of George III, and they joined Masonic lodges associated with the Opposition in England and the Illuminist underground in Europe. They were encouraged in these foreign Masonic interests by the Duke of Orleans, Grand Master of the Grand Orient system in France, who used his vast fortune to gain Masonic recruits in France and England.[16]

During a secret visit to London in 1776–7, Orleans sought instruction in Cabalistic magic from the Jewish Mason, Dr Samuel Falk, who consecrated a talismanic ring that would ensure Orleans's rise to the French throne. In 1784 Orleans returned to London, where he was pleased with the efforts of the Duke of Cumberland, elected Grand Master of the Moderns in 1783, to increase the power of the liberal Whigs in the London Grand Lodge.[17] In 1785 Orleans was fêted by Blake's friends in the Royal Academy, and he encouraged the Prince of Wales to visit taverns and meeting halls *incognito*, in order to 'see society in its various grades'.[18] When Blake was later offered (and refused) a position of drawing master to the royal family, it was probably through the Prince's influence. During the 1785 visit, Orleans also secretly introduced the Prince to occultist Freemasonry (Schuchard 1995).

In May 1786, while the Diamond Necklace trial rocked the throne of France, Orleans visited the Prince as part of his mission to build support for the defendants in the trial – Cagliostro, the 'Grand Cophta' of the Egyptian Rite of Masonry, and Cardinal Rohan, the Cophta's eminent disciple. Cagliostro had developed the rite out of the Cabalistic teachings of Dr Falk and Swedenborg, and he was now accused of being the 'Wandering Jew' and the anti-Christ. After suffering six months in the Bastille, Cagliostro was acquitted by the Parisian *Parlement* but banished from France by Louis XVI. Arriving in London in June, he was welcomed by the Prince of Wales who participated in his Egyptian rituals. However, his collaboration with the fiery Lord George Gordon provoked the British government into a campaign of persecution against those Masons who joined Cagliostro's rite.

By autumn 1788 the anti-Illuminist propaganda campaign pressured the Prince into backing off from public association with Cagliostro, but he was well aware that the 'Grand Cophta' continued to recruit Swedenborgians, artists and musicians from his circles of political supporters. Moreover, the Prince's uncle – the Duke of Gloucester – worked to secretly infuse Cagliostroan rituals into certain Illuminist lodges in London. Backed up by government-subsidized press attacks, Pitt ordered the arrest of Gordon in January 1787 for libel upon the Queen of France – a move that influenced the decision of the Prince of Wales in February to form a special, private lodge for his staff and supporters (Schuchard [in DiSalvo and Rosso] 1998). Many of Blake's Swedenborgian and artistic friends were affiliated with this lodge, which became a centre for political planning and recruitment by Opposition Whigs.

In autumn 1788, when George III's outbreak of mental illness provoked the Regency Crisis, the Prince and his party utilized their Masonic connections in their campaign to win an unrestricted Regency. However, by Spring 1789, when his father unexpectedly recovered, the Prince rapidly covered his Masonic tracks – as the angry King, Queen and Prime Minister determined to seek revenge on the Prince and his partisans. The hypocritical public displays of loyalty by the royal brothers and sons disgusted many of their Masonic associates, who resented their failure to support Cagliostro, Gordon and other persecuted Illuminists. In his unfinished poem *Tiriel* (1789), Blake sketched a Cabalistic satire of the Regency Crisis, in which he hinted at the early association of the royal brothers with Cagliostro's Egyptian Rite and their later cowardly retreat from its Illuminist political agenda (Schuchard [in DiSalvo and Rosso] 1998). The drawings of pyramids and Hebrew-derived names reflected the symbols and rituals used in the Egyptian lodges. Blake expressed an ambivalent attitude to the Prince of Wales (called 'Heuxos' in the poem), which combined sympathy for the Prince's miserable relationship with his parents and disenchantment with his greed and debauchery.

In 1788–9, as Blake responded to the intense arguments among
the Swedenborgians – arguments stimulated by political, sexual
and occultist controversies – he may have found Illuminist soul-
mates among the visiting Swedish, French and American Masons
who also participated in the society. The radical Swedes Augustus
and Carl Nordenskjold, Carl Wadstrom and Thomas Thorild
extended Swedenborg's theory of conjugal love (based on Cabalistic
techniques of 'genital respiration' and trance induction) into an
alchemical-occult theory of psychic-political equilibrium. In their
magical politics of desire, the intensification and liberation of sexual
energy would be used, not suppressed, by the Grand Architect
of the Universe in visionary creation. When Blake portrayed the
Masonic geometer and his compass as emblems of natural religion
and materialism, his Swedish colleagues would have interpreted
them as allusions to deistic, 'regular' Freemasonry, which disrupted
the cosmic equilibrium by repressing the forces of sexual and political energy. In *The Marriage of Heaven and Hell* (1790–1), as Blake
confidently ridiculed the conservative faction of Swedenborgians
at Great Eastcheap, who timidly backed away from Swedenborg's
advocacy of sexual magic and political millenarianism, his views
were shared by the Swedish Masons (Paley 1979).

In 1791 Blake utilized Joseph Johnson's liberal press to print the
first book of *The French Revolution*, in which he paid tribute to the
victims of tyrannous Church and State in France, England, and
Italy – and to the Masonic heroes of liberation. His portrayal of
prisoners in the Bastille was not based on the actual inhabitants
who were freed, but pointed to more recent victims of royal and
priestly tyranny. For example, Blake's seventh prisoner probably
represented Lord George Gordon (friend of Cagliostro and Orleans),
whom Burke had attacked and even Paine called 'mad'.[19]

> ... In the seventh tower, nam'd the tower of God, was a man
> Mad, with chains loose, which he dragg'd up and down;
>   fed with hopes year by year, he pined
> For liberty; vain hopes: his reason decay'd, and the world
>   of attraction in his bosom
> Center'd, and the rushing of chaos overwhelm'd
>   his dark soul. He was confin'd
> For a letter of advice to a King, and his ravings in
>   winds are heard over Versailles
>
>   (*FRev* 11.47–51, E1988, p. 188)

It was Gordon's scriptural harangues addressed to George III that provoked the paranoid king to order his extraordinarily prolonged confinement.[20] Blake was evidently aware of Gordon's many petitions for release, including one read before the National Assembly in France. In 1791, after three years in prison, Gordon's mental and physical health was deteriorating, and there was increasing public sympathy for his plight. Nevertheless, in February George III stonily rejected 'the application of the French Court for the liberation of Lord George Gordon from his confinement in Newgate'.[21]

The first prisoner was almost certainly a portrait of Cagliostro, in which Blake conflated the Grand Cophta's earlier imprisonment in the Bastille and his present plight in an Inquisition prison. Blake may have received the precise details from his friend George Cumberland, who visited Cagliostro in his cell in Italy in 1790:

> … and the den nam'd Horror held a man
> Chain'd hand and foot, round his neck an iron band,
>   bound to the impregnable wall.
> In his soul was the serpent coiled round in his heart,
>   hid from the light, as in a cleft rock:
> And the man was confined for a writing prophetic … '
>   (*FRev* 11. 26–9, E1988, p. 287)]

Because the Inquisition feared that Cagliostro would be liberated by a fleet of Freemasons in balloons, they chained him to the wall in a solitary cell perched on a high crag ('cleft rock') in the Appenines. Cagliostro's prediction (his 'writing prophetic'), issued in London in summer 1786, that the Bastille would be razed and an Illuminist prince (Orleans) rise to power was now seen as proof of his clairvoyant expertise. In Rome in autumn 1789, Cagliostro further predicted that Orleans would lead a mob against the tyranny of the French court, which led to the Cophta's arrest as a seditious Freemason in December. Among his confiscated papers were emblems of the revolutionary serpent, utilized by the Egyptian Rite.

In Blake's portrayal of the spirit of the French king Henry IV, he alluded to Orleans, a direct descendant of the pacifist monarch, and to the Orleanist-Masonic party which used Henry IV as a rallying symbol.[22] But, it was his portrait of Orleans as a magnetizing Grand Master that most clearly revealed Blake's Illuminist sympathies. Orleans, who supported the Whigs and Prince of Wales with secret loans and who recently refused the Regency of France, was 'generous as mountains' (*FrRev* p. 10 175–85 E294).[23] He 'put forth his benevolent hand' and then magnetized the assembly: 'He breath'd on them', and said: 'O princes of fire, whose flames are for growth, not consuming,/ Fear not dreams, fear not visions'. He then referred to the 'high breathing joy' sensated in hands, head, bosom and genitals. The Illuminist students of Animal Magnetism and of Swedenborg's theories of visionary sex would have recognized Blake's allusion to the breathing techniques that stimulate a state of ecstatic trance. Initiates of Cagliostro's Egyptian Masonry would have recognized the ritual in which the Master breathes on the face of the initiate, from forehead to chin, as he mesmerizes him (or her).

Unfortunately, the publication of the Inquisition biography of Cagliostro in spring 1791 meant that the enemies of the Revolution would also have recognized the ritual, which was luridly described by the Holy Fathers and repeated in the flood of articles and translations that disseminated the biography. Perhaps Joseph Johnson, who published a cautious review of *The Life of Joseph Balsamo, commonly called Count Cagliostro* in the *Analytical Review* (September 1791), decided that Blake's poem was too explicit and thus refused to publish the next instalments (despite the title-page 'advertisement' that 'The remaining Books of the Poem are finished, and will be published in their Order').[24] Johnson's reviewer noted that the *Life of... Cagliostro* included 'particulars of his trial before the Inquisition' and 'the History of his Confessions concerning Common and Egyptian Masonry'.[25] In December a contributor to the *Analytical Review* asserted his (or her) ignorance of 'the grand secret' of Freemasonry and pointed out the difference between 'what is technically called the regular lodges' and 'the Egyptian sect', of which Cagliostro was the founder.[26]

In the meantime, the Swedenborgians – both radical and moderate – continued to utilize Freemasonry to advance their causes. The more conservative wing was led by Robert Hindmarsh (printer to the Prince of Wales), who was determined to distance his faction publicly from the Illuminists by obtaining a Dissenter's Licence as a separate religious sect. Early in 1791 Hindmarsh asked Lord Francis Rawdon to study the separatists' publications and proposals, in order to present their petition to the House of Lords.[27] Rawdon was not only an intimate friend of the Prince of Wales but Acting Grand Master of the Moderns (as deputy to the Prince), which probably motivated Hindmarsh's choice of him as sponsor. Hindmarsh also solicited the support of Lord Chancellor Thurlow, another Modern Mason, who was simultaneously boon companion to the Prince and obsequious servant to the King. That Rawdon, a military martinet, had exercised extreme severity against the rebels in America, and that Thurlow advocated military repression of the Americans and Gordon rioters while supporting the slave trade must have galled many of the Swedenborgians.[28]

Thurlow, who had no apparent principles but greed, would later provoke Blake to satiric portraiture. Erdman argues that Blake's print, 'Our End is Come' includes a caricature of the Lord Chancellor, which was bound into a copy of *The Marriage of Heaven and Hell.*[29] The print, dated 5 June 1793, suggests Blake's awareness of Thurlow's earlier association with Hindmarsh's party, whom Blake lampooned in *The Marriage*. Thurlow may also appear in *Europe* (1794), among those politicians who attempt to 'bind the infinite with an eternal band' and 'to compass it with swaddling bands' – in the service of the repressive Grand Architect featured on the frontispiece (pl. 1:13–14 E61).

The determination of Hindmarsh's party to appear public and loyal was prompted by the activities of the radical Swedes, who returned to London and resumed their revolutionary campaign. In January 1791, Carl Nordenskjold arrived from Paris, where he had danced on the ruins of the Bastille. He immediately sought out Blake's friend J. A. Tulk in Lambeth, to launch a new Illuminist initiative. In March, Carl's brother Augustus came from Stockholm, where he had published incendiary propaganda for the revolution. Throughout May, Carl worked on a Swedish translation of Paine's *Rights of Man*, which he prefaced with a passionate indictment of Pitt's ministry and its transportation of dissidents to Botany Bay.[30] In the same month, Augustus inspired Tulk and the Universal Society to publish an appendix to their now defunct *New Jerusalem Magazine*, in order to praise the revolutionaries in France. Included in the issue was a letter from the Baron von Bulow, an Illuminist, who described the presentation of a new political constitution by a member of the New Church in London to the National Assembly in France.[31] In July, Augustus travelled north, visiting revolutionary societies in the industrial cities on his way to Scotland.[32] He evidently hoped to link up with those radical Scottish Masons who had long historical ties with the Swedish Rite. The proselytizing efforts of Swedish radicals in Scotland would later provoke a conservative Scottish Mason, Professor

John Robison, to publish a sensational exposé of the Swedenborgian Illuminists.[33]

The turbulent political and occultist controversies that wracked the Swedenborgians and Freemasons in 1791–2 raise provocative questions about Blake's *Song of Liberty*, the operatic coda that he added to *The Marriage of Heaven and Hell*. The 'Song' was first printed separately as a pamphlet, and Blake obviously hoped to get a public readership. The vexed question of dating is important, for the chorus contains Blake's most explicit reference to Freemasons (the free and accepted brethren), which would have quite a different significance if it were written in 1791 rather than 1792–3 (Peterfreund 1984, pp. 37–8). In the final Chorus, Blake proclaimed:

> Let the Priests of the Raven of dawn, no longer in deadly black, with hoarse note curse the sons of joy. Nor his accepted brethren whom, tyrant, he calls free: lay the bound or build the roof. Nor pale religious letchery call that virginity that wishes but acts not!
> For every thing that lives is Holy. (E45)

By examining the Masonic activities of our three Grand Masters from 1791 to 1793, we will see two different Illuminist messages emerge from the Chorus.

As the French Revolution intensified, the Prince of Wales and the royal brothers gradually shifted from their early enthusiastic support to a more wary attitude. Though the brothers stuck together against Pitt's policies in 1791, the accelerating attacks by the Jacobins on the basic principles of monarchy pushed them into a loyalist stance. In April 1792, when England declared war on France, the brothers vowed their support to the government. Even worse, for his former radical admirers, the Prince used his maiden speech in the House of Lords on 31 May to support the Proclamation against Seditious Writings. In August he wrote to his formerly despised mother that he now hated 'the damnable doctrines of the hell-begotten Jacobins'.[34] Inspired by the apostasy of his employer, the Prince's printer Hindmarsh utilized his *New Jerusalem Journal* (August–September 1792) to blast the *Illumines* and 'those who herd together like swine in *mobilo-equality*, aiming at republicanism'.[35] For the once-liberal Hindmarsh, it was now clear that 'the British government is perfect' and 'the king can do no wrong'.[36]

On 6 February the Modern Grand Lodge delivered an address of Masonic loyalty to George III before a huge crowd at Freemasons'

Hall. Signed and evidently written by Lord Rawdon, the speech assured our 'Most Gracious Sovereign' that the Freemasons shared the whole nation's disapproval of 'innovation and anarchy in other countries' and thus were willing to abandon their tradition of political neutrality:

> It is written, Sire, in the Institute of our Order, that we shall not, at our meetings, go into Political discussion ... A crisis, however, so unlooked for as the present, justifies to our judgement a relaxation of that rule ... [37]

Because the Prince of Wales, Rawdon and their party had unashamedly utilized Masonic lodges during their campaign for an unfettered Regency in 1788–9, the address was unashamedly hypocritical (Schuchard 1998). After painting the initiates as obsequious upholders of law and order, Rawdon concluded with a peroration that may have influenced Blake's negative portrayal of the Divine Architect in *Europe*:

> Having thus attested our principles, we have only to implore the SUPREME ARCHITECT OF THE UNIVERSE, WHOSE ALMIGHTY HAND HATH LAID IN THE DEEP THE FIRM FOUNDATION OF THIS COUNTRY'S GREATNESS, AND WHOSE PROTECTING SHIELD HATH PROTECTED HER AMIDST THE CRUSH OF NATIONS ... your Majesty-the immediate instrument of her present prosperity and power, to whom unblessed POSTERITY shall thus inscribe the COLUMN [of our Temple]: to GEORGE, the FRIEND OF THE PEOPLE and PATRON OF THE ARTS Which brighten and embellish life ...

On plate 11 of *Europe*, Blake portrayed a repressive monarch ('Albion's Angel ... upon the Stone of Night'), whose gross physiognomy was 'as close as Blake dared come to representing George III' (Erdman 1974, p. 169).

As attacks on the Illuminati issued from the conservative presses of England and Europe, the Prince of Wales and his party mounted a defensive action. In June 1793, they started publishing a monthly journal, *The Freemasons' Magazine*, which featured a portrait of the Prince as Grand Master surrounded by emblems of Masonry – the all-seeing eye, pyramid and cherubs with compasses. The first issue was dedicated to Lord Rawdon (now Earl of Moira), the

earlier supporter of Hindmarsh's party of Swedenborgian separatists. While continuing to defend traditional Whig causes, the
magazine repeatedly asserted its loyalty and devotion to law and
order. In speeches extolling the virtues of 'Free and Accepted
Masons', the editors stressed the importance of geometry as the
central Masonic art and praised the Grand Architect as 'Great
Nature's adorable and wonderous Geometrician'. When the
Prince of Wales received news of the execution of the Duke of
Orleans in November, the editors expressed their joy at the death
of lithe Monster Egalité, who at last paid the forfeit for his
crimes. In that same month, the editors ignored the death in
prison of Lord George Gordon, once the Masonic collaborator of
Cagliostro, Orleans and the Prince of Wales.

In December the *Analytical Review* discussed another defence of
'regulars' Freemasonry, published by the Prince of Wales's party
and entitled *An Important Discovery; or Revolution in Great Britain
and Ireland impossible* (London, 1793). The reviewer tried to down-
play current charges against the Illuminist Masons:

> To those who have caught the *alarm*, the present pamphlet must
> afford much consolation, for they are here assured, that there are
> no less than 140,000 Freemasons in Great Britain and Ireland,
> determined to resist any innovation whatever! ... We confess, it is
> now for the first time that we have ever understood free masonry
> to be a political institution. Were it known to be an engine for the
> preservation of ancient abuses, his holiness the pope, and all the
> despots of Europe, would be eager to propagate it in their respec-
> tive states.[38]

Though the cautious reviewer did not mention him, the pamphlet
devoted much of its propaganda to the role of the Prince of Wales
as loyalist Grand Master.

Thus, if Blake wrote *A Song of Liberty* in 1790–1, his chorus
seemed to express praise for the Free and Accepted Brethren, who
would no longer be cursed by priests or king, nor prevented from
building the Solomonic Temple. If the 'Song' were written in 1792–3,
then the increasingly conservative Free and Accepted Brethren
could no longer build the Temple, for only a tyrant would consider
them free. The resultant ambiguity feeds into Blake's portrayal of
Urizen. The Grand Architect may be seen as a Cabalistic transformation of Uriel, the angel of the sun, who praised 'the Grand

Master of the Skies' at the dedication of Freemasons' Hall in May 1776.[39] In *Europe* (1794), the portrait of Urizen with his compass was presented opposite a coiling serpent, suggestive of the emblematic serpent of Cagliostro's Egyptian Rite. As Erdman notes, Blake once thought to place the serpent on the title-page as a contrary to Urizen, who tries to write his laws while riding the curled monster (1974, pp. 156, 396). Though the Grand Architect assumes that his compass can 'bind the infinite' (E61), he forgets that there will always be a serpentine monster who needs binding.

In this positing of contraries, Blake perhaps reacted to the political defection of one of his Swedenborgian colleagues, George Adams, who served as optician and mathematical instrument-maker to the Prince of Wales. Blake almost certainly knew Adams, who was the mentor of his friend Dr John Birch and a learned scientist-theosopher.[40] In his more liberal Masonic days in 1789, Adams had written:

> the balance of the universe remains in equilibrium in the hands of the Ancient of Days. From the relations which exist betwixt all parts of the world and by which they conspire for one general end, results the harmony of the world.[41]

At that time, Adams followed Swedenborg in making the polarities and contraries equally important in the cosmic equilibrium. By 1794, however, Adams had become a staunch opponent of the French Revolution, and he published Swedenborgian tracts against the Illuminist Freemasons.

In a work dedicated to the 'princess royall' in early 1794, Adams discussed the identity of Jupiter with Jehovah, 'the God of Israel, the Creator of the Universe, I' who as 'the Great Architect necessarily presides over and directs every wheel of his machine.'[42] He then hinted at the Modern interpretation of the Masonic compass, urging the Lord to 'enable us to curb *desire*, and keep always within the bounds of rectitude'.

For Blake's former colleagues in the Swedenborg society, his portrayal in *Europe* of the 'Divine Architect' who tries to ride the unruly revolutionary serpent would have seemed a precise historical allusion to the recent struggles between Illuminists and loyalists. Moreover, Blake's caricature of Burke (on plate 1) harked back to the former's charges about foreign Illuminatist subversion in Britain; his portrait of the chained prisoner suggested Cagliostro's continued imprisonment; and his depiction of the bell-ringing plague warner reminded illuminated readers that Gordon died of pestilential fever in November 1793.[43] That the bell-ringer is dressed in the hat and robes of a Hasidic rabbi and looks very much like Gordon would have been recognized by Gordon's many admirers in the Ancient lodges and London Corresponding Society.[44] In January 1794, the latter society – led by Thomas Hardy, an intimate friend of Gordon – issued a resolution condemning the Earl of Moira (still Acting Grand Master) as a profiteering 'apostate from liberty'.[45]

Though Blake had watched the Grand Masters of England and France desert the Illuminist cause in 1792–4, he must also have known that another Grand Master – Duke Carl of Soudermania – was carrying on the revolutionary campaign. Younger brother of King Gustav III of Sweden, Duke Carl had known Swedenborg personally and infused Swedenborgian themes into the higher mystical degrees of Swedish Freemasonry. He and Gustav had received from Charles Edward Stuart, the Young Pretender, appointment as Grand Masters of Templar Freemasonry (Duke Carl for the northern lodges in 1776 and King Gustav for the whole system in 1788). Initially admired as a 'democrat couronne' by the *philosophes* in France and Whigs in Britain, Gustav III remained a staunch Jacobite to the end of his life.[46] His brother, however, shared in the peculiar transformation of Jacobite disaffection from the Hanoverian Georges to Jacobin disaffection from all kings – a shift that occurred in many Ancient lodges as the French Revolution progressed. As chief of the Swedenborgian 'Exegetic Society' in Stockholm, Duke Carl stayed in close touch with its affiliated initiates in London.[47] Blake's friend J. A. Tulk helped the Universal Society publish a journal that praised the Duke's Illuminist ardour.[48] Throughout the 1790s, the Swedenborgians in London were privy to the extremely secretive intrigues of the Swedish diplomats in Paris and London – Barons von Staël, Nolcken, Engestrom and Silfverhjelm – to spread the Illuminist creed.

The continuing campaign of the Illuminists was expressed in *The Conjuror's Magazine* (August 1793–January 1794), published by Cosway's friend Henry Lemoine. Fuseli, Cosway, Barlow and other artistic colleagues of Blake contributed, and rival Swedenborgians carried on their quarrels in lively articles. The eccentric William Gilbert (the correspondent 'B') lamented the death of the radical Gordon, recklessly praised the French revolutionaries, and issued predictions about the downfall of despots in England and abroad.

Gilbert's millenarial poetry would be greatly admired by Coleridge and Southey, and Cosway collected his works. That Blake probably also knew Gilbert makes the astrologer's political prophecies relevant to Blake's contemporary emblems.[49] Announcing himself as a Swedenborgian and Illuminist, Gilbert proclaimed in February 1792:

> The Free Masons are the only Corporation, whether under the name of a church, a nation, or a society, who have *melted* the *knowledge* possessed by the Ancients into the same fire with the knowledge of a Redeemer given to the Christians. May they shine with invigorated glories! They shall and shall give Rome the blow, it has always suspected and feared from their hands. As far as Cagliostro is a Free Mason, he shall revenge and triumph. LIBERTY IS SOLIDITY![50]

For this issue, Fuseli contributed a design of 'The Magician Balaam', which was 'purposely engraved for this work'. Gilbert also announced his plan to form special Masonic societies, which would include women and provide instruction in the occult sciences.

However, the magazine soon got into trouble, for the reckless Gilbert published (in December 1791) an astrological prediction of the death of Gustav III of Sweden:

> Kings will be privately tormented and conspicuously impotent and shamed. Women will be shamed too, and subject to men. The common people martial, and melancholy, and wicked... The Head of Sweden drowned cruelly...[51]

When Gustav was actually assassinated in March 1792, it was widely believed that his brother Duke Carl and the Jacobin Freemasons were responsible. In Stockholm, several Swedenborgians who had links with London were interrogated, and the Nordenskjold brothers were suspected of contributing to the conspiracy.[52] In April Gilbert boasted in *Conjuror's Magazine* that his prediction had come true, and then gave a detailed account of the assassination.[53] This situation so alarmed George Adams, who contributed to the magazine, that he wrote the editors in May and warned them against publishing any more revolutionary prophecies. From then on, the astrological predictions in the magazine would loyally support George III.[54] Adams's caveat was timely, for in August the British government received a detailed report on the assassination, in which the new Regent, Duke Carl of Soudermania, was described as 'deeply initiated in the mysteries of Freemasonry and the delusions of the modern illumination', and that his party means 'to carry their republican theories of government into execution'.[55]

Erdman suggests that Blake referred to the assassination of the Swedish king in an emblem picture that bears the caption, 'Rest Rest perturbd spirit' (1977, pp. 205 n. 20) Though the radical Swedes in England had earlier admired Gustav III, they were now relieved to have him removed from his self-appointed role as leader of the counter-revolutionary armies of Europe. They also welcomed the Regency of Duke Carl, who immediately initiated the young Crown Prince Adolph Frederick into an Illuminist lodge and steered the Swedish government towards support of the French Revolution. In February 1793, at a meeting of the London Corresponding Society, it was reported that Augustus Frederick Nordenskjold's translation of Paine's works was now published in Sweden (a move made possible by Duke Carl's declaration of press freedom).[56] Evidently referring to the Swedenborgian Universal Society, the LCS then praised a London religious society, 'whose sentiments lead strictly to republicanism', for 'beginning just now to organize themselveds ageeable to the principles of France'. Blake's friend Alexander Tilloch, a Freemason and Rosicrucian, reported favourably on the actions of the Swedish Illuminists and praised Duke Carl's Masonic action in his newspaper, *The Star* (15 March and 19 April 1793).[57]

At the same time, the Swedish Grand Master became increasingly immersed in the bizarre Cabalistic studies of the 'Asiatic Brethren', a strange antinomian sect of Jewish-Christian Masons, who claimed Dr Falk and Cagliostro as founders.[58] Several of Blake's Swedenborgian colleagues collected tracts about the 'Asiatics', who also sent emissaries to England. It seems plausible that Blake drew upon the 'Asiatic' themes of antinomian sexuality and millenarial politics for the occulted symbolism of *Europe* and *Urizen* in 1794. One important initiate of the sect was Duke Carl's protégé, Baron Lars van Engestrom, Swedish ambassador to London in 1793–5. Engestrom's revolutionary actions so alarmed Pitt's ministers that they characterized him as 'a determined Jacobin and a great *intriguant*', whose contacts in London should be watched closely.[59] It was probably no coincidence that Blake, who may have had direct contacts with the Swedish network, recorded his awareness of paid spies at this time: 'Why should I... shrink at the little blasts of fear / That the hireling blows into my ear?' (E1988, p. 473).

While an increasingly 'nervous' Blake worked on the manuscript of *The Four Zoas* at Lambeth, he infused his most radical Illuminist notions into its turbulent poetry and phantasmagoric drawings. The Swedenborgians who gathered at the Lambeth Asylum continued the polarizations that had earlier split the group. As the conservatives issued pamphlets disavowing the revolutionaries, the radicals received emissaries from the continental Illuminists in 1796 and 1798. Frightened by the collaboration of radical Masons with the 'United' brotherhoods (Irish, Scots and English), which seemed to confirm the charges of Barruel and Robison, Parliament passed the Secret Societies Act of 1799, which prohibited all oath–bound, clandestine fraternities.[60] However, the exertions of the Prince of Wales and Earl of Moira managed to exempt 'regular' Masons from the ban.[61] Those 'irregular' Masons who refused to register their names and detailed personal information with the government were subject to severe punishment. That year, as Pitt's spies intercepted correspondence from abroad and infiltrated lodge meetings, Blake's position became increasingly perilous. No wonder his friends wanted him out of Lambeth and removed to the relative safety of Hayley's parlour.

Notes

1. See Bernard Jones, *Freemasons' Guide and Compendium*, rev. edn (London: George Harrap, 1956), frontispiece; wall decorations in Scottish Rite lodges in Atlanta and Washington, D. C. Anthony Blunt first suggested Masonic imagery for this emblem (Blunt 1938, pp. 53–63. 26). The Masonic *Je ne sais quoi* club is alluded to in 'a Jaw / About freedom & Jenny suck awa' in his MS. Notebook, 1808–11 (E510, 869). See also, the present author's *Restoring the Temple of Vision: Cabalistic Freemasonry and British Literature* (New York: SUNY Press, 1997).
2. *Two Classics of the French Revolution: Reflections on the Revolution in France and The Rights of Man* (New York: Doubleday, 1989) p. 169.
3. *Reflections*, p. 171.
4. To substantiate his charges, Burke noted, 'See two books intitled *Einiae Originalechriften des Illuminatenordens. – System und Folgen des Illuminatenordens. Munchen 1787'*. Jan Rachold, ed., *Die Illuminaten: Ouellen und Texte zur Aufklfirungsideologie des Illuminatenordens (1776–1785)* (Berlin: Akademie-Verlag, 1984) pp. 111, 166–7, 177–8.

5.   Eugen Lennhoff and Oskar Posner, *Internationales Freimaurerlexikon* (Wien: Almathea, 1932) p. 242.
6.   On Paine and Freemasonry, see Mercure Conway, *The Life of Thomas Paine* (New York: G. Putnam, 1892) p. 229; Nicholas Hans, 'UNESCO of the Eighteenth Century', *Proceedings of the American Philosophical Society*, 97 (1953) pp. 518, 523; Jack Fruchtman, *Thomas Paine and the Religion of Nature* (Baltimore: Johns Hopkins University Press, 1993) pp. 53–4, 186 n. 41.
7.   Thomas Paine, 'The Origin of Freemasonry', in *The Theological Works of Thomas Paine* (Boston: the Advocates of Common Sense, 1834) pp. 273–91. The essay was meant to be a chapter in the third part of *The Age of Reason* (1794). A truncated version was published by Madame de Bonneville in 1811 and the full text in 1818.
8.   On the Moderns, see Margaret Jacob, *The Radical Enlightenment* (London: Allen and Unwin, 1981), and *Living the Enlightenment* (Oxford: Oxford University Press 1991).
9.   See Wright (1929) I, p. 2; Lowery (1940) pp. 14–15; Bogen (1968) pp. 509–20. On the Moravian–Masonic connection, see Erik Eriksson, *Emot Freymauererna* (1741) and *Emot Zinzendorffianer* (1741); also, Arthur E. Waite, *A New Encyclopedia of Freemasonry* (London: William Ryder, 1921), lg4.
10.   Grand Lodge, London: Atholl Register, Lodge #38.
11.   William R. Denslow, *Ten Thousand Famous Freemasons* (Transactions of the Missouri Lodge of Research, 1957) I, p. 155.
12.   Speech reprinted in *Principles and Practice of the Most Ancient and Honourable Society of Free and Accepted Masons* (London, 1786) pp. 150–6. Paine drew heavily on Dodd's speech in 'The Origins of Freemasonry'.
13.   *Principles and Practice of the Most Ancient and Honourable Society of Free and Accepted Masons* (London, 1786) pp. 165–6.
14.   For the accusation, see J. Frome Wilkinson, *Mutual Thrift* (London, 1891) pp. 12, 16; for a denial, see George Smith, *The Use and Abuse of Freemasonry* (London: G. Kearsley, 1783) p. 249. Smith was later accused of making Masons 'irregularly' and ejected from the Modern Grand Lodge. See also Robert Watson, *The Life of Lord George Gordon* (London: H.D. Symonds, 1795), on 'the grand fraternal union' that will overthrow despots of Church and State.
15.   According to archives and publications in the Grand Lodge, London, the following associates were definitely Freemasons – Stothard, Cipriani, Bartolozzi, Cosway, Loutherbourg, Humphry, Banks, Sandby, Chambers, Strange, Tilloch, Horne Tooke, Wolcot, Fittler, T. S. Duche, Astley, D'Eon; the rest were probably Freemasons – Fuseli, Flaxman, Cumberland, Johnson, Beckford, Hayley, West, Copley, Romney, Reed.
16.   Hubert La Marle, *Phillipe Egalité: 'Grand Maître' de la Revolution* (Paris: Nouvelles Editions Latines, 1989).
17.   Cumberland had been elected Grand Master of the Rite of Seven Degrees in 1774, a former Jacobite system that subsequently attracted supporters of the Opposition and students of the occult. This Rite may have influenced Blake's use of the symbolic term 'Los' (Schuchard 1992).

18. Robert Huish, *Memoirs of George IV* (London: Thomas Kelley, 1831) I, p. 166.
19. Burke, *Reflections*, pp. 97–8, and Paine, *Rights*, p. 287.
20. *Universal Magazine*, 80 (January 1787) pp. 51, 81 (December 1787) pp. 373–4; *Gentleman's* Magazine. 58 (1788) p. 1115.
21. *European Magazine*, 19 (May 1791) p. 157.
22. La Marie, *Egalité*, pp. 83 n. 292, 122.
23. La Marie, *Egalité*, p. 294.
24. Joseph Johnson may have been a Mason; the name appears on the Ancient's lodge registers #203 in 1792 and #20 in 1793. Despite Johnson's Whig principles, the *Analytical Review* was so dedicated to rational Unitarianism that it was hostile and often inaccurate in its reportage on Swedenborgianism, Animal Magnetism, mysticism and millenarianism.
25. *Analytical Review*, XI (September 1791) pp. 54–7.
26. *Analytical Review*, XI (September 1791) p. 463.
27. Robert Hindmarsh, *Rise and Progress of the New Jerusalem Church* (London: Hodgson, 1861), pp. 126–8.
28. For their reputations with contemporaries, see articles on Rawdon and Thurlow in *DNB*.
29. For Thurlow's career, see Lucyle Werkmeister, *A Newspaper History of England, 1792–1793* (Lincoln: Nebraska University Press, 1967); for Blake's satirical sketch of Thurlow, see Erdman (1974) p. 390; Erdman (1977) pp. 214–20, 512.
30. Thomas Paine, *Menniskans Rattigheter*, trans. C. F. Nordenskiold (Stockholm: C. G. Cronland, 11 July 1792); on the impact of this translation on Swedish political life, see Peter Hogg, 'Paine's *Rights of Man*, Swedenborgianism, and Freedom of the Press in Sweden: a Publishing Enigma of 1792', *British Library Journal*, 19 (1993) pp. 34–43.
31. *New Jerusalem Magazine* (May 1791) p. 274. Bulow's letter was dated 1 February 1791, and the presenter was evidently Edward Maubach, a member of Swedenborgian lodges in London, Paris and Avignon.
32. A. E. Arppe, *Antechningar om Finska Alkemister* (Helsingors, 1870) pp. 87–8.
33. John Robison, *Proofs of a Conspiracy against all the Religions and Governments of Europe, carried on in the Secret Meetings of Free Masons, Illuminati, and Reading Societies*, 4th rev. ed (London: T. Cadell and W. Davis, 1798) pp. 411, 479, 579–86.
34. John Van der Kiste, *George III's Children* (Wolfeboro Falls: Allan Sutton, 1992) p. 54.
35. *New Jerusalem Journal*, VI pp. 266–8, 311; X, p. 433.
36. *New Jerusalem Journal*, VIII pp. 329–35.
37. See *European Magazine*, 23 (June 1793) p. 441, and *Freemasons' Magazine* (June 1793) p. 17.
38. *Analytical Review*, XVII (December 1793) p. 454.
39. For discussion of possible indebtedness to Hebrew macaronics, see Spector (1988).
40. Thomas Spence Duche, a Swedenborgian *Illumine*, designed allegorical illustrations for Adams' earlier works, which Cosway owned.

41. George Adams, *Astronomical and Geographical Essays* (London: Robert Hindmarsh, 1789) p. 236.
42. George Adams, *Lectures on Natural and Experimental Philosophy* (London: Robert Hindmarsh, 1794) II, pp. 95–7, 136; III, pp. 1, 430–1.
43. Blake was probably aware of the government's identification of radical societies with pestilence. On 12 February 1793, when Thomas Powys seconded Pitt's motion for war, he blamed France for encouraging 'the combinations of bad men at home', who constitute 'the pestilence that walketh by night'. See Werkmeister, *Newspaper History*, p. 219.
44. See articles on Blake and Gordon in *Encyclopedia Judaica*.
45. Manoah Sibly, *The Genuine Trial of Thomas Hardy for High Treason* (London: J. S. Jordan, 1795), I p. 217. Sibly was a Swedenborgian Mason who almost certainly knew Blake.
46. Claude Nordmann, *Gustav III: un democrate couronné* (Lille: Presses Universitaires, 1986) pp. 209–61.
47. On relationships between Stockholm and London, see the series of articles by C. T. Odhner, 'Early History of the New Church in Sweden', *New Church Messenger* (1896–7).
48. *New Jerusalem Magazine*, IV (April 1790) pp. 178–9.
49. William Gilbert, *The Hurricane* (Bristol: Richard Edwards, 1796; facs. rat. Oxford: Woodstock Books, 1990). For Blake's probable acquaintance with Gilbert, see Schuchard, 'Rediscovering William 'Hurricane' Gilbert: A Lost Voice of Revolution and Madness in the Worlds of Blake and the Romantics' (forthcoming).
50. B. [William Gilbert], 'Cagliostro to Triumph as a Free Mason', *Conjuror's Magazine* (February 1792) p. 183.
51. B. [William Gilbert], 'Cagliostro to Triumph as a Free Mason', *Conjuror's Magazine* (February 1792) p. 144.
52. Hogg, 'Paine's *Rights of Man*', 38–9, 43; [C. F. Nordenskjold], *Considérations Générales sur le Christianisme Actuel et la Lumière Sue Mr. Emanuel Swedenborg Repand sur les Reloiouns* (1819), pp. 373–5, 400. This defence of Swedenborgian Masonry was banned in Sweden, but Nordenskjold smuggled a copy to J. A. Tulk.
53. *Conjuror's Magazine* (April 1792) pp. 396–7.
54. *Conjuror's Magazine* (May 1792) pp. 400–2.
55. Robert Liston to Lord Grenville (26 August 1792); in *The Manuscripts of J.B. Fortescue*. Historical Manuscripts Commission. 13th Report, Part III (London, 1892) V pp. 518, 520.
56. Sibly, *Genuine Trial*, II, 53. The correct name of the translator was Carl Frederic Nordenskiold (Augustus's brother).
57. On Tilloch, see 'Memoir of Alexander Tilloch', *Imperial Magazine*, 7 (1825) pp. 208–22; J. W. Hamilton Jones, ed., *Bacstrom's Alchemical Anthology* (London: J. M. Watkins, 1960) pp. 12–14.
58. On the Asiatic Brethren in Sweden, see Karl Frick, *Die Erleuchteten* (Graz: Akademische Druck-u. Verlagensanstadt, 1973) pp. 485–8; on their activities in Europe, see Gershom Scholem, *Du frankisme au jacobinism* (Paris: Le Seul, Gallimard, 1981); on their influence in England, see my 'Yeats and the Unknown Superiors: Swedenborg, Falk, and Cagliostro', in *Secret Texts: The Literature of Secret Societies*,

ed. Hugh Ormsby-Lennon and Marie Roberts (New York: AMS Press, 1995) pp. 114–68.

59. Lord Grenville to Lord St Helens (13 August 1794); *Fortescue*, II, p. 615.

60 Goodwin, *Friends of Liberty*, pp. 439–41; Brendan Clifford, *Freemasonry and the United Irishmen* (Belfast: Athol Books, 1992); A. T. Q. Stewart, *A Deeper Silence: The Hidden Roots of the United Irish Movement* (London: Faber, 1993) pp. 156, 164–85.

61. R. F. Gould, *The History of Freemasonry* (New York: Yorsten, 1885), III, pp. 204–5, 238–40. The threat of a complete prohibition of Freemasonry impelled the Duke of Atholl and Ambassador Silfverhjelm to publicly cooperate with their rivals in the Modern Grand Lodge, as they all vowed 'loyalty'. However, radical and breakaway lodges continued to operate clandestinely.

10

Blake and 1790s Plebeian Radical Culture

David Worrall

With the hindsight of twenty-two years of war, the anonymous author of *A Political Catechism* (1816) had no hesitation in providing radicalism's conclusive interpretation of the most far-reaching event of 1790s British politics:

Q. For what purpose did William Pitt enter into a war with France, in the year 1793?
A. To destroy liberty abroad, and to establish despotism at home.[1]

This verdict, expressed in the reductivist terms popularized by Hone's post-war political litanies, would have been an opinion familiar enough to many from the artisan class of Blake's origins. Such ideas, percolating in taverns and at firesides, might easily have been directly encountered by the elderly Blake, even as he lived out a dislocated career pieced together from a portfolio of skills among which might be included high-class independent painter and engraver, jobbing book illustrator, 'moonlighting' poet and print-maker and intermittent recipient of patronage.[2] This essay traces Blake's proximity to 1790s plebeian radical discourse in order to situate the social and political context of the illuminated books of the Lambeth period.

In 1793 there is evidence to suggest the existence of a plebeian radical culture whose rhetorics are assimilated in Blake's works. Before he turned to the more elaborate, less precisely controlled and probably more expensive books in colour-printing for 1794 and 1795, Blake worked with a degree of political provisionality reflected in the topicality of his works. Blake's October 1793 prospectus *To The Public* listed for sale *America, The Marriage, Visions of the Daughters of Albion, Innocence and Experience, The History of England* and (as he titled it) *The Gates of Paradise*, all with noticeably topical contents *(The Marriage's* Swedenborgian references, the *Songs'* social criticism, *Visions'* echoes of Wollstonecraftian feminism, the 1793 Gillray quotation in *For Children* 9 [Erdman 1977, p. 203]). This engagement with contemporary issues would be further strengthened by *The Book of Urizen's* relationship to Paine's *Age of Reason* (1794), save that the unpredictable fracturing of contemporary radical responses to Paine's book obscured the sharpness of Blake's agenda.

Our understanding of this provisionality is now greatly enabled by the unique copy L of *A Song of Liberty* (Collection: Essick) printed uncoloured, as Essick notes, on laid paper 'as an independent pamphlet'.[3] Illuminated books produced without the exacting dexterities of colour-printing are suggestive of Blake's wish to retain a degree of flexibility and immediacy to respond to shifts in the turbulent radical politics of 1793. Of the ten extant copies of *America* printed that year, nine were uncoloured monochrome. In this respect at least, they are similar to the five uncoloured copies of *For Children: The Gates of Paradise* which Blake declared published on 17 May.[4] In other words, two of the three Blake titles for 1793, or over half of that year's total illuminated book production, were uncoloured (a figure rising to three out of four if the abortive *The History of England* – selling at *For Children's* price – was intended to be uncoloured).[5]

Finding a big radical audience for Blake is a chimera (it didn't happen and even *America* was expensive for readers weaned on cheap editions of Paine). However, Keri Davies's crucial piece of evidence in this volume that works by Blake were available in Joseph Johnson's bookshop in late 1794, with their joint imprint in four out of five copies of *For Children*, puts his output in the midst of the most progressive elements of London's contemporary radical intelligentsia. In the momentous year of a suspension of Habeas Corpus and London Corresponding Society treason trials, Johnson's shop in St Paul's Churchyard was the perfect meeting place for those who wanted George dished, Paine honoured and, judging by two projected picture subjects for *The History of England*, to view 'The Cruelties used by Kings & Priests' with 'A prospect of Liberty' (E672).[6]

We can now more confidently engage with the echo of radicalism in Blake's works, but historical circumspection is essential. Just as that post-war *Political Catechism* probably distorts the actuality of the 1790s, the historical record throws up anomalies which makes

hindsight problematic and general overviews simplistic. Tom Paine's
hugely influential *Rights of Man* (1791–2) exemplifies a late, and
peculiarly Anglo-American, development of Enlightenment political discourse, but the range of issues crudely enlisted under the
banner of natural rights by his contemporaries included a much
wider set of economic, professional and moral claims. Writing as a
liberal protester in December 1792, the Charing Cross resident A.Z.
(someone 'not in an elevated sphere of life' but who claimed membership of 'several … [reformist] Societies') listed to Home Secretary
Henry Dundas a long series of grievances indicative of the breadth
of popular disaffection:

> The King's avarice, his riches, the extravagance of his family –
> the unnecessary places and pensions – the farce of an Opposition
> (formerly respected) – the truly diabolical practice of the Law,
> particularly of the exchequer Court, which robs both plaintiff
> and defendant, and fills our prisons. Upwards of 4000 regular
> attornies, besides pettifoggers. Every description of tradesmen
> pouring out bitter Curses on Government for suffering such a
> nest of hornets to exist by practices as disgraceful to good
> Government as it is repugnant to common sense. The abuse of
> the bankrupt Laws – Legislators screening themselves from their
> Creditors, and refusing payment of their just Debts. – The
> unequal representation of the people in parliament the truly
> farcical history of which is given in the three vols. – The persecu-
> tion which individuals undergo in voting against ministerial
> Candidates[;] by the farmers from the Clergy as to tythes – the
> most numerous and the most useful part of the Clergy (the
> Curates) starving[;] The English inquisition the Ecclesiastical
> Courts – the multiplicity of informers in consequence of the
> unconstitutional Extension of the Excise Laws – the inutility [*sic*]
> of and idle parade in repealing trifling taxes – the multiplicity
> of penal Statutes – the desertion of villages – the advanced price
> not only of provisions, but also of every article that is made use
> of. – High Rents – The profits of almost every description of
> tradesmen at least 20pr. cent less than they were within these 25
> years – The shameful and glaring monopolies – The clogs which
> a variety of trades experience in their business – the oppression
> which the publicans undergo. The rapacity and tricks of Navy
> agents – (the Seaman's Bill I thank you for). The abuse of the
> Poors' [*sic*] Rates – the swarms of beggars – the inability of the

middling Class to educate their children – the consequences to Society – Select vestries – the effects of them – innumerable host of gamblers, swindlers, thieves and pickpockets. The Shameful Traffic carried on from the justice down to the watchmen – the number of idle men and disorderly women.

A.Z.'s claim that these subjects were discussed 'in almost every beer house and Coffee house throughout the Kingdom' should be treated with caution, but his lengthy analysis offers a strong indication that an attack on 'Old Corruption' could not to be separated from a critique of the Government's poor grasp of structural economic conditions.[7] Significantly, A.Z. ranks the key rights issue of suffrage no higher than education, taxes and commerce. Even at that moment in late 1792, before national politics were riven by the anxieties of war, and when natural rights were most visibly on the public agenda following May's Royal Proclamation against seditious utterance (directly in response to Paine's *Rights of Man*), radicalism was always more than a debate which lamely mimicked the political implications of Enlightenment.

It is against the presence of such an extensive and complex set of contemporary disaffections that Blake's economic and intellectual position must be placed. If A.Z. is indicative of the 'background noise' of contemporary discontent, how can we adequately correlate Blake to 1790s radicalism on the basis of his sparse writings? Jon Mee (1992) has carefully traced Blake's adjacency to contemporary religious sects, but he still appears distant from mainstream political concerns and worryingly isolated from any conceivable peer group. Nevertheless, in December 1789 the Privy Council discussed a letter intercepted from a Swedenborgian visionary schismatic which replicates much of what Blake had to say in *The Marriage of Heaven and Hell* about Swedenborg.[8] On the 12 March 1789, almost a month to the day before William and Catherine Blake signed the register of the New Jerusalem Church Conference, Great East Cheap, the Londoner W. Brian wrote to a fellow Swedenborgian giving news of 'an immediate communication with Heaven' ('I am permitted to transcribe the following words of the Angell Gabriell') in which he offered to explain how 'Emanuel Swedenborg has erred'. Although Blake's trenchant annotations to *Heaven and Hell*, *Divine Love and Divine Wisdom* and *Divine Providence*, quite apart from *The Marriage of Heaven and Hell*, make it clear he had major doctrinal differences with Swedenborg, there is a noticeable degree of convergence in what Brian and Blake thought about the Swedish mystic. Indeed, there is evidence of a schism related to disputes about Swedenborg's quality as a visionary but which was occluded from Robert Hindmarsh's 'official' recollections of these years.[9]

Blake and Brian agree that Swedenborg's writings were insufficiently visionary and only disagree about the consequences of their inadequacy. Brian thought Swedenborg's writings overstatements of his actual prophetic insight: 'he has swelled out to many volumes that, which unmixed with his own, would have made one volume only'. Blake's view of Swedenborg's prophetic powers were similar, if more straightforwardly egalitarian: 'Any man of mechanical talents may ... produce ten thousand volumes of equal value with Swedenborg's' (*MHH* 21, E43). Both thought Swedenborg personally conceited. Brian wrote that pride had enabled the Devil to corrupt Swedenborg's divine revelations:

> unfortunately for E.S. & all his readers he would not believe, because it did not please the Lord to communicate it to him by the medium of his Angells, which pride opened a door for the grand deceiver of mankind to decieve [*sic*] him also, & much of his latter writings, are mixed with revelations from that source.

Blake's opinion was only slightly different: that Swedenborg had exclusively 'conversed with Angels who are all religious, & conversed not with Devils who all hate religion, for he was incapable thro' his conceited notions' (*MHH* 21, E43). While only Blake was innovative enough to make a polemical virtue of the contrarious rhetorics lurking in Swedenborg's 'conceited' works, their opinions are sufficiently coincident to suggest an identifiable London faith community which debated Swedenborg's writings and in which both Blake and Brian vigorously participated. The rare, but theologically specific, trace of late 1780s London Swedenborgianism allows us to figure Blake into a wider social grouping than that suggested by the immediate readership of *The Marriage*.

But the implications of Brian's letter do not stop there. However fine the schismatic turbulences in the New Church in the spring of 1789, they had gathered enough political resonance by December for Brian's letter to be discussed by the Privy Council. The Council might have initially turned with amusement to Brian's transcription of auto-prophetic dictation ('I am [said Gabriel] the angel of the

Eternal who am sent before the face of the Lamb to sound the trumpet on the mountains of Babylon to make known to the nations that the God of Heaven will soon come to the gates of the earth, to change the face of the world'), but what must have more seriously fixed their attention was the declaration that 'Human Blood will flow in large streams, that the enemies of God may subsist no longer'. Although the swish of the guillotine had yet to be heard, the Privy Council would have known the latest revolutionary news from France where, with varying degrees of violence, the Bastille fell in July and Parisian women marched on Versailles in October.

The spectre of domestic religious violence hinted at in Brian's letter precedes Robespierre's terror and the de-christianizing of France by some three years, but it would be a mistake to think the Government complacent or else solely reactive to subsequent French models of revolution. The authorities were engaged with unrest in London within a month of the fall of the Bastille when, in August 1789, a crude, threatening letter sent to the Lord Mayor of London warned that 'your Mantion [*sic*] House will be Burnt in a few Days and Liqwise [*sic*] the Albion Mills at Blackfryars [Road] unless you regulate the price of Bread & c'.[10] In fact, the well-known Lambeth flour mills were not burnt down (under suspicious circumstances) until March 1791 but, as is so frequently the case in late eighteenth-century Britain, ideological politics are underpinned by economic considerations.

Revealingly for our understanding of Blake's symbiosis with populist causes, the politics of bread provides a highly topical reference in *The Song of Los* (1795) where Blake wrote of the 'privy admonishers of men' who 'cut off the bread from the city' (6: 19, 7: 1, E68–9). As Roger Wells has shown, the Privy Council was closely involved in monitoring London unrest over the 1795 harvest.[11] Blake's injunction about how 'the Councellor throw[s] his curb / Of Poverty on the laborious' (*SofL* 6: 15–16, E68) is a highly concentrated commentary on that year's harvest failures. These were popularly believed to have been exacerbated by grain hoarding, which resulted in price rises even during the summer. Local authorities and Privy Council alike (Blake trickles both 'privy' and 'Councellor' into his text) found themselves torn between sympathy for the millers, factors and corn dealers and concern about a populace ready to take matters into their own hands to obtain what they believed was an ample wheat reserve (Blake's 'day of full-feeding prosperity', *SofL* 6: 13, E68). *The Song of Los* accurately reflects how crowds in the summer of 1795 in the grain regions of southern England detained shipments of outward-bound corn while food supplies to urban centres, and London in particular, were threatened by the near-total popular blockade of East Anglian ports. This highly untypical instance of a vivid topical allusion in Blake's text sets an extreme parameter for the possibility of the intimate relationship between poet and contemporary event.

Blake's illuminated books are integral with a complex artisan public sphere: the issues of moral economy, natural rights ideology and prophetic spirituality in *America, Europe* and *The Song of Los* may easily be paralleled elsewhere in contemporary records. The ex-Grafton Street, London, linen-draper Thomas Bentley's tract, *A Short View of some of The Evils and Grievances, which at this time oppress, The British Empire* (1792), was the subject of prosecution by the Treasury Solicitor and of informer activity by John Reeves's Association for Preserving Liberty and Property Against Republicans and Levellers (APLAP).[12] Bentley, by then removed to premises in Sudbury, Suffolk, kept a printing press in his home (just as Blake did) at a time when the new literary reviews still vied with such provisional types of publication. As well as protesting within a commonplace contemporary rhetoric about 'Thousands of rich, idle Gentlemen, Merchants, Factors, Farmers, and Tradesmen ... allowed to monopolize Lands, Provisions, and Goods' (p. 2), Bentley also offered a specifically agrarianist alternative ('lowering rents and dividing farms and Commons', p. 8) which was a persistent sub-theme of artisan radicalism and one to which Blake turned, albeit with a less politically specific agenda, in *The Four Zoas* (Lincoln 1995, chapter 8).[13] Despite the rationalist decoy of Bentley's sub-title, Bentley's *Short View* is striking for the prophetic idiom in which his political analysis is framed:

> ... the King is not 'religious and gracious', but covetous, oppressive and ungodly, – and if he dies in his present state, where God is[,] he will never come. In the same true names he [Bentley] also declares, That the Ministers of State, the Parliament, and the Judges are not 'men fearing God, and hating covetousness, and doing as they would be done by', but on the contrary, are in general destitute of the true fear of God, and may be fitly compared to Lions, Tygers, Foxes and Swine. And by the same authority he further declares, That the present Church of England is as really a Church of Antichrist as that of Rome is, or ever was ... (p. 7)

In a fashion analogous to concerns voiced about Blake's mental state, a Sudbury correspondent to the APLAP claimed that Bentley 'is not Considered here, as a person Insane – But a Man who is Capable of Arguing on almost every Topic ... an Enthusiast in Religion, but it seems a Religion of his own.'[14] Although the circulation of Bentley's pamphlet must have been tiny (his previous writings had been 'published' pasted to his window shutters), it is significant that the Treasury Solicitor thought it worthwhile convicting Bentley's obscure Kentish Town bookseller to two years' imprisonment for selling *A Short View*. It is also revealing that Bentley came to the attention of the APLAP. Prophets with printing presses and radical views could, and did, find themselves the subject of surveillance and prosecution.[15]

Scriptural texts themselves had, by the end of 1792, begun to figure in prosecutions for seditious utterance, a circumstance which makes the text of *America* plate 8 (E53) particularly vulnerable. The indictment against the Anabaptist William Winterbotham stated that he 'did preach speak utter and with a loud voice publish' a sermon on a biblical text ('The Night is far spent the Day is at hand; let us therefore cast off the Works of Darkness and let us put on the Armour of Light', Romans 13: 12) which Winterbotham prefaced by announcing that he intended 'to apply the Text Politically'. His sermon (with the Treasury Solicitor's indictments included here), is full of Biblical rhetoric: 'Darkness has long cast her Veil over the Land (*meaning amongst others this Kingdom*) ... The Yoke of Bondage among our Neighbours (*meaning the French*) seems now to be pretty-well broken and it is expected the same Blessing is awaiting Us (*meaning the Subjects of this Kingdom*).'[16] As D. W. Dörrbecker comments about *America* 8: 5–15, 'With this "prophecy" of universal liberation Blake joins the political to the Biblical' (Dörrbecker 1995, p. 131). Wintherbotham's successful conviction shows that in 1792–3 linking scripture with politics could no longer be done with impunity.

If *America's* religious idioms were sensitive, so too were its more overtly political nuances. As has long been recognized, when Blake removed from *America* a specific reference to 'George the third' (*America b*: 9, E58), he may have been acknowledging the legal dangers surrounding the use of the king's name in a republican context, though its excision also helped consolidate the poem's universal mythology which such a topicality compromised. By retaining a reference to Tom Paine (*America* 5: 4, E52), despite having revised significant visual details of plate 5 from the version known as pl. *a* (E802), Blake continued to court danger. It is difficult for us today to appreciate the extremity of the highly personalized attacks against 'the cloven-foot of Tom Paine', but one has only to read works like Robert Colville's poem *Atalanta* (1777) to realize the depth of the national trauma – economic, political and filial – brought about by America's secession from the empire.[17] Shielding *America*'s 1790s republicanism under the historical distancing of 1776–7 did not guarantee that it would escape cognizance as radicalism, especially to demonstrators who burned Paine's effigy in late December 1792.

Even in his minutiae, Blake reflects contemporary radical idioms. For example, Richard 'Citizen' Lee's *The Rights of Man ... Extracts from Pigott's Political Dictionary* (*c.* 1795) predictably defined America as 'a bright and immortal example ... proving the invincible energy and virtue of freedom', but Lee's definition of the single word '*Thirteen*' bluntly equated it with 'United States of America: which bravely threw off the English yoke; and, like all good Republicans, renounced the bug-bear of royalty'.[18] Blake's repetitious, if now obscure, allusions to *America's* 'Thirteen' angels, governors and states (*America*: 9: 1, 13, 21, 26; 10: 11; 12: 2; 13: 1, 6, E54–6) constitute a fragment of this intricate 1790s radical public sphere which was producing its own complex internal semiotics.

Artisan radicalism's generation of a separate public sphere was a collective reaction to restraints on the spoken word and print media, allied to the necessity for self reinvention within a linguistic space perceived to be distant from Burke's literary high ground. As Lee put it in the Preface to his revealingly titled *A Political Dictionary for the Guinea-less Pigs, or, A Glossary of Emphatical Words made use of by that Jewel of a Man, Deep Will. In his Administration, and his Plans for Yoking and Putting Rings in the Snouts of those Grumbling Swine, who raise such a Horrid Grunting, when Tyrannical Winds Blow High* (*c.* 1795), 'The prostitution of language has lately, been so glaring, and notorious that in my opinion, it requires a nice discrimination, to distinguish, even in our own Language, the true intent, and signification, of many Phrases, now in general use.'[19] Thrown up in Blake's works are many such redefinitions which are the fragments of a still partially recoverable radical ideology.

A phrase of Lee's about 'the cobweb'd charters of state' (p. 9) in *A Summary of the Duties of Citizenship! Written Expressly for Members of the London Corresponding Society; including Observations on the Contemptuous Neglect of the Secretary of State with Regard to their late*

Address to the King (1795), is an independent conflation of several verbal and visual images already exploited by Blake in 'London', *Europe* and *The Book of Urizen*.[20] Similarly, Blake's memorable piece of anti-clericalism in *America* ('What crawling villain preaches abstinence & wraps himself / In fat of lambs?' 'Till pity is become a trade...' [11: 10, 14–15, E55]) is part of a widespread sentiment typified in Lee's *Summary* and re-echoed on *Urizen*'s title-page: 'The priest prepares youth for subjection... he seals our abjection and his own exclusive indulgence... and turns religion into a trade: ignorance and fear are the agents of his fraud; his right hand holds persecution, and his left superstition' (p. 9).

Neither would the combination of poetry and design in the illuminated books have shielded Blake. Unguarded comments and anti-George visual images, under some circumstances, merited prosecution and persecution. Although prints of a seditious tendency were only infrequently prosecuted they still encountered a degree of surveillance and repression. Prints were not mentioned in the actual indictment of Charles Pigott's *Jockey Club* libel of 1793, but the Treasury Solicitor's notes detailed how his Birmingham bookseller James Belcher was found 'Exhibit.g [*sic*] in his window for sale a variety of Caracture [*sic*] Prints' of the king.[21] In London one informer at the end of 1792 urged the APLAP 'to put a Stop to' 'the many shameful & libellous Prints upon our Gracious Sovereign and his Family which are to be seen in the Printshops in Piccadilly Bond Street, Oxford Road & c.', while another complained about 'Print Shops... fill'd with Revolution Representations imported from France'.[22] Blake's carefully modulated excursions into semi-caricatures of Edmund Burke and George III in *Europe* plates 3(4) and 12(14) should be placed into a contemporary context where political expression through visual imagery carried real, if low-level, threats from the courts and semi-official organizations like the APLAP.[23] Even references to the king in relation to royal attitudes to painting were open to legal indictment if not handled with due deference. When the Royal Academy was between presidents in the spring of 1792, the owners of *The Morning Post And Daily Advertiser* were prosecuted for publishing an anonymous article entitled 'To the Royal Academicians' which attacked George's alleged neglect of the late Sir Joshua Reynolds ('the Alfred of the Arts'). *The Morning Post* was convicted of seditiously contrasting Charles I's 'magnificent' patronage of the arts with that of 'the malignant eye of a sordid Hanoverian'.[24]

Such prosecutions were part of a pervasive climate in which political unrest was accompanied by physical violence. One APLAP correspondent urged them to 'employ a few stout fellows' to 'knock down' radicals who stuck up handbills.[25] Blake's poignant image in 'London' of 'How ... / ... the hapless Soldiers sigh / Runs in blood down Palace walls' (E27) may not be specific to a particular event but we can gain some inkling of how such an image functioned in a brutalized society. A year before the war there was an important legal test case concerning the court-martial of Samuel George Grant, a civilian 'Recruiting Agent' who received army pay. The case had implications for every male citizen. In a seditious pamphlet published by Joseph Johnson and the soon to be indicted Paine publisher James Ridgway, Grant's lawyer John Martin based the defence on whether a court-martial had jurisdiction over a person not actually enlisted. Martin lost, the case went to appeal, the conviction was upheld and Grant was sentenced to an incredible 'one thousand lashes on the bare back, with a cat-o'-nine tails'.[26] Who then was *not* a soldier if the 'hapless' citizen could be made subject to a court-martial?

Political songs played a prominent part in the conflict between these increasingly polarized ideologies. The social criticism of *Songs of Innocence and of Experience* (1794) is symptomatic of how song became activated for ideological purposes.[27] One Cheapside correspondent, arguing that 'It was the Ancient as well as modern custom to excite Men to Good or Bad actions by songs', enclosed his own loyalist effort and urged the APLAP to 'employ some fellow creatures to recommend it Viva Voce in the Streets'.[28] The urban streets, which so vividly feature in the designs of 'London', 'The Chimney Sweeper' and 'The Little Vagabond', were sites of political confrontation in which songs played a substantial role. One Associationist personally intervened when 'two women were singing a very loyal song ... under the piazza at Covent Garden' when 'a man ... cried out, It was a lie, a damned lie – which he so often repeated that the women could not go on.'[29] These were not just private disputes within public spaces. In Edmonton, Middlesex, a loyalist procession dragooned the church band to accompany a 'triumphal Arch' supported by five men on which a dove held the motto 'No Revolution', while 'the rear was brought up by Women and Children; before night they were *half Seas over* and sang God save the King & c.'[30] Children, songs and socializing were all enlisted in scenes of social conviviality glimpsed at in the text and design of 'Laughing Song' and 'The Little Vagabond' whose 'Ale-house' is not only 'healthy & pleasant & warm' (*Songs* 45: 2, E26) but likely to be a place where political meetings were held.[31]

The rhetorics of this communal culture are reflected in the *Songs*. The chapel with 'Thou shalt not. writ over the door' in 'The Garden of Love' (*Songs* 44: 5–6, E26) is a trenchant rejoinder at a time when 'Thou Shalt Not Read' could be satirized as the 'Eleventh Commandment'.[32] Church and ale house were sites for competing gestures of appropriation. In Sheffield a pro-Paine festival lacked a peal of bells because of 'a refusal to give up the keys of the church to the ringers – who are in general staunch liberty boys', while, at the nearby Lion and Lamb tavern, there was greater fun when 'an Effigie of the Duke of Brunswick was dressed up and filled with combustible matter, fired at several times, and then consigned to the flames. The sacrifice of whole sheep on this occasion was twelve, ten roasted, and two boiled … '[33] Blake was clearly not the only 1790s radical with a pugnacious sense of humour. A Dubliner sent the Association a polemical 'counter address … And as it may a little depress your Spirits, I also send you a merry Glee, Tune Billy Pitt … ', while another enclosed a little story adapting Blake's favoured 'lost-and-found' *Songs* formula in which 'A poor Woman' searching for a lost coin finds, instead, 'Paine Rights of Man – A verity [which] for Ages, has laid hid. – at length, it is found – Men & Angels, sing to the Eternal immortal Praises. I am Mr Reeves, Not your humble Servant, but the Contrary.'[34]

Blake's *Songs* are reflective of this groundswell of political contrariety in which songs, pamphlets, anonymous letters and other ephemera competed for ideological supremacy in a society undergoing rapid political polarization.[35] Amongst collections such as John Devonshire's *Songs, Political, Satyrical, and con vivial, dedicated to the laughter loving goddess, Vestina; calculated to inspire mirth and set the festive table on a roar* (1794), Blake's 'Laughing' *Songs of Innocence* (15, E11) have a similar range from gentle to satiric good humour because, prior to the depths of the war, song-making was still fun. At the Revolution Club, Leicester, in November 1792, 'The utmost hilarity prevailed, several constitutional and patriotic toasts were given, and the SONS OF FREEDOM sang the praises of their "ever smiling goddess;" with chearful voices; [and] that admired song "O'er the vine cover'd hills" was sung, in a superior style.'[36] Contemporary radicals composed political songs, *extempore,* with little regard for permanence. A spy sent to a reform meeting in the Borough picked up a list of five 'Songs' plus four 'Original Songs', the latter 'Superlatively adapted for the purposes in view', but which he was not quick enough to get down.[37]

Nearly as ephemeral and fugitive were the fragile tobacco paper broadsides and pamphlets produced by the printer Robert Hawes at the Constitutional Liberty Press operating in Whitechapel and Spitalfields in the early 1790s, whose 'very improper ballads' circulated in Kennington taverns at reformist 'Clubs numerously attended by the Lower Classes'.[38] Hawes shared with Blake and Thomas Spence that heady contemporary mix of radical politics, Biblical citation, self-promoted distribution and a fondness for innovative presentation (Mee 1992; Worrall 1995). Although much less visually aware than Blake or Spence, twelve crude woodcuts or typeset pictures adorned Hawes's slip *Libertas Dei Gratia! The Proclamation of LIBERTY! A SONG* (1792), and his political acrostics invited the reader to search out the pacifist message 'swine O may God from henceforth bind the monster war and man all acts but acts of grace abhor amen amen' concealed in the text of his four page pamphlet, *PEAS FOR SWINE! AND GRAPES FOR CITIZENS! OR The Monster! An ACROSTIC* (c. 1793).

Hawes and Blake shared the culture of 1790s plebeian radicalism. Using contemporary 'illuminist' rhetorics cognate with *The Marriage*, Hawes asked, 'Who from thick films will clear *Sol's* once *free* Ways, / And through long *blinded* WINDOWS lead his Rays?' while *PEAS FOR SWINE!* employed a rich counterpoint of political puns ('Pain'd by Oppression'), woodcut pictures of Christ, Mary, grapes and vines with a 'PEACE' acrostic.[39] Blake's *A Song of Liberty* (especially in copy L) is idiomatically related to Hawes's broadside or four-page pamphlets *The Triumph of LIBERTY: OR, The RIGHTS of MAN* (c. 1792), *PEAS FOR SWINE!* and *The Proclamation of LIBERTY! A SONG*.[40] Interestingly, Hawes's rationalism ('Let Reason be heard, and let Reason go round') is counterbalanced by religious enthusiasm ('Chorus … *Hail, RELIGION! Cross the Waves*: Ah, charm Mankind! With Thy Right Mind – EASE, unconfin'd, *Serve all Nations! FREE all Slaves! Amen.* Huzza!'), quoting Ezekiel, Isaiah, Psalms and Proverbs in support of 'the Gospel's friendly Plan, / Divine Decorum, and THE RIGHTS of Man!'[41] Like Thomas Bentley and Blake, Hawes used the prophetic stance to question the religious integrity of monarchy and state. His belief that

'All christian [*sic*] Legislators, must be good, / Consistent, liberal, not men of blood' led to the pointed query 'GEORGE! Art thou King? – A CHRISTIAN King, indeed?' Significantly, all three squibs were separately prosecuted.[42]

Some of the rhetorical patterns of this emergent plebeian radical culture are also common to Blake. The 'Chorus' of Hawes's *The Proclamation of LIBERTY! A SONG* ('LIBERTY's Reign is begun, Sirs! = ECHO. "Dun-Zirs!"') reminds us that Blake specified a 'Chorus' in *A Song of Liberty*. In the convivial atmosphere of working-class taverns, roisterers would actually have sung '"Dun-Zirs!"' (probably very loudly), but Blake's 'Chorus' also recalls the raucous radical toasting which alternated with political songs at these meetings. Loyalist toasts were long established, but their 1790s radical versions were more assertive, more ideologically elaborate and, for that reason, frequently collected by spies who realized they crisply summarized prevailing sentiment. The prose pattern of *A Song of Liberty* and its 'Chorus' with its crucial opening verb ('Let the Priests ... ') repeats the format of early 1790s radical songs and toasts. At the Bear Inn, Bath, in November 1792, radicals heard 'Many excellent songs, some of which were composed for the occasion ... and the following ... toasts: The encreased, increasing, and sacred flame of liberty. May the tree of liberty flourish in every part of the globe, and every human being partake of its fruit'. On the same day at the Tontinic Inn, Sheffield, the toast was 'May the empire of the mind be free'.[43] A printed *List of Toasts, & c.* found by the Borough spy shows songs alternating with numbered toasts in a layout similar to the numbered 'verses' or declarations in *A Song of Liberty*. The Borough meeting ended with toast '16. The Virtue of Revolutions; and may Revolution generate Revolutions till Despotism is extinct', a sentiment similar to Blake's '20. ... Empire is no more! and now the lion & wolf shall cease' (*MHH* 27, E45).[44]

It has not particularly been the concern of this essay to argue that Blake was a radical, although we may guess that he was. Rather, what has been demonstrated is Blake's proximity to the artisan public sphere of discourse in 1790s London; no more, no less. There is something uncanny in the precision with which Blake's texts accommodate themselves to these neglected radical rhetorics but in exceedingly complex ways. Blake declared his large colour prints of *Nebuchadnezzar* 'inv' in '1795' (Butlin 1981, nos. 301–5), some five years after he had used a similar figure (with spiked crown) in

The Marriage, plate 24.[45] 1795 was the year of the food shortages and 'bread' imagery in *The Song of Los*. Whatever Nebuchadnezzar's earlier resonances, a biblical grass-eating king, when the current king ate well and the country starved, was an obvious target for the indefatigable Richard Lee, whose *Rights of Nobles. Consisting of Extracts from Pigotts Political Dictionary* (?1795) included an explanation of the Babylonian king's name, adding pointedly that 'It is thought by physiologists that it would greatly conduce to the welfare of his People if the king of Georgia was turned out to grass before the meeting of every session of Parliament.' A year later, the caption accompanying the original *Marriage* design ('One Law for the Lion & Ox is Oppression' [E44]), as well as the main compositional features of the image itself, were strikingly echoed in *The Civil Citizen* going on all fours, a Thomas Spence political token coin and etching captioned, 'If The Law requirs [*sic*] it we will Walk Thus!'[46]

These cognates of text and design are too chronologically problematic to be directly related to each other yet they reveal, implicitly, a common rhetoric concerning law, oppression and brutalization. Blake, Lee and Spence are neither influences nor sources of one another's work but, rather, they share the common vocabulary of an emerging artisan public sphere persisting across two generations.

In Lambeth, on 5 June 1793, Blake published a separate etched plate entitled 'Our End is come' (Collection: Bodleian Library, Oxford), showing three armed figures looking off-stage in horror. Blake declined to put voice 'balloons' into their mouths in the manner of contemporary caricature prints, but his title is suggestive of speech and redolent of other representations in text and design from the violent contrariness of 1790s ideological struggle. In early 1793 it was possible to purchase, suitable to one's political persuasion, token coins showing lynched figures with the mottoes 'End of Pain' or 'End of P*tt' (Bindman *et al.* 1989, nos. 54.a,c; 206.s). This is the 'End' Blake's figures foresee, captioned in a quasi-biblical language politicized by anti-Painites and pro-revolutionaries alike. Such was persistence of this rhetoric that, almost twenty-five years later, the millenialist ex-print colourer and revolutionary Spencean activist, Thomas Evans Senior used a cognate discourse in *Christian Policy, the Salvation of the Empire* (1816), 'The end is come, and a new era arrived…establish Christianity and abolish paganism' (p. 20).

Evans's manner is recognizably Blakean, not because they knew each other but because they shared the idioms of an emergent, assertive, innovative and long-lasting artisan public sphere. It is not surprising that Blake absorbed so much, so often – and so haphazardly – from this vibrant radical culture.

Notes

1. Anon. [An Englishman], *A Political Catechism. Dedicated (without Permission) to this Most Serene Highness Omar, Bashaw, Dey and Governor of the Warlike City and Kingdom of Algiers; the earl of Liverpool; lord Castlereagh, & Co.*, 4th edition (Manchester: Wardle and Pratt, 1816) p. 8.
2. For post-war political litanies chanted by working-class audiences in taverns, see David Worrall, '*Mab* and Mob: The Radical Press Community in Regency England', *Romanticism, Radicalism, and the Press*, ed. Stephen Behrendt (Detroit: Wayne State University Press, 1997) p. 144.
3. Blake usually worked on woven rather than the cheaper laid paper (Essick 1994, pp. 110–11).
4. *America* copies C, D, E, F, G, H, I, L and R (Viscomi 1993, pp. 262–6, 376).
5. For *The History of England*, see E672, 693. A suggestive monochrome model for Blake's *History* was his copy of anon., *A Political and Satirical History of the Years 1756 and 1757, In a Series of Seventy-five Humorous and Entertaining Prints* (?1757) (Bentley 1995, p. 313).
6. See Leslie F. Chard, II, 'Joseph Johnson: Father of the Book Trade, *Bulletin of the New York Public Library* 79 (1975–6) pp. 51-82; and G. P. Tyson, *Joseph Johnson: A Liberal Publisher* (Iowa: Iowa University Press, 1979).
7. 3 December 1792; Public Record Office (PRO), H[ome] O[ffice] 42/23. 89.
8. 13 December 1789; PRO P[rivy] C[ouncil] 1/18/19. It is significant that Brian's letter (I can find no first name) went up to Privy Council level, a government body roughly equivalent in stature to today's Cabinet but having the power to interrogate suspects directly, as they did in preparation for the 1794 Treason Trials.
9. See Robert Hindmarsh, *Rise and Progress of the New Jerusalem Church* (1861). For other schisms amongst the Swedenborgians in 1789, see Schuchard (1992).
10. 8 August 1789, HO 42/14. 311.
11. Roger Wells, *Wretched Faces: Famine in Wartime England, 1793–1801*, (Gloucester: Alan Sutton; New York: St. Martin's Press, 1988), Chapter 7. On the role of Privy Council, see pp. 187–91.
12. *A Short View of some of The Evils and Grievances, which at this time oppress, The British Empire, through The Corruption of its Government: And which are utterly contrary to the Spirit and Precepts of REASON and Christianity.* See PRO T[reasury] S[olicitor] 11/579/1904; B[ritish] L[ibrary] Add. Ms. 16922. 141, 16 December 1792.

13. Blake's agrarian utopianism is based on a Hebraic model popularized in radical circles by Spence and Irish anti-colonialists.
14. BL Add. Ms. 16922. 141, 16 December 1792.
15. I have been unable to find evidence of Bentley's prosecution. The Treasury Solicitor's case-notes hint he disappeared.
16. TS 11/458/1524. My italics.
17. BL Add. Ms. 16925. 15, (c. 1792). As well an avalanche of pamphlets, anti-Painite propaganda circulated as political prints, token coins, and even transfer printed ceramic mugs, see David Bindman, Aileen Dawson and Mark Jones, *The Shadow of the Guillotine: Britain and the French Revolution* (London: Trustees of the British Museum, 1989).
18. Richard Lee, *The Rights of Man. Consisting of Extracts from Pigott's Political Dictionary* (n.d. 1795?).
19. 'Deep Will.' is William Pitt, that is, William of the deep pit.
20. Lee's *A Summary of the Duties of Citizenship!* echoes Paine's *Age of Reason* (1794) in attacking the Bible as 'interpolated … sometimes contradictory, sometimes unintelligible' (p. 9).
21. TS 11/578/1893. The caricatures referred to were 'the Farm House of Windsor Farmer George & Ch-l-tte going to Market a Voluptuary under all the horrors of Digestion'. Identifiable or representative prints are *The Thieves Detected at Last. Or, A Wonderfull Discovery at the Windsor Farm!!!*, by Newton, 8 November 1792; *Going to Market*, attributed to James Gillray, 21 November 1791 and *A Voluptuary under the horrors of Digestion*, James Gillray, 2 July 1792, all satires on King George, usually on the subject of his farming hobby.
22. BL Add. Ms. 16922. 200, 19 December 1792, 16921. 125, 10 December 1792.
23. Blake returned to caricature later in his career (Read 1988).
24. *The Morning Post And Daily Advertiser*, 17 March 1792, TS 11/1080/5512. Blake would not have agreed with the anonymous author ('Fresnoy') about Reynolds, but they shared similar views about Charles and the arts, see *Public Address* (E580) and (Eaves 1992, pp. 13–14, 141). 'Fresnoy' alludes to Charles Du Fresnoy, author of *The Art of Painting of Charles Alphonse Du Fresnoy*, trans. William Mason with annotations by Sir J. Reynolds (York, 1783).
25. BL Add Ms. 16921. 69, 8 December 1792.
26. John Martin, *An Account of the Trial Of Sam. George Grant, Before a General Court Martial, Held at Chatham Barracks, On Wednesday, March 21, 1792, and Seven Following Days, for having advised and persuaded Francis Heritage and Francis Stephenson, Two Drummers of the Coldstream Regiment of Guards, to Desert* (1792). A civilian charged with 'seducing' soldiers would normally have been tried in a civil court. Martin's pamphlet is at TS 11/457/1519. The appeal case is *The Genuine Account of the Proceedings of a General Court-Martial on the Trial of Serjeant Samuel George Grant (published by Authority) and with the Consent of the court-Martial; together with the Judgment of the Court of Common Pleas, On an Application to them for a Prohibition* (1792).
27. For liberal song collections relevant to Blake, see Mee (1992, pp. 113–17).

28. BL Add Ms. 16920. 119, 5 December 1792.
29. BL Add Ms. 16923. 127, 28 December 1792.
30. BL Add. Ms. 16924. 58, 8 January 1793.
31. Iain McCalman, 'Ultra-radicalism and Convivial Debating-clubs in London, 1795–1838', *English Historical Review*, 102, 1987, pp. 309–33.
32. *The Manchester Herald*, 3 November 1792.
33. *The Manchester Herald*, 27 October 1792.
34. BL Add Ms. 16921. 31, 6 December 1792; 16922. 143, 16 December 1792.
35. Compare Anon., *The Anti-Gallican and Anti-Levelling Songster; being a selection of curious political songs* (1793) and R. Thompson, *A Tribute to Liberty; or new collection of Patriotic Songs, entirely original ... Sacred to the Rights of Man* (1793).
36. *The Manchester Herald*, 17 November 1792.
37. 10 December 1792, HO 42/23. 292.
38. BL Add Ms. 16920. 57, 3 December 1792; 16922. 12, 11 December 1792.
39. *PEAS FOR SWINE!* was allegedly a 'Prologue to "The Star of PEACE"', which, as in Blake's trailing of the 'Bible of Hell' (*MHH* 24, E44), is a reminder that printing Devils puffed works they had yet to write.
40. I am not suggesting that *A Song of Liberty* was printed in 1792. The radical rhetorics discussed in this essay originate earlier than the 1790s but were only systematically collected by the authorities post-1791.
41. Hawes obviously exploits, as Spence did, his extensive biblical knowledge but in *PEAS FOR SWINE!* he declared himself 'a Member of the Church of England'.
42. TS 24/3/129; TS 24/3/174; TS 24/3/168.
43. *The Manchester Herald*, 17 November 1792.
44. 10 December 1792, HO 42/23. 292. By the mid-1790s, radical toasts had become more long-winded, viz. Richard Lee's, *At a Meeting of the Society of the Friends of Liberty, at Shacklewell ... July 20, 1795:* '2. May the blossoms of Liberty survive the cutting blasts of Despotism, and ripen into the fruit of which the whole Earth may partake. 3. May England be speedily divided into small farms, by which the industrious poor may live, and monopolozing be done away'. Blake's numbering of statements (eg. '20.') in *A Song of Liberty*, seems to intentionally conflate biblical versification with contemporary political toast listing.
45. Watermarking on the Tate Gallery impression suggests a date of *c.* 1805 for the printing.
46. Reproduced, Marcus Wood, *Radical Satire and Print Culture, 1790–1822* (Oxford: Clarendon Press, 1994) figs. 11 and 12. Unlike Spence's durable token coins in the British Museum Department of Coins and Medals, *The Civil Citizen* etching appears only to have survived in a 1917 facsimile.

11

Mrs Bliss: a Blake Collector of 1794

Keri Davies

It has been a perennial problem for Blake criticism to establish an original context of reception for his illuminated books. In this essay I hope to establish not only the identity of Blake's earliest known collector, hitherto known only as 'Mrs Bliss', but also to delineate his relations with Joseph Johnson's publishing house and to offer a reconstruction of an early audience for Blake's work rather different from the male radical intelligentsia with which he is customarily associated.

It will be shown that Rebekah Bliss's library is not only of great importance to Blake studies, but also to the history of book-collecting in Britain as one of the earliest female collectors. As a bibliophile contemporary of Wollstonecraft and Austen, her collection of sumptuous printed books and over 70 illuminated manuscripts, including missals, psalters and Books of Hours, provides and extraordinary example of a dissenting, woman-centred, female connoisseur. Feminist assessment of Blake has grown increasingly sceptical over the past two decades, but attention to Rebekah Bliss and her milieu obliges us to reassess the appeal of his works to a contemporary female audience.

The earlier Blake scholars Keynes and Bentley note little more than that *BIBLIOTHECA SPLENDIDISSIMA. A CATALOGUE OF A SELECT PORTION OF THE LIBRARY OF MRS. BLISS, Deceased, Removed From Her Residence At Kensington* was auctioned in April 1826 in 814 lots sold over four days (Keynes 1968, p. 47; Bentley 1977, p. 654).[1] The Blake lots were *For Children: The Gates of Paradise, Songs of Innocence and of Experience*, Blair's *Grave* (1808) and one coloured and one uncoloured copy of Young's *Night Thoughts* (1797). This essay will demonstrate that the 'Bliss Blakes', as we might call them, were collected at dates from 1794 (*For Children: the*

Gates of Paradise), through 1802 (the supposed date of her copy of *Songs*) and at least up to 1808 (Blair's *Grave*).

On the basis of Bentley's evidence one may conjecture that Bliss acquired her Blakes directly from the poet-painter himself (1977, pp. 187, 191, 384, 419, 643, 654). Her copy of *For Children: the Gates of Paradise* is a proof before either Blake's or Johnson's imprints were added. Her copy of *Songs* (Copy P) is distinctive with, unusually, *Innocence* and *Experience* separately paginated in Blake's hand, suggesting he possibly knew they were intended to he bound in two volumes. Bliss's plain and coloured copies of Young's *Night Thoughts* are also significant. There are around twenty copies of the hand-coloured *Night Thoughts* and Bentley has suggested that 'the plan was always for Blake to be given copies of the *Night Thoughts* to colour, as part of his share of the profits of the work' (1988b, p. 302). In other words, even in the example of Bliss's ownership of a relatively extensively produced work like *Night Thoughts*, circumstances suggest a purchase made directly from Blake.

Mrs Bliss's library of illuminated manuscripts may also have had a more general aesthetic influence on Blake. Anthony Blunt claimed that Blake's apprenticeship years provided his 'first contact with medieval art, which was to remain a powerful influence and source of inspiration for the whole of his life' (1959, p. 4). Jean Hagstrum has argued that specific Books of Hours in the collection of the bookseller James Edwards inspired Blake in the late 1780s (1964, pp. 31–3). To these possibilities must now be added the medieval illuminated mansucripts in the library of Mrs Bliss. If Blake saw the collection, we cannot doubt the quality of the items at his disposal. For example, her Psalter for Franciscan usage, acquired by the Bodleian Library with the bequest of the antiquary Francis Douce (MS. Douce 48), is a manuscript of the late thirteenth century with fifteen fine miniatures and painted capitals.[2]

In other words, Mrs Bliss was a bibliophile of national importance who collected medieval illuminated manuscripts alongside Blake's illuminated books. But who was she? Hitherto, the sale catalogue has been the sole source of information. Bentley thought Mrs Bliss connected with Philip Bliss, an Oxford antiquary, perhaps because it was relatively easy to find information about him.[3] Joseph Viscomi identified 'Mrs Bliss' as Anne Bliss, the mother of Philip (1993, p. 425 n. 28). Unfortunately, the dates do not match up for either of these possibilities. Philip Bliss was born in 1787. His parents were Rev. Philip Bliss, rector of Dodington and Frampton

Cotterell in Gloucestershire (born 1742, died 1 February 1803), and
Anne Mitchell of Conham, in present-day Bristol (born about 1751).
After her husband's death, Mrs Anne Bliss lived at Taunton.[4] The
younger Philip Bliss died at St Mary Hall, Oxford, on 18 November
1857. His wife Sophia, whom he married in 1825, survived him.
They had one son and one daughter.[5] The very wording of the
1826 sale catalogue with its reference to 'The Library of Mrs Bliss,
Deceased, Removed from her Residence at Kensington' means that
'Mrs Bliss' was dead by 1826 but that she had resided at Kensington.
This rules out both Philip Bliss's wife (newly wed in 1826) and his
mother, who continued to reside in Taunton after her husband's
death in 1803. It also seems unlikely that Francis Douce, who
meticulously documented his collection – and acquired at least one
manuscript with a 'Mrs Bliss' provenance – failed to note a connection with Philip Bliss's family.[6]

   Douce himself was an important Blake collector, owning copies
of *The Marriage of Heaven and Hell* (Copy B with the separate plate,
'Our End is come'), and *The Book of Thel* (Copy I), plus *A Descriptive
Catalogue* (Copy H), a third state of the *Canterbury Pilgrims*, and
Hayley's *Poems* (1802) (Bentley 1977, pp. 118, 122, 128, 134, 138, 289,
298, 658). Douce had begun in 1779 a correspondence with Richard
Twiss, a wealthy, older fellow antiquary, traveller and miscella-
neous writer. Their correspondence covers such varied topics as the
history of chess (the subject of one of Twiss's publications), botany,
entomology, the tuning of harpsichords, children's toys, mathematical recreations and many books – books bought, read, borrowed
and lost.[7] There are 86 letters from Twiss preserved amongst the
Douce papers in the Bodleian Library.[8] Joan K. Stemmler was the
first Blake scholar seriously to examine Douce's correspondence
(1992, pp. 9–19). The earliest extant letter from Twiss to Douce
dates from 1779, the last is from 1807, with the majority written in
the 1790s. Unfortunately, Stemmler's transcripts are significantly
incomplete and, importantly, omit a crucial reference to Blake. Two
letters written in September 1794 are of particular interest.

   Twiss wrote the first letter from 'Bushhill Edm[onto]$^{n'}$ on 13
September 1794. Typically, as for much of their correspondence, the
(highly compressed) substance of his first paragraph is largely concerned with books on entomology Douce lent Twiss:

> I rec^d Barbut & 3 tokens &c. safe last Sat^y, & am oblig'd I have
> sent it to Enf^d to be bound, & I shall be oblig'd further to you if

you will lend me your Barbut for a few days, next Saturday 20th, for me to colour the insects from which I have not got. if that day will suit you, I shall send your Mouffet &c back on the same morning; will be only one Errand for your Man: if that day does not suit, mention any day in the following week. I shall send Curtis On insects. & Mandevilles treatise on Stews, which is Mr Taylor's (the surgeon).[9]

Amidst this learned outpouring can be identified the writers on entomology, Jacques or James Barbut (fl. 1780–91), Thomas Moufet (1553–1604) and William Curtis (1746–99); 'Mandeville' is the Dutch-born Bernard Mandeville (1670–1733), whose books anatomizing the hypocrisy of a prosperous society's moral foundations were much relished by Twiss and Douce.[10] The letter continues with references to 'Drury the silversmith in the Strand', 'S^ir Jos Banks', and 'Pr Pindar'. At the beginning of the second page are the first of the Blake references:

A Lady here has just shown me a little book 'the Pleasures of memory' 5th Ed^n Poems. (by Mr Rogers the Banker!) 1793. Cadell. 12mo, with four beautiful plates, and two curious works of Blake N° 13 Hercules Build^s Lambeth. One 'the gates of Paradise', 16 etchings. 24mo the other 'Songs of Innocence' prin[ted in] colours. I suppose the man to be mad; but he draws very well have [you] any thing by him?[11]

Since the letter is written from Bush Hill, Edmonton, the 'Lady here' clearly lives in, or has some connection with, the Edmonton neighbourhood.[12] This is the earliest reference to either *For Children* or the *Songs*.

There are only five extant copies of *For Children: The Gates of Paradise*. One of them belonged in 1826 to 'Mrs Bliss'. The 1826 sale catalogue also indicates that she owned a copy of *Songs of Innocence and of Experience*. The coincidence is so striking that one must consider if the 'Lady here' and Mrs Bliss are not one and the same person. If Mrs Bliss owned these works in September 1794, this makes her the earliest identifiable owner of works by Blake.[13] Twiss's remark, 'I suppose the man to be mad', could have come from sight of Blake's work, but also through report of his eccentricities from Mrs Bliss or some other mutual acquaintance.

The next letter (dated '25 Septr 94') continues the entomological discussion:

> On <u>Saturday next, 27</u>th any time after 12 o'Clock, if you will be so good as to send to the Black Bull Holborn, you will find there ready your Barbut, Mouffet, 3 imposteurs, Donovans insects &c. Jere. Taylor, Mandeville on Stews, & my Curtis insects & Blakes Paradise. and also a very curious <u>Caterpillar</u>, which will produce next May Linnaeus's *Phalena Pudibunda*:[14] this is the large one with four brushes, on its back; black velvet rings, & near the purple brush on the tail, a hole like a nipple from whence issues green matter; no other Caterp^r has this. It has been painted & described by Madam Merian & also by Sepp. It eats walnut & Lime Leaves. a small <u>Caterpillar</u> which feeds on Plumb leaves not is Sepp but probably in Roesel, & two more <u>large ones</u> like the one you have these will produce the *Phalena Rubi.* (the little *Pupa* I sent before is the *jacobœa*.) Some <u>Cynips's</u> nests on a Rose branch, & some <u>Cynips</u> at the undersurface of oakleaves, each of these contains a maggot, the black ones are almost ready to come out files: should be put in a bottle with gauze. or in a box & glass: the bottle is best, as the files can't get out. the Larva of the Beetle is dead & rotten.

The muddle of bibliography and entomology is typical of Twiss's letters. Listed first are books being returned to Douce ('Barbut, Mouffet, 3 imposteurs, Donovans insects'), then books borrowed from some third party ('Jere. Taylor, Mandeville on Stews'), and finally books being lent by Twiss ('my Curtis insects & Blakes Paradise').[15] This breathless letter almost suggests Twiss sorting out his books to be parcelled up, or else checking the parcel as he writes. It clearly implies Twiss has arranged to show Douce his own copy of Blake's *Gates of Paradise.*

The second paragraph of the same page contains an important Blake reference unaccountably missed by Stemmler:

> Letsoms b^k was printed by Dilly. I have read the article about Earwigs in Valmont: there is no hole from the Ear to the Brain. See what Valmont says about Mandragora. there are <u>no</u> neuters in *Blattœ p.* 102 *Barbut*; those you thought so, are the *Larva.* You will see several more of Blakes books at Johnsons in St. P^s Ch. y^d — inclosed your Dutch MS. I shall explain it to you when we meet, 'tis dated 1286. religious nonsense, but curious for its antiquity.[16]

The presence of 'several more of Blakes books at Johnsons in St. P^s Ch. y$^{d'}$ is highly significant. Largely on the basis of his well-known letter to Dawson Turner in 9 June 1818, it has been assumed Blake had no means of publicizing or distributing his works in illuminated printing other than by word of mouth.[17] In much the same way *For Children's* imprint, '1793 Published by W. Blake No 13 Hercules Buildings Lambeth and J. Johnson St Paul's Church Yard', has also been dismissed as wishful thinking. Bentley, for example, points out that 'There is no evidence beyond that on the title-page that Joseph Johnson ever sold the book; in particular, he never advertised it in his journal, *The Analytical Review*' (1977, p. 187). Moreover, not only does Twiss's letter suggest *For Children* was on sale, it also suggests other works by Blake were available at Johnson's shop in late 1794.

Taken together, the implication of these extracts is that Johnson was displaying 'samples' of illuminated printing in order to attract orders; and that Twiss saw 'several more of Blake's books' when he purchased his copy of *For Children*. Johnson would presumably have handled the copies which bore his own imprint, but there are further conundrums. The absence of an imprint in Mrs Bliss's copy suggests she either acquired it directly from Blake himself or, alternatively, the imprint's absence may imply it was a 'display copy'. If so, when it was sold to Mrs Bliss, it may have helped Blake realize the book's market potential, leading in turn to Johnson's participation into the enterprise.

However, Twiss's letter of 13 September 1794 yields further evidence with its references to the 'Lady here' and her 'two curious works of Blake N° 13 Hercules Build^s Lambeth'. One item is ' "the gates of Paradise" ... the other "Songs of Innocence" '. This implies that Mrs Bliss – if she is the 'Lady here' – had some connection with Enfield or Edmonton. A search of the Middlesex parish registers for the years 1750–1800 disclosed no Bliss marriages in Edmonton, Tottenham or Monken Hadley, and just one in South Mimms (Sarah Bliss to Thomas White in 1768). However, in the neighbouring parish of Enfield, the registers of St Andrew's Church show a long-established Bliss family in the Enfield area throughout the eighteenth and nineteenth centuries. Contemporary directories were unhelpful, but Jennifer Claridge, a descendant of the Enfield Blisses, and herself an experienced family history researcher, recalled a 'stray' entry amongst her family records. Her notes helped suggest a connection between the bibliophile Mrs Bliss of 'Kensington' and the death in 1819 of a 70-year-old Rebecca Bliss of Kensington, buried at St Nicholas, Loughton.[18] The brief recording of her death was filled out slightly by an obituary in the *Gentleman's Magazine* notifying 'At Kensington, Mrs. Rebekah Bliss, niece of the late John Gorham'.[19] The age of the deceased tallied exactly with the Rebecca Bliss whose birth on 9 March 1749 is listed in the *Register* of the Independent Chapel at Carey Street, New Court.[20]

Mrs Bliss's social position was confirmed by the will of 'Rebekah Bliss of Kensington in the Country of Middlesex Spinster' in the Public Record Office.[21] It is clearly the will of a keen book-collector. This is a typical bequest:

> List of Books with the Parlor Book Case for M[r] Ebenezer Maitland to have at mine or Mrs. Whitakers decease as she shall direct a set of Gentlemans Mag from 1731 to the present time and which I have kept up purposely for him Harleian Miscellany 8 Vol[s] Gross's Antiquities 8 Vol[s] Rapins History of England 5 Darts Westminster Darts Canterbury Dugdale S[t] Pauls Evelyns Sylva Ogilvys Esop Montfaucons Antiquities 2 vol Hales Husbandry Richardsons Iconology Arthurian Oracle 3 Vol the Alcoran Roma Patria 2 vol Dictionary of all Religious to the above list I give him of my own purchasing S[ir] W[m] Hamiltons Roman and Grecian Antiquities in 4 vol folio also a Book of Prints called incantations both which were bought by me & if there are any other Book or Books he may particularly wish to have & are not specifically devised I request that he may have them.

And another:

> I also give to Mrs. Fuller Maitland's Daughters 2 vols of Les Oiseaux dorees & 2 vols of Le Vaillant's Birds as a Token though a small one of my Remembrance to them.

Mrs. Fuller Maitland's grandson was J. A. Fuller Maitland, music critic and editor. In his autobiography, he reminisces:

> In Church Street there stood two beautiful old houses side by side, close to what is now Kensington Palace Gardens; I am not sure which of may forbears gave the name of Maitland House to one of them, but I know there was a connection, as one of my uncles remembered being taken as a boy to pay his respects to

two cousins, old ladies, to whom it had come, who were styled 'Mrs' Whittaker and 'Mrs' Bliss. (The statelier designation was a survival of old custom adopted when maiden ladies attained a certain age.)[22]

The difficulty of the library of the 'Late' Mrs Bliss not being sold until seven years after Rebecca Bliss died is explained by a codicil in her will bearing out Fuller-Maitland's recollection of '"Mrs" Whittaker'. Bliss's library was kept substantially intact, even though so many books are bequeathed in her will, because her residuary legatee was the woman with whom she shared her home, Ann Whitaker. The codicil will states:

I give and bequeath the Use and Enjoyment of all my Library of Books Book-Cases Cabinets of Shells Minerals Pictures and all other Articles of Furniture Glasses &c. which belong to me and are standing in the House at Kensington to Mrs. Ann Whitaker for and during her Life and after her Death I give and bequeath them as under written unless she chooses to give them in her Lifetime.

The collection apparently survived until Ann Whitaker's death. Again we find an entry amongst the burial records in Loughton Library:

1825 …2 *December* WHITAKER Anne; *Loughton;* aged 84 years
(& of Kensington).[23]

together with another corresponding obituary in the *Gentleman's Magazine* for 1825 noticing: '[*Lately*] At Kensington, aged 83, Mrs. Anne Whittaker.'[24]

The owner of the *Bibliotheca Splendidissima* can be identified as Rebekah Bliss (1749–1819). Further evidence linked Mrs Bliss with the Enfield or Edmonton neighbourhoods and the 'Lady here' referred to by Twiss. Once again, the will is informative. She leaves to:

M[rs.] Walker Southgate the Minerals & case with Contents standing in chimney Recess also a Book of Chinese Drawings of Flowers folio & 6 v[ols] of Flora Danica a Persian Manuscript contain[g] 5 Poems & a smaller one of the Turkish Wars of the Emperor Babur & Gulistan to M[r] Walker the three latter Books.[25]

John Walker was born in 1765; his wife Sally in 1774. Walker's father Isaac bought the Arnos Grove estate in 1777 and it remained the home of the Walker family for over 130 years. In 1794, Walker also had a town house in Upper Gower Street, where he was a near neighbour of Francis Douce. If Mrs Bliss showed her Blake books to Richard Twiss at Bush Hill, it may have been while visiting her friends the Walkers at the neighbouring estate of Arnos Grove.[26]

Not only do these dates, baptisms, deaths and wills all match up, they cumulatively provide a vivid picture of Rebekah Bliss's life and the milieu in which she moved. She was only fourteen when her father died in 1763 and nineteen when her mother died.[27] Her father's will, made in the month of his death, is brief and formal. In common with many such wills written *in extremis* and bearing the mark rather than signature of the dying man, it makes no attempt to itemize his estate, and makes a single nominal bequest: 'Item I give to my wife Sarah Bliss the Sum of One Shilling'.[28] The *Register* of the Independent Chapel at Carey Street New Court additionally recorded the births of Anne Bliss in 1750, John Bliss in 1751, and William Bliss in 1753, but none of her siblings reached adulthood.[29] She found herself, at an early age, not quite alone in the world because her uncle and cousins were part of the same Independent Chapel congregation, but perhaps with a freedom to determine her own future denied to most of her female contemporaries.

Ordinarily, the pressures to marry would have been considerable, but Rebekah Bliss remained a spinster throughout her life: how did she escape what Blake condemned as 'the marriage hearse'? Some time before 1780, she met another orphan heiress, Ann Whitaker, the only child of the second marriage of Alderman William Whitaker of Loughton in Essex, and they set up home together in Church Street, Kensington, in a house built by Rebekah's uncle, John Gorham. Social historians have documented the profoundly homosocial nature of contemporary middle- and upper-class English life where the sexes were highly segregated, and powerful emotional (and sometimes physical) ties between persons of the same sex were common and often expressed in romantic terms.[30] Passionate same-sex friendships were commonplace amongst middle-class women in the eighteenth century with the establishment of an independent home often being its fondest expression.[31] The Bliss–Whitaker household may have been just such a friendship. In their wills, both women repeatedly invoke 'my much cherished Friend', 'my

Friend', 'my late d^r Friend' and it is revealing that the women not only lived together for 35 years but also were buried together at Loughton.

The role of John Gorham, her mother's brother, and her oldest close relative was probably crucial.[32] He was sufficiently convinced of his niece's ability to make her his sole executrix and included clauses in his will imposing penalties on any beneficiary who challenged her judgement. The legatees are all relatives or servants of the deceased with the exception of Ann Whitaker:

> Also I give to my said Niece Rebecca Bliss for her own All my Household Goods Plate Linen Books and every thing of every kind that is moveable in and about my Dwellinghouse in the Kings Road aforesaid (except my two Rose Wood Tables which I have hereby given to Mrs. Ann Whitaker).[33]

This is a telling example of how Rebakah Bliss's partner was adopted into the Bliss–Gorham–Maitland clan. In turn, she acknowledged this recognition by making the Maitland family principal heirs of her own estate.[34]

The couple were able to resist the heterosexual imperative, partly because they had no close male relatives to force them into marriage, and partly because their background respected female autonomy. The domestic arrangements of their Kensington home were shaped according to their own inclinations. They had been partners since the 1780s but around 1800 they took in a much younger woman, Harriet Barnes, to act as a companion. In this role, Barnes could enjoy sociability without rivalry and financial security without the shame of being merely a servant. The household exemplified the best ideals of companionship. Rebekah Bliss made bequests in her will to her new companion, 'now residing with the said Ann Whitaker', providing 'an annuity of One Hundred Pounds' and 'Two thousand pounds three p^r Cent Consolidated Bank Annuities'.[35] Harriet Barnes was not long to enjoy her new wealth, dying at Kensington in April 1823, aged 42 to be buried at Loughton alongside her benefactor.[36]

From details of their bequests, it is possible to reconstruct the strata of well-to-do dissent in which they moved and were prominent. Rebekah Bliss was a lifelong member of the congregation at Carey Street New Court and left a substantial legacy to its minister ('to the said Revd Dr Winter One thousand Pounds like 3 p^r Cent

Annuities').[37] The registers of the Chapel record the births of all the
Bliss children and their cousins the Maitlands. Together they form a
tightly knit clan of wealthy Dissenters. John Clayton (a dissenting
minister left legacies by both Rebekah and Ann) married Mary
Flower, a niece of William Fuller, the banker, and sister to the radical journalist Benjamin Flower. Ebenezer Maitland, a director of the
Bank of England, married Mary Winter, sister of Robert Winter, the
minister at Carey Street New Court. Rebekah Bliss's cousin's son
Ebenezer Fuller Maitland married Bethia Ellis, who was a grand-
daughter of William Fuller.[38] Thus, her entire extended family
adhered to this dissenting community over several generations.
Like so many Christian sects, the congregation at Carey Street New
Court preferred endogamy, following the biblical prohibitions 'Be
ye not unequally yoked with unbelievers' and 'Thou shalt not plow
with an ox and an ass together'.[39] Ann Whitaker also became part
of this dissenting community, for 'he that is joined unto the Lord is
one spirit'.[40]

The 1826 sale contents of Rebekah Bliss's library does not represent
its likely totality. Evidence of other books and manuscripts she
owned may be found in her will and in that of Ann Whitaker as
well as in sales of the books inherited by her relatives. It is from
these sources that one can piece together something of the scope of
the library of England's earliest female bibliophile.[41] Not everything in her will can be identified with certainty, but many gifts of
books are identifiable. Robert Winter was left 'Magna Charta in Gold
Letters a token of Remembrance in boards' identifiable as *Magna
Charta Regis Johannis, xv die Juni, mccxv, anno regni xvii*. (London: John
Whittaker, 1816), perhaps the most sumptuous book published in
England during the nineteenth century and almost certainly the
first to be printed in gold. It is tempting to read into the presence of
this publication in her library an expression of her political sympa-
thies that may also account for the number of works relating to
Napoleon Buonaparte sold with the *Bibliotheca Splendidissima*.[42]
Ebenezer Maitland was left 'Sir Wm Hamiltons Roman and Grecian
Antiquities', that is *Antiquités Etrusques, Grecques et Romaines. Tirées
du cabinet de M. Hamilton. Collection of Etruscan, Greek and Roman
antiquities from the Cabinet of the Honble. Wm. Hamilton* (Naples:
[Francesco Morelli], 1766–7), four folios of great importance in the
development of neoclassical design.[43] Maitland was also bequeathed
'Ld Nelsons Naval Victories atlas folio', with illustrations by P. J. de
Loutherbourg.

But the finest printed volumes in her library were natural history books, including spectacular folios:

Buffon Histoire Naturelle des Oiseaux, 14 vols. LARGE PAPER; ... Storia Naturelle degli Uccelli, 5 vols; ... Sepp's Birds, 2 vols; Scheuchzer's Natural History, 15 vols; ... Plenck Icones Plantarum, 6 vols; Thornton's Sexual System of Linnæus; ... Roxburgh's Plants of the Coast of Coromandel; ... Abbot and Smith's Insects, 2 vols; ... Bulliard Historie des Champignons de la France, 7 vols; Vieillot Histoire Naturelle, 3 vols, LARGE PAPER; ... Brookshaw's Pomona; ... Buchoz Historie Naturelle, 5 vols, ... &c. &c.

This collection reflects a widespread female interest in natural philosophy which developed during the eighteenth century, her wealth enabling her to fill her library with the grandest publications in that field.

While Rebekah Bliss's printed books can often be traced, very few of the manuscripts, missals and Oriental books can be positively identified. A small part of her collection was subsequently listed in Ann Whttaker's will, but a remarkably informative source for the manuscripts of *Bibliotheca Splendidissima* is a sale catalogue including items from the library of Samuel Roffey Maitland, the son of Rebekah's cousin Alexander. The sale was held on 21 April 1842 and for three following days.[44] A copy of the catalogue survives in the British Library Department of Manuscripts, annotated by Sir Frederic Madden:

Those MSS. to which M. is prefixed belonged to the Rev. S. R. Maitland, Librarian to the Abp. of Canterbury. He inherited them from his father, who had them from a Mrs. Bliss the widow [*sic*] of a Collector of that name of Kensington.[45]

Madden marked 30 lots as originating in the Bliss collection.[46] Of these, three acquired by Madden for the British Museum illustrate the collection's superb quality:

698 Chinese costume. – A volume containing upwards of forty figures, representing the costume etc. of the Natives, with descriptions in Chinese, *finely executed*[47]

720   HORAE BEATAE VIRGINIS, A BEAUTIFUL MANUSCRIPT
UPON VELLUM … containing THIRTEEN LARGE PAINTINGS
OF SINGULAR CHARACTER AND EXTRAORDINARY CARE-
FULNESS OF FINISH, (*in the same style as one in the Bibliotheque
Royale des Manuscrits at Paris, executed for Anne of Britanny,*)
THIRTY-ONE BORDERS OF FRUITS, FLOWERS, AND INSECTS,
AND MANY HUNDRED CAPITAL LETTERS, *an exquisitely fin-
ished and beautiful Manuscript, bound in crimson velvet* … 8vo[48]

758   CHARLES III. KING OF SPAIN. – Original grant by King
Charles III. of the title of Marquis of Sobre Monte to Don Joseph
de Sobremonte and his heirs 1761 … MOST BEAUTIFULLY
WRITTEN UPON VELLUM WITHIN A VERY RICH BORDER
MOST HIGHLY FINISHED IN GOLD AND COLOURS … folio[49]

As these catalogue entries indicate, Rebekah Bliss collected over a
wide field, both geographically and temporally. The distinguishing
feature ofs her manuscripts is their high quality illustrations,
emphasized by the auctioneer's by the auctioneer's 'puffs' and confirmed by the high prices they fetched.

Where were these books acquired? One clue comes from Thomas
F. Dibdin, but it is not completely reliable. His *Bibliographical
Decameron* (1817) relates that lot 720 'was purchased at the sale of
Mr. Edward's library', but adds:

My respectable neighbour, (and indefatigable collector of 'rich
and rare' gems, in the department of book-illuminations) Mr. Bliss,
is the present possessor of the volume here alluded to. … It is a
thick broad duodecimo of HOURS OF THE VIRGIN; containing
13 larger illuminations – … and thirty-one borders of fruits and
flowers, &c. … The condition of this curious little volume is most
desirable. It was sold for 56*l*. 15*s*.[50]

Dibdin pretends to more knowledge than he had. Having seen no
more than the name 'Bliss' against an entry, he supposed the collector to be male.

The source of Rebekah Bliss's Blake books are even more
problematic. Did she acquire her Blakes directly from the artist?
The principal evidence in support of this speculation is her proof
copy of *For Children: The Gates of Paradise*. It would have been strange
for her to have acquired this from Johnson when the remainder of

the edition specifically bears his imprint. A possible hypothesis is that Johnson displayed other works by Blake (including works in illuminated printing) but directed prospective purchasers to deal with the artist himself.

One might speculate that Rebekah Bliss's dissenting circle were fellow worshippers with Blake's family at Carey Street chapel. New Court is conveniently near Lincoln's Inn Fields and Blake could have known the chapel from his apprenticeship days with Basire when he lived at Great Queen Street. Additionally, Blake's friend Alexander Tilloch had business premises at 1 Carey Street in the 1790s. Robert Winter, the minister at New Court, was born on 25 March 1762 at Brewer Street, Golden Square, just around the corner from the Blake family. Although Blake is said not to have attended public worship for the last forty years of his life (1788–1827), he could have met Rebekah Bliss through the social circle of the Carey Street chapel even if, in so far as there is evidence, he seems to have associated with Baptists, or else with Muggletonians (Bentley 1969, pp. 7, 8; Thompson 1993, pp. 102–5, 121). It may be misguided to seek a single allegiance given the rich variety of religious experi- ence on offer in London. After all, in 1789 William and Catherine signed the manifesto of the Swedenborgian New Jerusalem Church, but when he died in 1827, he was buried, like his father, mother, brothers and aunt, at Bunhill Fields, the dissenters' burial ground with, at his own request, a service following the Anglican Prayer Book (Gilchrist 1863, p. 361).

Clearly the copy of Blake's *Songs of Innocence and of Experience* (Copy P, *c.* 1802), which appeared in the 1826 sale, could not have been the book shown to Twiss in 1794. Rebekah Bliss's cousin, Ebenezer Maitland, was one of the joint executors of her estate and by curious coincidence, his great-grandson J. A. Fuller Maitland owned some leaves of the *Songs* (Copy G) (Bentley 1977, p. 415). It is tempting to assume that these leaves came from her library. She may thus have owned two copies (G and P) of *Songs of Innocence and of Experience* to put with her two copies of *Night Thoughts*. Given that Viscomi allots copy G a date of 1794, this could have been the one Twiss saw that year. The evidence is meagre, but the implication is that Bliss possessed a second, currently unidentified or lost, copy of *Songs*.

Twiss's correspondence with Francis Douce also provides evidence of how Blake advertised his works in illuminated printing, at least during the period of his friendship with Joseph Johnson. When

Blake inscribed the *Gates* as 'Published by Blake & Johnson' the imprint has a real meaning: Johnson was involved in the distribution of Blake's work. Similarly, Blake's methods of publicizing and distributing his work, at least for 1794, were not solely reliant on word of mouth. Although Blake's letter of 1818 to Dawson Turner implies he never left a stock of his works in illuminated printing with a 'regular publisher', it allows the loophole that he left display-copies at Johnson's. This would be consistent with the phrasing of Twiss's letter which says 'You will see' rather than 'you may buy'. The publisher would not have had nothing to gain financially but he was known for this kind of generosity. A contemporary recorded, without irony, that he 'often shewed kindness to needy authors, was not over hard in his bargains with them, and ... would often give them a dinner.'[51]

The availability of Blake's works at Johnson's shops also provides a context for his Prospectus *To the Public* of 10 October 1793.[52] The single-leaf flyer recorded by Gilchrist could have been prepared to accompany display copies at Johnson's and other friendly book-sellers. It also establishes a precedent Blake may have followed for flyers advertising his 'Exhibition of Paintings in Fresco' and 'Descriptive Catalogue' in 1809 (Bentley 1977, pp. 133, 164).

Irrespective of her significance as an early female bibliophile, Rebekah Bliss's milieu represents a vivid example of a contemporary homosocial society and also of a rather different kind of dissenting community from that customarily associated with Blake. She owned copies of the *Songs of Innocence and of Experience* and *For Children: the Gates of Paradise* as early as September 1794 which she may have acquired directly from Blake himself. It is also highly probable Richard Twiss acquired a copy of *For Children: The Gates of Paradise* that same year. Additionally, the Twiss–Douce letters, with their evidence of 'Blakes books at Johnsons.' make it now possible to specify a precise mode for their dissemination during this peak year in his creative talents. Taken together, these new pieces of evidence should compel a revision of the traditional assumption that Blake lacked any significant contemporary audience.

Notes

1. The title is, *BIBLIOTHECA SPLENDIDISSIMA. A CATALOGUE OF A SELECT PORTION OF THE LIBRARY OF MRS. BLISS, Deceased,*

Removed From Her Residence At Kensington; ... the Whole in the Finest Condition, Many on Large Paper, with Proof, and Early Impressions of the Plates, the Works on Natural History and Botany Most Beautifully Coloured, Sumptuously and Tastefully Bound in Morocco and Russia, by Kalthoeber, Staggemeier, C. Lewis, Bohn, Welcher, C. Smith, Murton, and Other Eminent Binders, Regardless of Expence, and Finished in Their Best Style. Which will be Sold by Auction, By SAUNDERS & HODGSON, At Their Great Room, 'The Poet's Gallery,' 39, Fleet Street. On Wednesday, April 26th, 1826, and Three Following Days, At Half-Past Twelve O'Clock Precisely. To Be Viewed, Three Days Preceding, and Morning of Sale, and Catalogues had, (price 1s. each.) Keynes and Bentley wrongly give the title as "Bibliotheca Splendissima." The correct Latin superlative is "Splendidissima". The Blake books were:

'10 Blake's (W.) Gates of Paradise, 16 *plates, red morocco, gilt leaves*

11 ————Songs of Innocence and Experience, 2 vols, *coloured engravings, red morocco, gilt leaves*

41 Blair's (Robt.) Grave, a Poem, *illustrated by 12 etchings, by Schiavonetti, from designs by W. Blake, calf extra, gilt leaves* 1808

370 Young's (Edw.) Night Thoughts, *with engravings from Blake's designs, half bound, red morocco* 1797

371 Young's (Edw.) Night Thoughts, *with engravings from Blake's designs, coloured calf extra, marble leaves* 1797.'

2. The entry reads:

'470 HEURES GOTHIQUE, MS. ON VELLUM, 15 miniatures, Life of Joseph, and Calendar, with painted capitals, *red morocco, gilt edges*'

See *The Douce Legacy: an Exhibition to Commemorate the 150th anniversary of the Bequest of Francis Douce, 1757–1834* (Oxford, 1984) no. 237; Bod[leian] L[ibrary], *Latin Liturgical Manuscripts and Printed Books: Guide to an Exhibition* (Oxford: Clarendon Press, 1952) no. 51; BodL. *Summary Catalogue of Western Manuscripts* (Oxford: Clarendon Press, 1953) no. 21622; R. Branner, *Manuscript painting in Paris during the reign of St. Louis* (Berkeley: University of California Press, 1977) pp. 211, 246; Otto Pächt and J. J. G. Alexander, *Illuminated Manuscripts in the Bodleian Library* (Oxford: Clarendon Press, 1966–73) i, no. 532 and plate XL; J. F. Willard, "Occupations of the Months in Mediaeval Calendars", *Bodleian Quarterly Record*, VII (1932), 38.

3. G. E. Bentley, Jr., personal communication, 12 April 1994.

4. Verses written by her on her 64th birthday in 1825 are in B[ritish] L[ibrary] Add. Ms 34569 (fols. 221–2). I have been unable to find a date of death for Anne Bliss.

5. On Philip Bliss (1787–1857), see *DNB* and Strickland Gibson and C. J. Hindle, 'Philip Bliss (1787–1857) editor and bibliographer', Oxford Bibliographical Society. *Proceedings & papers*. Vol.3 (1931–3) pp. 173–260, 387–8. For an obituary of Rev. Philip Bliss, Sr., see *Gentleman's Magazine*, March 1803, p. 284. A pedigree of the Bliss family of Market Harborough, is in J. Nichols's *History and antiquities of Leicestershire* ii, p. 693.

6. Douce and Philip Bliss had a number of mutual friends and acquaintances including J. P. Collier and Frederic Madden (see, for example, BodL, *The Douce Legacy*, xi).
7. Richard Twiss, *Chess* (London, 1787–9).
8. BodL MS. Douce. d.39.
9. BodL MS. Douce d.39 fol.70^r. Words underlined by Twiss are italicized in these transcripts. Words underlined in red by Douce are underlined here.
10. See E. J. Hundert, *The Enlightenment's Fable: Bernard Mandeville and the Discovery of Society* (Cambridge: Cambridge University Press, 1994).
11. BodL MS. Douce d. 39 fol.70^v.
12. Bush Hill was an estate within the ancient parish of Edmonton adjoining the parish boundary with Enfield. The house at Bush Hill that Twiss occupied in the 1790s as tenant of a Mr Wilkinson was demolished during the period I was researching this essay.
13. 'There is no earlier reference to either (or, I believe, to any book by Blake) in *Blake Records* (1969), *Blake Records Supplement* (1988a), or in any of the information I have collected since.' G. E. Bentley, Jr, personal communication, 2 February 1995.
14. At this point Stemmler's transcript ends.
15. 'Your Barbut' can be identified as Jacques Barbut, *Les genres des insectes de Linné* (London, 1781), Douce (B 800). 'Mouffet' is Thomas Moffett, Moufet, or Muffet, (1553–1604) physician and surgeon. There are four books by Thomas Moufet in the Douce collection. The reference is probably to his *Insectorum sive Minimorum Theatrum* (London, 1636) (Douce W, subt. 52). The '3 imposteurs' (*Les Trois Imposteurs*) was anonymously published, *c.* 1775. A copy is in Douce (I 69). The three imposters are Moses, Jesus, and Mohammed. 'Jere. Taylor' presumably Jeremy Taylor, Anglican bishop of Down & Connor although there are no books by him now in Douce. 'Mandeville on Stews' is an unidentified edition of Bernard de Mandeville, *A Modest Defence of Public Stews: Or, An Essay Upon Whoring As it is Now Practis'd in These Kingdoms*. No copy is in Douce but, according to his previous letter (13 September 1794), Twiss borrowed it from 'Mr Taylor the surgeon'. 'My Curtis insects' must be Twiss's copy of William Curtis, *Instructions for Collecting and Preserving Insects, Particularly Moths and Butterflies* (London, 1771). Stemmler interprets the quoted lines as implying that Douce had a copy of *For Children: the Gates of Paradise*, but this contradicts the syntax and grammar of the sentence.
16. BodL. MS. Douce d.39 fol.72^r.
17. 'I have never been able to produce Sufficient number for general Sale by means of a regular Publisher It is therefore necessary to me that any Person wishing to have any or all of them should send me their Order to Print them on the above terms.'(E771).
18. '1819[;] 9 March ... BLISS [,] Rebecca; Kensington; *aged 70 years.*' '*Loughton burials*, 1674–1830. (n. pub., n.d.) p. 48. Typescript in Loughton Library.
19. *Gentleman's Magazine*, vol. 89 (1819) p. 284.

20. P[ublic] R[ecord] O[ffice] RG 4/4228 (Baptisms 1707–57).
21. PRO PROB 11/1614 ff.58–61 (Will of Rebekah Bliss). All wills are quoted from the Prerogative Court of Canterbury probate copies. I have corrected obvious errors of copying.
22. J. A. Fulller Maitland, *A Doorkeeper of Music* (London: John Murray, 1929) p. 15.
23. *Loughton burials*, 50.
24. *Gentleman's Magazine*, vol. 95, part 2 (1825) p. 646.
25. *PRO* PROB 11/1614 ff. 58–61 (Will of Rebekah Bliss)
26. John Walker and Richard Twiss were part of a local antiquarian circle of the 1790s which included Richard Gough and Isaac d'Israeli.
27. [December 1768] '14 Mrs. Sarah Bliss from Little Moorfields in a grave $00 = 13 = 6'$ PRO RG 4/4633 (Bunhill Fields Registers. vol. 11) 99.
28. PRO PROB 11/893, q. 498 (November 1763: Will of William Bliss).
29. PRO RG 4/4228 (Baptisms 1707–57).
30. Discussed by G. S. Rousseau, *Perilous Enlightenment: Pre- and postmodern discourses, sexual, historical* (Manchester: Manchester University Press, 1991) chapters 3 and 4.
31. Lillian Faderman, *Surpassing the Love of Men: Romantic Friendship and Love between Women from the Renaissance to the Present* (New York: Morrow, 1981; London: Junction Books, 1982. Reprinted London: Women's Press, 1985) p. 125.
32. PRO PROB 11/1361, q. 528. Probate was granted for the estate of John Gorham in August 1801.
33. PRO PROB 11/1361, q. 528, fols. 288^r–291^v.
34. PRO PROB 11/1709 fols. 172–181 (Will of Ann Whitaker).
35. PRO PROB 11/1614 fols. 58–61 (Will of Rebekah Bliss).
36. Ann Whittaker was also buried alongside them after her death in 1825, aged 84. *Loughton burials*, 49, 50. See also William Chapman Waller, *Loughton in Essex* (Epping: Alfred B. Davis, 1889–1900) ii, 48, who notes that a (now lost) memorial was raised to the three friends.
37. PRO PROB 11/1614 ff. 58–61 (Will of Rebekah Bliss).
38. Fuller's unmarried daughter Sarah, Bethia Fuller Maitland's aunt, was another inhabitant of Enfield.
39. 2 Corinthians, ch. 6, v. 14; Deuteronomy, ch. 22, v. 10.
40. 1 Corinthians, ch. 6, v. 17.
41. Prematurely, Seymour De Ricci, *English collectors of books and manuscripts* (Cambridge: Cambridge University Press, 1930) awarded this title to Miss Richardson Currer (1785–1861).
42. Lots 117, 147, 319, 320, 342, 409.
43. See, Francis Haskell, 'The Baron d'Hancarville: an Adventurer and Art Historian in Eighteenth-Century Europe', *Past and Present in Art and Taste: Selected Essays* (New Haven: Yale University Press, 1987).
44. *'Valuable Books and Manuscripts. A Catalogue of the Very Select and Elegant Library, Printed & Manuscript, of A Private Gentleman, Together with Another Collection, Including the Most Beautiful and Valuable Collection of Missals, and Other Richly Illuminated Manuscripts, Which Have Been Offered for Sale During Many Years; Some of the Delicately and*

Highly Finished Paintings in Which, Have Been Engraved in Dr. Dibdin's Decameron. Also Some Splendidly Illuminated Manuscripts in the Hebrew, Chinese, Arabic, Persian, Burmese, Hindostan, Sanscrit, Singalese, Japonese, Russian, Italian, French and English Languages, with Curious Specimens of Ancient Music. Which Will Be Sold by Auction, by Mr. Fletcher, At His Great Room, 191, Piccadilly, on Thursday, April 21st, 1842, and 3 Following Days, (Sunday Excepted.) At Twelve O'clock. To Be Viewed Four Days Previous, Catalogues Had At Mr. Fletcher's Office 191 Piccadilly. Price One Shilling Each.'

45. BL Department of Manuscripts P.R.2.c. 14(3).
46. Lots 690–3, 695, 697–700, 715–22, 739–41, 744–5, 753, 758.
47. It sold for £9.15s.
48. The manuscript is now BL MS. Egerton 1149. It sold for £45.13s.6d.
49. Now BL Add. 17,059. It sold for £4.14s.6d.
50. Thomas Frognall Dibdin, *The Bibliographical Decameron* (London, 1817) clxi–clxii.
51. William Beloe, *The Sexagenarian, or, The Recollections of a Literary Life* (London, 1817) ii, p. 253.
52. No copy is extant but Gilchrist (1863, ii. 263) provides a transcript. See also (Bentley 1977, p. 450).

Bibliography

Ackroyd, Peter, *Blake* (London: Sinclair-Stevenson, 1995).

Ault, Donald, *Visionary Physics: Blake's Response to Newton* (Chicago: Chicago University Press, 1974).

Behrendt, Stephen C., *Reading William Blake* (London: Macmillan, 1992).

Bellin, Harvey and Darrell Ruhl, eds., *Blake and Swedenborg: Opposition is True Friendship* (New York: Swedenborg Foundation, Inc., 1985).

Bentley, G. E. Jr., *Blake Records* (Oxford: Clarendon Press, 1969).

Bentley, G. E. Jr., *Blake Records Supplement: being New Materials relating to the Life of William Blake discovered since the Publication of* Blake Records *(1969)* (Oxford: Clarendon Press, 1988a).

Bentley, G. E., Jr., 'Richard Edwards, Publisher of Church-and-King Pamphlets and of William Blake', *Studies in Bibliography*, 41 (1988b) pp. 283–315.

Bentley, G. E., Jr., *Blake Books Supplement: A Bibliography of Publications and Discoveries about William Blake 1971–1992 being a Continuation of* Blake Books *(1977)* (Oxford: Clarendon Press, 1995).

Bentley, G. E., Jr., *Blake Books: Annotated Catalogues of William Blake's Writings in Illuminated Printing* (Oxford: Clarendon Press, 1977).

Bindman, David, *Blake as an Artist* (Oxford: Phaidon, 1977).

Blackstone, Bernard, *English Blake* (Cambridge: Cambridge University Press, 1949).

Blake, William, *Jerusalem* [reproduction of copy C], forward by Geoffrey Keynes (London: Trianon Press for the William Blake Trust, 1952).

Bloom, Harold, *Blake's Apocalypse: a Study in Poetic Argument* (London: Gollancz, 1962).

Blunt, Anthony, 'Blake's "Ancient of Days": the Symbolism of the Compasses', *Journal of the Warburg and Courtauld Institute*, 2 (1938) pp. 53–63.

Blunt, Anthony, *The Art of William Blake* (London: Oxford University Press, 1959).

Butlin, Martin, *The Paintings and Drawings of William Blake* (New Haven: Yale University Press, 1981).

Butlin, Martin, review of Eaves (1992) *Burlington Magazine*, 136 (1994) p. 119.

Cantor, Paul A., *Creature and Creator: Myth-Making and English Romanticism* (Cambridge: Cambridge University Press, 1984).

Carr, Stephen Leo, 'Illuminated Printing: Toward a Logic of Difference', in Hilton and Vogler (1986) pp. 177–96.

Clark, Lorraine, *Blake, Kierkegaard, and the Spectre of Dialectic* (Cambridge: Cambridge University Press, 1991).

Clark, S. H., 'Blake and Female Reason', *Sordid Images: the Poetry of Masculine Desire* (London: Routledge, 1994) pp. 138–87.

Clark, S. H., 'Blake's *Milton* as Empiricist Epic: "Weaving the Woof of Locke"', *Studies in Romanticism* 36: 3 (1997) pp. 457–82.

Clark, S. H., 'Locke and the Poetry of the Early Romantics', in Thomas Woodman (ed.) *The Early Romantics* (London: Macmillan, 1998) pp. 30–54.

Cooper, Andrew M., *Doubt and Identity in Romantic Poetry* (New Haven and London: Yale University Press, 1988).

Cox, Stephen, *'The Stranger Within Thee': Concepts of the Self in Late Eighteenth-Century Literature* (Pittsburgh: Pittsburgh University Press, 1980).

Cox, Stephen, *Love and Logic: the Evolution of Blake's Thought* (Ann Arbor: Michigan University Press, 1992).

Crehan, Stewart, *Blake in Context* (Dublin: Gill and Macmillan, 1984).

De Luca, Vincent Arthur, *Words of Eternity: Blake and the Poetics of the Sublime* (Princeton: Princeton University Press, 1980).

Dörrbecker, D. W., ed., *William Blake: The Continental Prophecies* (London: The William Blake Trust/Tate Gallery, Princeton: Princeton University Press, 1995).

Eaves, Morris, 'Blake and the Artistic Machine: An Essay in Decorum and Technology', *PMLA* 92 (1977) pp. 903–27.

Eaves, Morris, *The Counter-Arts Conspiracy: Art and Industry in the Age of Blake* (Ithaca and London: Cornell University Press, 1992).

Eaves, Morris, Robert N. Essick and Joseph Viscomi (eds.), *William Blake: The Early Illuminated Books* (London: The William Blake Trust/Tate Gallery, Princeton: Princeton University Press, 1993).

England, Martha Winburn and John Sparrow, *Hymns Unbidden: Donne, Herbert, Blake, Emily Dickinson and the Hymnographers* (New York: New York Public Library, 1966).

Erdman, David V., *Blake, Prophet Against Empire: A Poet's Interpretation of the History of His Own Times* (Princeton: Princeton University Press, 1954; 3rd edn, revised 1977).

Erdman, David V., '"Terrible Blake in his Pride": An Essay on *The Everlasting Gospel*', in Frederick W. Hilles and Harold Bloom (eds.), *From Sensibility to Romanticism: Essays Presented to Frederick A. Pottle* (London: Oxford University Press, 1965).

Erdman, David V., *'America*: New Expanses', in David V. Erdman and John E. Grant (eds.), *Blake's Visionary Forms Dramatic* (Princeton: Princeton University Press, 1970) pp. 92–114.

Erdman, David V., *The Illuminated Blake* (New York: Doubleday, 1974).

Erdman, David V., ed., *The Complete Poetry and Prose of William Blake*, with Commentary by Harold Bloom (Berkeley and Los Angeles: California University Press, 1966, 3rd edn, revised, 1982).

Essick, Robert N., 'Blake and the Traditions of Reproductive Engraving', *Blake Studies* 5 (1972) pp. 59–103.

Essick, Robert N., *William Blake Printmaker* (Princeton: Princeton University Press, 1980).

Essick, Robert N., *The Separate Plates of William Blake: A Catalogue* (Princeton: Princeton University Press, 1983a).

Essick, Robert N., 'John Linnell, William Blake, and the Printmaker's Craft', *Huntington Library Quarterly* 46 (1983b) pp. 18–32.

Essick, Robert N., 'How Blake's Body Means', in Hilton and Vogler (1986) pp. 197–217.

Essick, Robert N., *William Blake and the Language of Adam* (Oxford: Clarendon Press, 1989).

Essick, Robert N., 'William Blake's "Female Will" and its Biographical Context,' *Studies in English Literature* 31 (1991a) pp. 615–30.

Essick, Robert N., 'William Blake, Thomas Paine, and Biblical Revolution', *Studies in Romanticism* 30 (1991b): 189–212.

Essick, Robert N. and Joseph Viscomi (eds.) *Milton, a Poem, and the final illuminated works, The Ghost of Abel, On Homer's Poetry, On Virgil's Laocoön* (London: The William Blake Trust/Tate Gallery, Princeton: Princeton University Press, 1993).

Essick, Robert N., 'Blake in the Marketplace, 1993, Including a Report on the Sale of the Frank Rinder Collection', *Blake/An Illustrated Quarterly* 27 (1994) pp. 104–29.

Esterhammer, Angela, *Creating States: Studies in the Performative Language of John Milton and William Blake* (Toronto: University of Toronto Press, 1994).

Ferber, Michael, *The Social Vision of William Blake* (Princeton: Princeton University Press, 1985).

Ferber, Michael, 'Blake's *America* and the Birth of Revolution', in Stephen C. Behrendt (ed.), *History and Myth: Essays on English Romantic Literature* (Detroit: Wayne State University Press, 1990) pp. 73–99.

Ferber, Michael, 'The Finite Revolutions of *Europe*', in Jackie Di Salvo and Anthony Rosso (eds.), *Blake, Politics, and History* (Hamden, CT.: Garland Press, 1998) pp. 212–34.

Frosch, Thomas A., *The Awakening of Albion: The Renovation of the Body in the Poetry of William Blake* (Ithaca: Cornell University Press, 1974).

Frye, Northrop, *Fearful Symmetry: a Study of William Blake* (Princeton: Princeton University Press, 1947).

Gaunt, William, *Arrows of Desire: A Study of William Blake and his Romantic World* (London: Museum Press, 1956).

Gilchrist, Alexander, *Life of W. Blake, 'Pictor Ignotus*, 2 vols (Cambridge and London: Macmillan, 1863).

Gillham, D. G., *Blake's Contrary States: The Songs of Innocence and of Experience as Dramatic Poems* (Cambridge: Cambridge University Press, 1966).

Glausser, Wayne, 'Atomistic Simulacra in the Enlightenment and in Blake's Post-Enlightenment', *The Eighteenth Century: Theory and Interpretation* 32 (1991) pp. 73–88.

Hagstrum, Jean, *William Blake, Poet and Painter: An Introduction to the Illuminated Verse* (Chicago: Chicago University Press, 1964).

Helms, Randel, 'The Genesis of *The Everlasting Gospel*', *Blake Studies* 9 (1980) pp. 122–40.

Heppner, Christopher, *Reading Blake's Designs* (Cambridge: Cambridge University Press, 1995).

Hilton, Nelson, *Literal Imagination: Blake's Vision of Words* (Berkeley and Los Angeles: University of California Press, 1983).

Hilton, Nelson and Thomas A. Vogler (eds.) *Unnam'd Forms: Blake* and *Textuality*, (Berkeley and Los Angeles: University of California Press, 1986).

Hilton, Nelson, '"I" Sings Blake's *Songs'*, in *Symposium on Romanticism* (Adelaide: Centre for British Studies, 1990).

Hirsch, E. D., Jr., *Innocence and Experience: An Introduction to Blake* (New Haven: Yale University Press, 1964).

Holloway, John, *Blake: The Lyric Poetry* (London: Edward Arnold, 1968).

Keach, William, 'Blake, Violence, and Visionary Politics', in James A. W. Heffernan (ed.), *Representing the French Revolution: Literature, Historiography, and Art* (Hanover, NH: University Press of New England, 1992) pp. 65–88.

Keynes, Geoffrey, *The Gates of Paradise. For Children. For the Sexes, etc.* (Clairvaux: Trianon Press, 1968).

Kittel, Harald A., 'The *Book of Urizen* and *An Essay Concerning Human Understanding'*, in Michael Phillips (ed.), *Interpreting Blake* (Cambridge: Cambridge University Press, 1978) pp. 111–44.

Larrissy, Edward, *William Blake* (Oxford: Basil Blackwell, 1985).

Larrissy, Edward, '"Self-Imposition", Alchemy, and the Fate of the "Bound" in Later Blake', in Steve Clark and David Worrall (eds.), *Historicizing Blake* (New York: St. Martin's; Basingstoke: Macmillan, 1994) pp. 59–72.

Larrissy, Edward, '"Deposits" and "Rehearsals": Repetition and Redemption in *The Anathemata'*, in Paul Hills (ed.), *David Jones: Artist and Poet* (Aldershot: Scolar Press, 1997) pp. 132–40.

Lincoln, Andrew, *Spritual History: A Reading of William Blake's Vala or The Four Zoas* (Oxford: Clarendon Press, 1995).

Lister, Raymond, *Infernal Methods: A Study of William Blake's Art Techniques* (London: G. Bell & Sons, 1975).

Lowery, Margaret Ruth, *Windows of the Morning. A Critical Study of William Blake's Poetical Sketches, 1783* (New Haven: Yale University Press, 1940).

Mann, Paul, 'The *Book of Urizen* and the Horizon of the Book', in Hilton and Vogler (1986) pp. 49–68.

McGann, Jerome J., 'The Text, the Poem, and the Problem of Historical Method', *New Literary History* 12 (1981) pp. 269–88.

McGann, Jerome J., 'The Idea of an Indeterminate Text: Blake's Bible of Hell and Dr. Alexander Geddes', *Studies in Romanticism* 25 (1986) pp. 303–24.

Mee, Jon, *Dangerous Enthusiasm: William Blake and the Culture of Radicalism in the 1790s* (Oxford: Clarendon Press, 1992).

Mellor, Anne Kostelanetz, *Blake's Human Form Divine* (Berkeley: University of California Press, 1974).

Miller, Dan, Mark Bracher and Donald Adult (eds.) *Blake and the Argument of Method* (Durham, NC: Duke University Press, 1987).

Mitchell, W. J. T., 'Poetic and Pictorial Imagination in Blake's *The Book of Urizen'*, *Eighteenth Century Studies* 3 (1969) pp. 83–107.

Mitchell, W. J. T., *Blake's Composite Art: A Study of the Illuminated Poetry* (Princeton: Princeton University Press, 1978).

Moskal, Jeanne, *Blake, Ethics, and Forgiveness* (Tuscaloosa and London: University of Alabama Press, 1994).

Otto, Peter, 'Time, Eternity and the Fall in *The Book of Urizen'*, *Philological Quarterly* 69 (1990) pp. 359–76.

Otto, Peter, *Constructive Vision and Visionary Deconstruction: Los, Eternity and the Productions of Time in the later Poetry of William Blake* (Oxford: Clarendon Press, 1992).

Paley, Morton D., *William Blake* (Oxford: Phaidon, 1978).

Paley, Morton D., '"A New Heaven is Begun": William Blake and Swedenborgianism', *Blake/An Illustrated Quarterly* 13 (1979) pp. 64–90. Reprinted in Bellin and Ruhl, pp. 15–34.

Paley, Morton D., *The Continuing City: Blake's Jerusalem* (Oxford: Clarendon Press, 1983).

Pechey, Graham. '1789 and After: Mutations of 'Romantic' Discourse', in Francis Barker et al. (eds.), *1789: Reading Writing Revolution. Proceedings of the Essex Conference on the Sociology of Literature July 1981* (Colchester: University of Essex, 1982) pp. 52–66.

Peterfreund, Stuart, 'Blake, Freemasonry, and the Builder's Task', *Mosaic*, 17 (1984), pp. 37–8.

Phillips, Michael, 'Blake and the Terror 1792–93', *The Library*, 6th series, 16 (1994), pp. 263–97.

Pinto, Vivian de Sola, 'William Blake, Isaac Watts, and Mrs. Barbauld', in Vivian de Sola Pinto and Allan Edwin Rodway (eds.), *The Divine Vision. Studies in the Poetry and Art of William Blake* (London: Victor Gollancz, 1957, reprinted New York: Haskell, 1968) pp. 65–88.

Punter, David, 'Blake: Creative and Uncreative Labour', *Studies in Romanticism* 16 (1977) pp. 535–61.

Punter, David, '"Blake: 'Active Evil' and 'Passive Good'"', in David Aers, Jonathan Cook, and David Punter (eds.) *Romanticism and Ideology: Studies in English Writing 1765–1830* (London and Boston: Routledge Kegan Paul, 1981) pp. 7–26.

Punter, David, *Blake, Hegel and Dialectic* (Amsterdam: Rodopi, 1982).

Raine, Kathleen, *Blake and Tradition*, 2 vols. (Princeton: Princeton University Press, 1968).

Read, Dennis M., 'The Rival Canterbury Pilgrims of Blake and Cromek: Herculean Figures in the Carpet', *Modern Philology*, 86 (1988) pp. 171–90.

Rogal, Samuel J., 'Blake's "And did those feet" as Congregational Hymn', *The Hymn* 44 (1993) pp. 22–5.

Rose, Edward J., 'Blake and the Double: The Spectre as Doppelganger', *Colby Library Quarterly* 13 (1977) pp. 127–39.

Rosenberg, Marc, 'Style and Meaning in *The Book of Urizen'*, *Style* 4 (1970), pp. 197–212.

Rothenberg, Molly Anne, *Rethinking Blake's Textuality* (Columbia: University of Missouri Press, 1993).

Sandler, Florence, 'The Iconoclastic Enterprise: Blake's Critique of "Milton's Religion"', *Blake Studies* 5 (1972) pp. 13–57.

Schuchard, Marsha Keith, 'The Secret Masonic History of Blake's Swedenborg Society', *Blake/An Illustrated Quarterly* 26 (1992) pp. 40–51.

Schuchard, Marsha Keith, 'William Blake and the Promiscuous Baboons: A Cagliostroan Seance Gone Awry', *British Journal for Eighteenth-Century Studies*, 18 (1995) pp. 185–200.

Schuchard, Marsha Keith, 'Blake's *Tiriel* and the Regency Crisis: Lifting the Veil on a Royal Masonic Scandal', in Jackie DiSalvo and Anthony Rosso (eds.), *Blake Politics, and History* (Hamden, CT.: Garland Press, 1988) pp. 115–35.

Scrimgeour, J. R., '"The Great Example of Horror & Agony": A Comparison of Søren Kierkegaard's Demonically Déspairing Individual with William Blake's Spectre of Urthona', *Scandinavian Studies* 47 (1975) pp. 36–41.

Shrimpton, Nick, 'Hell's Hymnbook: Blake's *Songs of Innocence and of Experience* and their Models', in R. T. Davies and B. G. Beatty (eds.), *Literature of the Romantic Period, 1750–1850* (New York: Barnes & Noble, 1976) pp. 19–35.

Simpson, David, 'Reading Blake and Derrida – Our Caesars neither Praised nor Buried', in Hilton and Vogler (1986) pp. 11–25.

Smith, Donald M., 'Blake's *Songs of Innocence and Experience* [sic] and Eighteenth-Century Religious and and Moral Verse for Children', *Essays in Arts and Sciences*, 20 (1991) pp. 1–16.

Spector, Sheila A., 'The Reasons for "Urizen"', *Blake: An Illustrated Quarterly* (1988), pp. 147–48.

Spector, Sheila A., 'Sources and Etymologies of Blake's "Tirzah"', *Blake: An Illustrated Quarterly* 23 (1990) pp. 176–83.

Stemmler, Joan K., '"Undisturbed Above Once in A Lustre": Francis Douce, George Cumberland and William Blake at the Bodleian Library and Ashmolean Museum', *Blake/An illustrated Quarterly* 26 (1992) pp. 9–19.

Swinburne, Algernon Charles, *William Blake: a Critical Essay* (London: J. C. Hotten, 1868; reprinted New York: Arno Press, 1980).

Tannenbaum, Leslie, *Biblical Tradition in Blake's Early Prophecies: The Great Code of Art* (Princeton: Princeton University Press, 1982).

Thompson, E. P., *Witness Against the Beast: William Blake and the Moral Law* (New York: The New Press, 1993; Cambridge: Cambridge University Press, 1993).

Villalobos, John C., 'A Possible Source for William Blake's "The Great Code of Art"', *English Language Notes* 26 (1988) pp. 36–40.

Vine, Stephen, *Blake's Poetry: Spectral Visions* (Basingstoke and London: Macmillan, 1993).

Viscomi, Joseph, *Blake and the Idea of the Book* (Princeton NJ: Princeton University Press, 1993).

Viscomi, Joseph, 'The Evolution of William Blake's *The Marriage of Heaven and Hell*', *Huntington Library Quarterly* 58 (1997).

Viscomi, Joseph, 'Lessons of Swedenborg; or, the Origin of Blake's *The Marriage of Heaven and Hell*', in Robert Gleckner and Thomas Pfau (eds.), *Lessons of Romanticism* (Durham, NC: Duke University Press, 1998) pp. 173–212.

Witke, Joanne, 'Blake's Tree of Knowledge Grows out of the Enlightenment', *Enlightenment Essays* 3 (1972) pp. 71–84.

Worrall, David (ed.), *The Urizen Books: William Blake* (Princeton: Princeton University Press and William Blake Trust/Tate Gallery, 1995).

Index